Preface Books

A series of scholarly and critical studies of major writers intended for those needing modern and authoritative guidance through the characteristic difficulties of their work to reach an intelligent understanding and enjoyment of it.

General Editor: MAURICE HUSSEY

Branwell Brontë, 'The Brontë Sisters', c. 1834. The blur in the centre of the picture shows where Branwell has painted over his portrait.

A Preface to the Brontës

Felicia Gordon

Longman, London and New York

Longman Group UK Limited,
Longman House, Burnt Mill, Harlow,
Essex CM20 2JE, England
and Associated Companies throughout the world.

First published 1989
Second impression 1992 **LEARN**

British Library Cataloguing in Publication Data
Gordon, Felicia
  A preface to the Brontës.
  1. Brontë. *(Family)*   2. English fiction –
  19th century – History and criticism
  I. Title
  823.8'09   PR4169
  ISBN 0-582-35464-1

Library of Congress Cataloging in Publication Data
Gordon, Felicia.
  A preface to the Brontës/Felicia Gordon.
    p.   cm. – (Preface books)
  Bibliography: p.
  Includes index.
  Summary: Biographical material and a critical survey of the
  works written by the Brontë family.
    ISBN 0-582-35464-1
    1. Brontë family.   2. Brontë, Charlotte,
  1816–1855.   3. Brontë, Emily, 1818–1848.   4. Brontë,
  Anne, 1820–1849.   5. Authors, English – 19th century –
  Biography.   6. Yorkshire – Biography.
  [1. Brontë family.   2. Authors, English.   3. English
  literature – History and criticism.]   I. Title.
  PR4168.G64   1988
  823'.8'09 – dc19
  [B]
  [920]   87–29881

Set in 10/11 point Baskerville Linotron 202
Produced by Longman Singapore Publishers Pte Ltd
Printed in Singapore

823.7

ISBN 0 582 35464 1

Contents

List of illustrations

To the memory of Shiras Morris

Foreword

The most impressive early changes in the development of fiction into the dominant Victorian literary form may be understood if we compare the works of the distinguished daughter of the Rev. George Austen and those of the three principal survivors of the family of the Rev. Patrick Brontë. The great strength of Jane Austen lies in humane and satirical classical comedies which are economical in their treatment of natural imagery. The Brontës operate quite differently: the human scenes are passionate and sensational, and their images intensify the striking scenery on the borderland between the Yorkshire moors and the new industrial zone. Out of such filaments, a fresh Romantic art and mythology came into existence. For the Brontës, one of the greatest poets was Lord Byron (Jane Austen, we remember, favoured the Rev. George Crabbe), and the key artist was possibly John Martin, one of whose large apocalyptic canvases provides the present cover. The effects of such changes in observation, sensibility and technique must, it seems to me, be identified by all serious students of the novel as well as of painting. In order to select the central ideas here, Felicia Gordon draws upon a wide experience of European literature. Taken together, her observations have produced a discerning and varied Part Two; later chapters, in Part Three, upon individual novels and passages, provide fine models for the student and lay down helpful guidelines.

Because the Brontës shared a common life for a long period, their writings and their relationships intertwine, and they must inevitably be seen all together, even if it is to relegate Anne, who is a distinctive if small voice, to a lower place in the hierarchy. The tensions and tortures suffered by Branwell, the only one of his children of whom Patrick had high expectations, mean that the horrendous life story and little writing and painting of merit he left behind may take on a higher place than, finally, he deserved. One recognizes that however close Charlotte and Emily were, they wrote quite differently one from the other. *Jane Eyre* (1847) is strongly autobiographical where *Wuthering Heights* (1847) is not. In the former, universal themes like romantic love, nervous impulses, madness and frustration are all there together with one more specific issue that grew into prominence in the 1840s: the role of the governess. Without Charlotte's experience of this role, *Jane Eyre* might seem a matter of individual dream-like scenes from about the year 1800. Anne's *Agnes Grey* (also 1847) is equally a governess novel, where *Wuthering Heights*, the greatest of all these works of fiction, is not. In every way it stands out and forms the climax of the present book. It is plotted very sharply and logically, after an opening in 1801 before the writer's birth. It then, as we may note from the time-chart on p. 193, returns to the 1770s and moves forward with the help of two contrasting narrators to scenes upon two estates, balancing old country ways with newer social habits and economic ideas. Some critics have detected an ideological purport in these aspects of what is also a most passionate and free human document, much of which existed purely in the imagination of the author and not in her direct experience.

The final segment of Preface Books is always given to a variety of brief matters suggesting various ways of taking studies further. Felicia Gordon's Part Four could have no more practical response than for the student to take an old-fashioned literary pilgrimage to Haworth. Outside Stratford, there is no better shrine of its type in the country.

MAURICE HUSSEY
General Editor

Acknowledgements

The writer owes many debts to friends who have listened to anecdotes or borne with her discoveries about the Brontës. Maurice
Hussey, as editor of the series, has been most helpful with sugges-
tions, emendations, and occasional constructive disagreements. I
would like to thank John Purkis for his illuminating reading of *Jane
Eyre*, Judy Bibbins for visiting Haworth with me and pointing out
the writing on the wall, as well as doing picture research in
Cambridge, Massachusetts, Bill Greenwell for his perceptive
comments on John Martin and the Brontës' visual imagination and
especially Ian Gordon for having encouraged me at every stage.
His detailed and constructive reading of the early drafts of my
manuscript have been invaluable and his support made the whole
project seem worthwhile. Thanks are also due to my college,
CCAT, for having granted me research time to finish the book, and
to John Blanchfield and David Pearson of the CCAT Computer
Centre for their advice and help on the presentation of the text.

We are grateful to the following for permission to reproduce
photographs: British Library, pages 21, 101, 112 (2), 113 (2); The
Brontë Society, pages 12, 18, 23, 25, 45, 47, 57 (above), 62, 97, 103,
172, 192; Syndics of Cambridge University Library, page 159; The
Church of Scotland's Board of Practice and Procedure, Edinburgh,
page 117; Courtauld Institute of Art, page 170; Kunsthistorisches
Museum, Vienna, page 163; Suzanne and Edmund J. McCormick
collection, page 123; National Portrait Gallery, London, pages ii,
53, 57 (below); The Schlesinger Library, Radcliffe College, page
166; Sowerby Bridge Public Library, page 29; The Toledo Museum
of Art (Gift of Edward Drummond Libbey) page 50; Victoria &
Albert Museum, London, page 32; David Daiches & John Flower:
Literary Landscapes of the British Isles, Paddington Press, 1979, pages
137, 199.
Cover: Painting of Belshazzar's Feast by John Martin (1821) from
the collection at the Laing Art Gallery, Newcastle upon Tyne.
Reproduced by permission of Tyne and Wear Museums Service.

FELICIA GORDON is a graduate of Radcliffe College, Cambridge, Massachusetts, and took her Ph.D. in comparative literature from the University of California at Berkeley. She is a senior lecturer in European Thought and Literature at the Cambridgeshire College of Arts and Technology. She is currently writing a biography of Dr Madeleine Pelletier, an early twentieth-century French feminist and medical doctor, to be published by Polity Press.

Chronological table

1824 Tabitha Aykroyd engaged at the parsonage.
Maria, Elizabeth, Charlotte and Emily sent to Cowan Bridge School.

1825 Maria dies.
Elizabeth dies.
Charlotte and Emily brought home.

1824 Charlotte writes her first recorded story, 'There once was a little girl and her name was Ane' [sic].

1829 Roman Catholic Relief Act passed, ended disabilities against Roman Catholics.

1830 Belgian Revolution.

1831 Jan., Charlotte enrolled at Roe Head.

1831 Reform Bill defeated by Bishops in House of Lords.

1832 May, Charlotte leaves Roe Head, begins correspondence with Ellen Nussey and Mary Taylor.

1832 Reform Bill passed.

1833 Mr Brontë buys Moore's *Life of Byron*.

1833 Newman of Oxford publishes first *Tract for the Times*, launches Oxford Movement.

1834 Branwell's portrait of self and sisters, in which he later painted himself out and substituted a pillar.

1835 Branwell writes to editor of *Blackwood's*.
Leeds painter, William Robinson, gives Branwell lessons.
Branwell's abortive trip to London to enrol in Royal Academy of Arts.
July, Charlotte and Emily return to Roe Head.
Oct., Anne replaces Emily.

1836 Emily goes as teacher to Law Hill, Halifax.
Dec., Charlotte writes to Robert Southey.

1837 Branwell writes to Wordsworth, no reply.
March, Charlotte receives reply from Southey.
Dec., Anne and Charlotte return to Roe Head.

1838 Branwell goes to Bradford as a portrait painter.

1839 Feb., Henry Nussey proposes to Charlotte.
March, refused.
April, Anne governess to Ingham family, Mirfield.
May, Branwell returns home.
June–July, Charlotte governess to Sidgwicks at Stonegappe, near Skipton.
Aug., William Weightman becomes curate.
Dec., Anne leaves Inghams.
Branwell takes up post as tutor with the Postlethwaites, Ulverston.

1840 May, Anne engaged as governess by Rev. and Mrs Robinson of Thorp Green.
June, Branwell dismissed by Postlethwaites.
Aug., Branwell appointed Assistant Clerk at Sowerby Bridge Railway Station.

1841 March, Charlotte governess to Whites of Rawdon, near Bradford.

1836 Norton vs. Norton case won by defendants, Caroline Norton and Lord Melbourne.

1839 Infant Custody Act passed.

1841 April, Branwell promoted
to Chief Clerk,
Luddenden Foot.

1842 Feb., Charlotte and
Emily go to Brussels
with financial help from
Aunt Branwell, arrive at
Pensionnat Heger.
March, Branwell sacked
from Luddenden Foot for
financial irregularities.
Sept., William
Weightman dies.
Oct., Martha Taylor dies
in Brussels.
Oct., Aunt Branwell dies,
leaves £1,500.
Nov., Emily and
Charlotte return to
Haworth.

1843 Jan., Charlotte returns to
Brussels. Branwell goes
with Anne to Thorp
Green as tutor.
Sept., Charlotte goes to
Catholic confession.
Dec., Charlotte leaves
Brussels for home.

1843 Governesses' Benevolent
Institution founded.

1844 Plans made to open
school at Haworth come
to nothing.

1845 May, Rev. A. B. Nicholls
becomes curate of
Haworth.
Charlotte visits North
Lees Hall Farm, which
has 'mad woman's
room'; home of Eyre
family.
June, Anne leaves Thorp
Green.
July, Branwell dismissed
by Robinsons.

1845 Lunatics Act passed.

1846 Aug., Patrick has operation for cataracts in Manchester, Charlotte attends him.

1846 Charlotte, Emily and Anne publish *Poems* of 'Currer, Ellis and Acton Bell' with Aylott and Jones.

1847 July, *Wuthering Heights* and *Agnes Grey* accepted for publication by Newby.
The Professor rejected.
Aug., Smith and Elder accept *Jane Eyre*.
Oct., *Jane Eyre* published.
Dec., *Wuthering Heights* and *Agnes Grey* published.

1848 July, Anne and Charlotte go to London to reveal their identities to Smith and Elder.
Sept., Branwell dies.
Dec., Emily dies.

1848 June, *Tenant of Wildfell Hall* published.
Queen's College, London, founded for educating governesses.

1849 May, Anne dies at Scarborough.
Dec., Charlotte meets Thackeray and Martineau.

1849 Oct., *Shirley* published.

1850 May, Charlotte visits London, sees Duke of Wellington, portrait painted by Richmond.
June, trip to Edinburgh.
Aug., meets Mrs Gaskell.
Dec., stays with Martineau at Ambleside.

1850 Roman Catholic Church reinstated in Britain, Cardinal Wiseman appointed to Westminster.

1851 April, Mr Taylor proposes to Charlotte.
May–June, Charlotte in London, sees Great Exhibition, hears Wiseman preach.

1851 'On the Enfranchisement of Women', Harriet Taylor Mill.

1852 Dec., Mr Nicholls proposes to Charlotte.

1853 April, Charlotte visits Mrs Gaskell. Sept., Mrs Gaskell returns visit.

1854 April, Charlotte and Arthur Nicholls engaged. June, wedding.

1855 Jan., Charlotte falls ill. Feb., Tabby dies. 31 March, Charlotte dies. Mrs Gaskell invited to write *Life* by Mr Brontë.

1853 Jan., *Villette* published.

1857 *The Professor* published. Mrs Gaskell's *The Life of Charlotte Brontë* published.

1861 June, Patrick dies.

Introduction

When recounting her first meeting with Charlotte Brontë in August 1850, Mrs Gaskell wrote to a friend:

> Such a life as Miss Brontë's I never heard of before. Lady Kay-Shuttleworth described her home to me as in a village of a few grey stone houses, perched up on the north side of a bleak moor – looking over sweeps of bleak moors. There is court of turf and a stone wall, – (no flowers or shrubs will grow there) a straight walk, and you come to the parsonage door with a window on each side of it. The parsonage has never had a touch of paint, or an article of new furniture for 30 years; never since Miss B.'s mother died. . . . The sitting room of the parsonage looks in to the Church-yard filled with graves. Mr B. has never taken a meal with his children since his wife's death, unless he invites them to tea, – never to dinner. . . . The poverty of home was very great.
>
> (to Catherine Winkworth, 25 Aug. 1850)

Part of the value of Mrs Gaskell's biography lies in its testimony, from a contemporary writer, as to the strangeness of the Brontës' lives. It is this view which has set the tone for subsequent accounts of the Brontës. Even for Mrs Gaskell, who knew the industrial north of England well, the combination of mill town and isolated moorland as a setting for the Brontës' genius seemed chilling. It must be remembered that she first met Charlotte after the deaths of Branwell, Emily and Anne, who had all died within the space of one year, and at a time when Charlotte was a prey to loneliness and depression. Still, it would be true to say that the Brontës had always experienced social if not cultural isolation. Too poor to mix with local gentry, too well-educated to mix with farming families, they were entirely dependent for intellectual and imaginative stimulus on reading and on one another. For the four Brontë children who survived into adult life, Charlotte, Branwell, Emily and Anne, the chief consequence of this isolation was to throw them upon their own resources, to encourage voracious reading, a precocious imaginative development and to cement family ties. Though this early isolation had effects both on their physical health and mental stability, especially pronounced in the case of Branwell, it was also extraordinarily fruitful for their development as creative writers.

Today it is impossible not to be swayed by the myths surrounding the Brontë phenomenon. Even during Charlotte's lifetime, their lives had become legendary. Their straitened Yorkshire upbringing, the originality of their few novels and poems, their early deaths and even the botched tragedy of their brother Branwell's life contributed to the transformation of Haworth, the Yorkshire village where they lived, and their father's parsonage, into literary shrines, soon after Charlotte's death in 1855. Her father, Patrick Brontë, and her husband, the Reverend Arthur Bell Nicholls, were badgered by literary visitors; the next incumbent at Haworth, the Reverend John Wade, admitted to being 'incommoded by enthusiasts'. Every scrap of paper written by, or any object belonging to the Brontës that could be saved or collected has been accorded the status of an almost holy relic. In 1928, Haworth Parsonage was given to the Brontë Society by Sir James Roberts and is now one of the most visited literary shrines in Britain. The immense and continuing interest of tourists in Haworth and its now famous former inhabitants testifies to the power of the Brontës' works but also to the fascination and pathos of their lives. In itself, the Brontë myth is a remarkable phenomenon.

From a biographical perspective, another difficulty when approaching the Brontës lies in the problem of sources. Though there exists a wealth of historical and biographical detail (as chronicled, for example, in the *Transactions of the Brontë Society*), there are really two major first-hand sources. The first is Elizabeth Gaskell's *Life of Charlotte Brontë* (1856), one of the great examples of biographical literature. Mrs Gaskell knew Charlotte but never knew Anne or Emily. She visited Haworth and met Mr Brontë and Mr Nicholls. Her account of Charlotte's life dwells particularly on the Brontës' tragic destinies, stressing Charlotte's self-sacrifice and familial devotion. The second principal source is Charlotte's very extensive correspondence (including letters to her school friend, Ellen Nussey, her headmistress, Miss Wooler, and her publisher, George Smith), a record of her daily life ranging from accounts of her housekeeping duties to reflections on contemporary literature, politics and religion. In addition, some letters by Branwell remain, a few short and formal notes by Emily and Anne, and four very lively but unfortunately brief 'diary papers' by Emily and Anne. There exists no large body of independent correspondence by Charlotte's two younger sisters; it appears that she may have destroyed many of their personal papers after their deaths. Charlotte, therefore, is the principal, indeed the only major witness to the lives and characters of her sisters and brother. A further exception can be made in the reminiscences of Charlotte's two school friends, Mary Taylor and Ellen Nussey. However, their accounts, while immensely valuable, were written in the knowledge that their subjects were already famous, in that they wrote their memoirs after Charlotte's death, prompted by Mrs Gaskell.

So it is Charlotte who serves as the primary interpreter of the lives and works of her sisters and brother. Though her perspective is a priceless source of first-hand knowledge, it is necessarily partial. Charlotte was at pains to create a particular image of Emily and Anne; she was the first artificer of the Brontë legend. After her sisters' deaths, we know that Charlotte saw it as a labour of love to present them to the public in the best possible light. Emily's taciturn disposition and her religious unorthodoxy, for example, are to some extent smoothed away by Charlotte, who had an unqualified admiration for her sister's genius. 'Stronger than a man, simpler than a child, her nature stood alone' (1850 Biographical Notice to *Wuthering Heights*). Though Charlotte was clearly troubled by the violence and strangeness of *Wuthering Heights*, she defended it vigorously against its detractors:

> I have just read over *Wuthering Heights*, and for the first time, have obtained a clear glimpse of what are termed . . . its faults; have gained a definite notion of how it appears to other people. (Editor's Preface to the New 1850 Edition of *Wuthering Heights*)

Charlotte described Emily as living in a kind of imaginative innocence:

> Her imagination, which was a spirit more sombre than sunny, more powerful than sportive, found in such traits material whence it wrought creatures like Heathcliff, like Earnshaw, like Catherine. Having formed these beings, she did not know what she had done.
>
> (1850 Preface to *Wuthering Heights*)

Anne, on the other hand, suffered from the faint praise of Charlotte's characterization:

> Anne's character was milder and more subdued, she wanted the power, the fire, the originality of her sister, but was well-endowed with quiet virtues of her own. Long-suffering, self-denying, reflective and intelligent, a constitutional reserve and taciturnity placed and kept her in the shade, and covered her mind, and especially her feelings, with a sort of nun-like veil, which was rarely lifted.
>
> (1850 Biographical Notice to *Wuthering Heights*)

One suspects that Anne was somewhat patronized by Charlotte, and has been patronized by critics ever since. Charlotte strongly disapproved of *The Tenant of Wildfell Hall*, Anne's second novel; 'the choice of subject' (the decline of a rake into alcoholism, a painful echo of Branwell's career) 'was an entire mistake', and she may have destroyed the manuscript of a novel by Anne after the latter's death. Reacting with understandable defensiveness to the disgrace that Branwell brought on the family, Charlotte constructed her own version of the Brontë legend.

The note of sadness that emerges from many of Charlotte's letters, inspired by her disappointments in love and her loneliness after her sisters' deaths, can easily create an impression of unrelieved bleakness and repression dominating the Brontës' entire lives. However, the contrary would seem to have been the case. Their childhood and youth were unusual, but characterized by practical and imaginative activity. The close family bonds forged by the four children were an enduring consolation. Charlotte's testimony, then, is of enormous value, but it is essential to bear in mind that it represents the point of view of the surviving sister, shaken by the tragedies which had overwhelmed the family, and who wished to ennoble her sisters for posterity.

The Brontë manuscripts

The fate of the Brontës' letters and other manuscripts, such as the juvenilia, has proved a source of frustration to scholars. Unscrupulous collectors bought up collections, dispersed them and altered or forged important letters. Mrs Gaskell gives us the first glimpse of the excitement associated with the Brontë manuscripts. She and Sir James Kay-Shuttleworth had succeeded in borrowing various papers from Mr Nicholls, Charlotte's husband, who was normally reluctant to part with anything:

> I came away with *The Professor*, the beginning of her new tale 'Emma' . . . and by far the most extraordinary of all, a packet about the size of a lady's travelling writing case, full of paper books of different sizes, from the one I enclose upwards to the full on half sheet size, but all in indescribably fine writing . . . they are the wildest and most incoherent things, as far as we have examined them, *all* purporting to be written, or addressed to some member of the Wellesley family. They give one the idea of creative power carried to the verge of insanity.
>
> (to George Smith, 25 July 1856)

These 'paper books' were the juvenilia (see pp. 95–108).

Brontë scholarship has suffered from the fact that the earliest guardians of the Brontë memorabilia who sought to protect the sisters' memory (Ellen Nussey and Mr Nicholls in particular) suppressed material. The next generation of supposedly professional scholars seemed largely concerned with profit. The first edition of Charlotte Brontë's letters was published by J. Horsfall Turner between 1885 and 1889 and was incomplete. The manuscripts and other correspondence belonging to Mr Nicholls were eventually purchased from him by T. J. Wise, who with J. A. Symington edited *The Shakespeare Head Brontë* (19 volumes, Oxford, 1931–38). This edition, comprising novels, poems and letters, is not accurate or complete. Portions of correspondence, such as Charlotte's letters to Ellen Nussey, had already been destroyed by Ellen or others, and Wise was not above tampering with dates and even forging letters. His editing was neither rigorous nor reliable. Brontë scholars, in particular T. Winnifrith, have condemned him as dishonest and slovenly. Two earlier collections of letters by C. K. Shorter, *Charlotte Brontë and her Circle* (1896) and *The Brontës' Life and Letters*, are also limited in accuracy. One of the many sad ironies of the Brontës' lives, haunted as they themselves were by the fear of poverty, is that their manuscripts and letters provided a source of rich financial reward for unscrupulous editors.

The Yorkshire setting

From the 1880s on, guidebooks on the 'Brontë Country' began to proliferate. Every walk the Brontës might have taken, every village they might have visited or had connection with has, in the course of time, been charted. Mrs Gaskell, in her *Life of Charlotte Brontë*, first recognized the importance of the Yorkshire setting, by devoting an extended introduction to the history, people and landscape surrounding Haworth. She evidently felt the need to explain to her contemporary audience what would have seemed to them a wild and little-known part of England.

Yorkshire, a north-eastern county of England, was formerly divided into three areas called 'ridings'. Haworth lay in the West Riding (see map, p. 137). Historically, the Yorkshire moors, an upland heath region, was a wool-producing area. Mrs Gaskell was impressed by the singularity of the Yorkshire landscape and by its proverbially dour inhabitants. Describing a walk over Penistone Moor with Charlotte, she remarked:

> the sinuous hill seemed to girdle the world like a great Norse serpent. . . . [Miss Brontë] told me such wild tales of the ungovernable families who lived or who had lived therein that Wuthering Heights even seemed tame comparatively. Such dare-devil people, – men especially, – and women so stony and cruel in some of their feelings and so passionately fond in others.
>
> (to John Forster, Sept. 1856)

The *Life* stresses the self-sufficiency and independence of the Yorkshire character. Certainly in the Brontës' novels one finds little of the spirit of deference of servants to masters, children to parents or of women to men, that would have been the norm in much nineteenth-century fiction. The isolated lives of the hill

Mrs Elizabeth Gaskell, 'Haworth Church and Parsonage', 1857

farmers and wool merchants produced, in Mrs Gaskell's view, 'irregularity and fierce lawlessness'. In this context, the domestic excesses of Hindley Earnshaw or of Heathcliff seem plausible, not to say natural. Yorkshire farmers, in Mrs Gaskell's account, united considerable wealth with a kind of savage rusticity more reminiscent of the Middle Ages than of nineteenth-century England.

From the literary rather than the biographical point of view, the Yorkshire setting forms an interesting chapter in landscape aesthetics. During the Brontës' lifetime the moors were not considered to be traditionally picturesque. *Wuthering Heights*, indeed, stresses the prosaic, unromantic nature of life in a remote farmland community, inhabited by unsociable country people like Joseph and Zillah; it is the city dweller, Lockwood, who attempts, unsuccessfully, to find picturesque elements at the Heights. Unlike the Lake District, Yorkshire in the first half of the nineteenth century had no tourist or aesthetic following. Whereas by the 1820s and 30s, the Cumberland fells and lakes, long the home of Wordsworth, Southey and Coleridge, had become a recognized Romantic landscape, Yorkshire was simply thought of, if people outside Yorkshire thought of it at all, as an uncultivated waste. The moors were bleak, without dramatic peaks; there were no lakes to reflect the light; and manufacturing towns sprouting in the valley were not aesthetically pleasing. Yet it is this setting and landscape which the Brontë legend has helped to romanticize. What is presented in *Shirley* and *Wuthering Heights* as a deliberately unpicturesque landscape, inhabited by stubborn and undeferential rural people, became for post-Brontë enthusiasts a new Romantic landscape.

One reason, perhaps, that the physical setting of Haworth captures readers' imaginations is the sense one gets, even today, of clarity of demarcation. The village of Haworth lies on the north side of a green valley dominated from above by the moors. Haworth has expanded to fill the valley with extensive mill works. However, clear divisions between the human and the natural environment still persist. The parsonage, where the Brontës lived, faces the churchyard, crowded with huge raised gravestones. (The present church is a late Victorian replacement for the building in which Mr Brontë preached.) Immediately behind the parsonage lie fields, and rising steeply behind them, the moors. The Brontës' house was at the upper extremity of the village, abutting on the church and tight clusters of village houses in the front, and completely open to the fields to the rear. Thus the physical setting presents striking contrasts. On the one hand, one sees the village's narrow, cobbled streets and the stone houses hunched on the edge of the steep hillside, and on the other, above the village, the seemingly limitless expanse of moor. The field system around Haworth creates a similar impression of oppositions. The fields, divided by dry-stone walls, extend up the valleys until they meet the moorland top. There the delineation of landscape into man-made enclosures abruptly changes into seemingly trackless bog and heather. The physical setting in which they lived fortuitously created a system of oppositions or Romantic contrasts that informed the Brontës' novels. For example, *Wuthering Heights*, the novel most closely ident-ified with the landscape in its structure, depends on a series of physical, psychological and symbolic polarities; moor and valley, Wuthering Heights and Thrushcross Grange, freedom and constraint, heaven and hell. The natural setting of Haworth offered Emily Brontë a physical basis for the dynamics of her novel.

A final opposition lies in the contrast between rural and urban worlds in the West Riding of Yorkshire in the first half of the nine-teenth century. Bradford, Leeds and Halifax (all near Haworth), were, when the Brontës were young, cities undergoing rapid indus-trial transformation. The sense of a timeless rural culture in and around Haworth contrasted forcibly with the bustle and change of life in the new booming mill towns. The railway that linked Keighley, four miles from Haworth, with Leeds put the Brontës in touch with city life. They were by no means simple country folk. Rather they were acquainted from an early age both with the reali-ties of rural England, and with the transformations effected in the cities by the Industrial Revolution.

Part One

The Brontës and their Background

1 A parsonage childhood

Patrick Brontë

The Brontës' father, Patrick Brontë, was the eldest son of an Irish labourer. He was born on 17 March 1777, St Patrick's Day, at Drumballyroney-cum-Drumgooland, County Down, Ireland. His mother, of Catholic stock, had renounced Catholicism to marry a Protestant, Hugh Brunty. The family lived in a two-room thatched cottage with a dirt floor. Patrick Brontë was born into the experience of the Irish labouring poor. His struggles to educate himself, to become a schoolteacher and at length to enter St John's College, Cambridge, in 1802 to read theology, appear little short of miraculous in an age of still rigid social divisions. Patrick's rapid rise to the status of a gentleman, albeit a poor one, may go some way to explaining his daughters' sensitivity about social status, as well as their ambition and perseverance in pursuing a writing career.

At Cambridge, Patrick began the transformation of his name into something more appropriate to his change in social status, from Brunty, Bronte (with alternating accents), finally settling on the spelling Brontë. His theological views also evolved at Cambridge under the influence of Charles Simeon, an Evangelical leader in the Anglican Church. The Evangelical strain which Patrick imbibed at university became a significant influence in his children's lives (see pp. 73–8). Patrick, though associated with Presbyterians as a young man in Ireland, may have heard the Methodist leader, John Wesley, preach there. Evangelicalism strongly coloured his theology and affected the religious atmosphere in which his children grew up. After his ordination as an Anglican clergyman in 1806, he was appointed curate at Wethersfield in Essex, and subsequently at Wellington, Shropshire, and Dewsbury, Yorkshire. Remaining in Yorkshire, he was moved to Hartshead, Thornton, and finally, in 1819, he was awarded the permanent incumbency of Haworth.

In 1812, while at Hartshead, Patrick met and married Maria Branwell, then visiting her cousin, Jane Fennel, at a Wesleyan school, Woodhouse Grove, where Patrick had been appointed examiner. Maria Branwell came from a well-to-do Wesleyan Methodist family in Penzance, Cornwall. Little is known of her apart from a series of letters she wrote to Patrick during their engagement. These are lively and full of piety on the question of marriage and of wifely duty. After her marriage, Maria published one essay in a religious journal, on the advantages of poverty for the religious life. Her own married life was composed of a series of pregnancies. She bore six children in the space of nine years: Maria, April 1814; Elizabeth, 8 February 1815; Charlotte, 21 April 1816; Patrick Branwell, 26 June 1817; Emily Jane, 30 July 1818; and Anne, 17 January 1820. Maria Brontë died of cancer a year after Anne's birth. Her illness was prolonged and agonizing; she was only 39 when she died. Mrs Gaskell says of her:

> She had six children as fast as could be: and what with that, and the climate, and the strange half mad husband she had chosen, she died at the end of nine years. An old woman at Burnley who nursed her at last, says she used to lie crying in bed, and saying, 'Oh God, my poor children – oh God, my poor children!' continually.
>
> (to C. Winkworth, 25 Aug. 1850)

We observe that Mrs Gaskell was not an admirer of Patrick Brontë. In *The Life*, however, she greatly modified her strictures on his character, though even there she was criticized as painting too exaggerated a portrait.

In the absence of their mother, Mr Brontë's influence over his children's upbringing was crucial. His eccentricity of character was immortalized by Gaskell, who related possibly apocryphal stories told her by an old servant, to the effect that Mr Brontë once cut off the sleeves of his wife's dress because he disapproved of the style, and that he was in the habit of indulging in pistol practice every morning out of his bedroom window. Patrick undoubtedy was an unusual man and did become increasingly odd, especially in his old age when Mrs Gaskell met him. He appears, however, to have been energetic and physically courageous. Living in the industrial north-east of England at a time of poverty, unemployment and industrial unrest, and representing high Tory principles and the Established Church within a largely dissenting community, he found himself politically at odds with radicals and religiously at odds with dissenters. While minister at Hartshead, he had first-hand experience of the Luddite rebellion when, in 1812, a group of rioters attacked Cartwright's Mill. This story, which he told his children many times, was transposed by Charlotte into her novel *Shirley*. It was at Hartshead that Patrick adopted the habit of carrying pistols wherever he went on his parish duties.

Mr Brontë has aroused conflicting emotions in Brontë scholars. He was a man of considerable ability who, thanks to his relative poverty and humble origins, was never a natural part of the Anglican establishment. The cadences of his speech, a tendency to pomposity and bombast, noted by Mrs Gaskell, were probably a consequence of being largely self-taught and, like his children, of

The Reverend Patrick Brontë, c. 1860

developing his intellect in isolation. His passionate interest in politics, which led him to subscribe to, or borrow, an unusual number of newspapers and periodicals, undoubtedly enriched the culture of his children. He seems to have encouraged them in a wide and impressive range of miscellaneous reading from his own library and from the Mechanics' Institute Library at Keighley. Patrick's admiration for the Duke of Wellington fired his children's imaginations, and he kept an awareness of political and social events in the forefront of their minds. Thanks to their father, the Brontë children were better informed about current events than many of their more conventionally educated contemporaries.

There were other aspects of Patrick's paternal rule that were less fortunate. After his wife's death and two unsuccessful attempts to remarry, he brought his sister-in-law, Elizabeth Branwell, from Penzance to Haworth to look after his children. She was a woman of limited imagination and puritanical views who imposed a strict régime of household tasks and plain sewing on the girls and indulged Branwell, whose education was left to his father. Within the family, Patrick followed the rôle of the Victorian father, keeping his distance from the six children in the none-too-large house. He ate his meals alone and spent much of his time, when not directly engaged in parish duties, by himself. Whereas when his children were young, this benign neglect allowed them to develop in remarkably unfettered ways, the endless paternal silence was felt as a crushing burden on Charlotte, and in Emily and Anne produced the legendarily shy and silent creatures whom we know only through their novels and poems.

A final important and positive way in which Patrick Brontë may be seen to have influenced his children's ambitions was the fact that he was a published, if unsuccessful, author. He had written both poems and short tales, five volumes in all. When Mr Brontë gave the children a present of toy soldiers in 1826, they followed their father's example by turning their dramatized plays with the soldiers into written records, from which a remarkable and sustained series of juvenilia developed. The Brontës' apprentice-ship as writers was virtually continuous, involving the production of novels about linked characters, which took on epic dimensions. The quality and the importance of the juvenilia will be discussed below (pp. 95–108) but the fact of its existence reveals a literary culture and ambition that the children undoubtedly owed to their father.

School experience

Branwell was largely educated at home, in the classics, by his father, and in drawing and painting by masters imported from

Bradford. The girls, however, were all sent away to school for varying periods. Their home education consisted in learning household management from their Aunt Branwell, helping the servant, Tabitha Aykroyd, in the kitchen, and having lessons in general subjects with their father. Anne, for example, learned Latin sufficiently well to be able to teach it when she became a governess, an unusual accomplishment for a girl at that period. Mrs Gaskell is almost certainly mistaken when she says that 'their father never taught the girls anything – only the servant taught them to read and write' (to C. Winkworth, 25 Aug. 1850). Much of their education, however, was derived from miscellaneous and undirected reading.

In 1824, the year after their mother's death, the four eldest girls, Maria, Elizabeth, Charlotte and Emily, were sent to Cowan Bridge School, Emily, the youngest, then being four years old. Cowan Bridge had been founded by a clergyman, the Reverend Carus Wilson, for the education of poor clergymen's daughters, and could boast among its eminent patrons William Wilberforce and Charles Simeon. Because the future prospects in life of the girl pupils at Cowan Bridge were unpromising, belonging as they did to a genteel but impoverished class, the school was run on spartan lines, designed to encourage resignation and humility. Cowan Bridge School lives in the public memory because it was pilloried by Charlotte in *Jane Eyre*, and because Mrs Gaskell explicitly identified Lowood School of *Jane Eyre* with Cowan Bridge. What seems certain is that the school régime was harsh, the food was often poor and contaminated, and that on Sundays the children walked two miles to church where they remained all day, huddled together in the pews between services to keep warm and suffering agonies of boredom, in addition to cold and hunger. During the Brontës' sojourn there, typhus broke out, assisted by the poor hygienic conditions and the undernourished state of the pupils. The combined effect of ill-health and malnutrition on the Brontë girls was dramatic. In 1825, Maria developed consumption and died at home in May, aged eleven. Elizabeth was next brought home and died in June, aged ten; Charlotte and Emily were finally withdrawn in the course of the summer. The death of Maria, who, young as she was, had become the children's substitute mother, appears to have been particularly felt by the family. She was reputedly one of the most intelligent of the children. Living as they did in Haworth next to the graveyard, 'terribly full of upright tomb stones' (Mrs Gaskell), the presence of death was graphically before them. This first-remembered loss, the double deaths of two loved sisters, strongly coloured the imaginations of the two eldest remaining children, Branwell and Charlotte.

Clergy Daughters' School, Cowan Bridge, an engraving by O. Jewitt of Derby, 1824

The four surviving Brontë children spent the next six years at home. This was perhaps their happiest period. Emily and Anne, the two youngest, became inseparable as twins. Charlotte allied herself with Branwell; their juvenile writing, which they began soon after their sisters' deaths, accordingly followed the same pattern. Their stories were written as joint productions, Emily and Anne composing the Gondal saga, Charlotte and Branwell the Angrian adventures. Charlotte's often anthologized poem, 'Retrospection', commemorates this time of relative liberty and intense imaginative activity, and her subsequent sense of the shadows over their adult lives:

> We wove a web in childhood,
> A web of sunny air;
> We dug a spring in infancy
> Of water pure and fair;
>
> We sowed in youth a mustard seed,
> We cut an almond rod;
> We are now grown to riper age:
> Are they withered in the sod?
>
> Are they blighted, failed and faded,
> Are they mouldered back to clay?
> For life is darkly shaded,
> And its joys fleet fast away!

(19 Dec. 1835)

In 1831, when she was fifteen, Charlotte, now the eldest child, was entered as a pupil at Miss Wooler's school at Roe Head, near Dewsbury, Yorkshire, where she remained until May of the following year. Mary Taylor, the friend whom she first met at Miss Wooler's, has described her arrival at the school:

> I first saw her coming out of a covered cart, in very old-fashioned clothes, and looking very cold and miserable. . . . She looked a little, old woman, so short-sighted that she always appeared to be seeking something, and moving her head from side to side to catch sight of it. She was very shy and nervous and spoke with a strong Irish accent. When a book was given her, she dropped her head over it till her nose nearly touched it, and when she was told to hold her head up, up went the book after it, still close to her nose, so that it was not possible to help laughing.

(18 Jan. 1856)

Though a short period of formal schooling, her stay at Roe Head was to influence Charlotte profoundly. She surprised her teachers and fellow pupils by a combination of erudition, especially in

Miss Ellen Nussey

Miss Mary Taylor

literary and political subjects, and ignorance of areas of general knowledge, or at least of those areas of knowledge, such as simple geography, thought appropriate to the education of young ladies of that period. Nevertheless, she soon established herself as intellectually pre-eminent at the school. Ellen Nussey's reminiscences are revealing about the sort of impression Charlotte made on her fellow pupils:

> Some of the elder girls, who had been years at school, thought her ignorant. This was true in one sense; ignorant she was indeed in the elementary education which is given in schools, but she far surpassed her most advanced school-fellows in knowledge of what was passing in the world at large, and in the literature of her country. She knew a thousand things unknown to them.
> (quoted in Gérin, *Charlotte Bronte*, p. 65)

Roe Head School was a humane institution and Charlotte in later years became a close friend of its headmistress, Miss Wooler. But initially, Charlotte found the adjustment to school routine and communal living agonizing. Nevertheless, the desire to qualify herself for financial independence and her real love of knowledge led her to learn everything that the school had to teach. Perhaps, more importantly, it was at Roe Head that she made her first friends outside her family; Ellen Nussey, the daughter of a Tory land-owning family near Birstall, Yorkshire; and Mary Taylor and her sister Martha, daughters of a formerly prosperous but now somewhat impoverished Yorkshire cloth manufacturer of radical political opinions. A great deal of our knowledge of the Brontës derives from Charlotte's correspondence with Ellen Nussey and from some telling recollections of Mary Taylor. Charlotte's description of Mary Taylor as Rose Yorke, in *Shirley*, seems taken from life:

> Rose, the elder, is twelve years old; she is like her father, – the most like him of the whole group, – but it is a granite head copied in ivory; all is softened in colour and line. Yorke himself has a harsh face; his daughter's is not harsh, neither is it quite pretty; it is simple, – childlike in feature. . . . Rose is a still, sometimes a stubborn girl now: her mother wants to make of her such a woman as she is herself, – a woman of dark and dreary duties, – and Rose has a mind full-set, thick-sown with the germs of ideas her mother never knew. It is agony to her often to have these ideas trampled on and repressed. She has never rebelled yet; but if hard driven, she will rebel one day, and then it will be once for all.
> (*Shirley*, Ch. 9)

24

Anne Brontë, a pencil drawing of Roe Head School

It was noticeable to Charlotte's contemporaries at school that, partly due to her short sight and partly to her intense shyness, she did not know how to join in games. None of the Brontës had ever learned the usual children's pastimes. They lived in their imaginary worlds of Gondal and Angria, which seemed more real and infinitely more satisfying than normal childish pursuits. As a consequence, they all experienced difficulty in adapting to the demands of adult life in terms of social ease, and, in Branwell's case, of responsible behaviour. Branwell, when sent to London to enrol at the Royal Academy to study painting in 1835, panicked, drank up his money and never presented his letter of introduction to the Academy. He came back disgraced to Haworth after only a few weeks. In their turn, Emily, Anne and Charlotte suffered agonies of shyness at school and as teachers and governesses. Emily, indeed, became a virtual recluse and appears to have abandoned any wish to engage with the world outside Haworth. Charlotte and Branwell, in their different ways, did seek friends; Branwell found disreputable drinking companions at Haworth and at Luddenden Foot, where he worked as a railway clerk between April 1841 and March 1842, when he was dismissed for financial irregularities. Charlotte, more fortunate, made enduring friendships at school and other important friendships after she became known as an author. Apart from her ties with her last employers, the Robinson family, Anne, like Emily, seems to have made few bonds outside the family. One major exception was their father's curate, the Reverend William Weightman, who served at Haworth from 1839 to 1842 when he died of cholera. Weightman had the unique gift of overcoming the Brontë family reserve. Biographers have suggested that both Emily and Anne were in love with him, though there is no conclusive evidence. Charlotte appears both to have liked him and to have been exasperated by his tendency to flirt with all available ladies. But he was a good friend, especially to Branwell. Weightman's death removed the most sociable influence ever to break into the Brontës' isolation.

2 The path to maturity

The choice of a profession

It was always evident to the Brontë children that they would be thrown on their own financial resources in the event of their father's death, since the small income from his living would end with him. Branwell, who showed signs of talent, was encouraged to become a painter. It was assumed, by his too sanguine family, that he would make the family fortune. Emily, Anne and Charlotte followed his artistic interest, and turned to drawing as a medium of self-expression. They were largely self-taught, copying engravings in the magazines and books that came their way. An interest in the visual arts may be traced in all their works but perhaps most strikingly in Charlotte's (see below, pp. 109–18). Of Emily we have some well-observed sketches of domestic animals. Branwell, after his unsuccessful trip to London, did study painting in Bradford with Leyland and, in particular, has left two paintings of his sisters which are valuable as historical records. Overall, his lack of artistic success and his inability to pursue any settled career was arguably the spur that led to his sisters' eventual determination to become published authors.

Branwell's growing incapacity for useful employment meant that Charlotte, Emily and Anne had early to face the necessity of taking up careers, either as schoolteachers or as governesses, the only employment open to middle-class women of the period. Their inexperience with children outside of their own family rendered them singularly ill-equipped to teach average, healthy and undisciplined children of the upper-middle classes. They found life both at school and as governesses, where every moment of their time was strictly organized, to contrast painfully with their relatively free existence at Haworth. Further, their extreme shyness and hypersensitivity made them poorly adapted for a rôle that could only have been filled successfully by individuals of more robust temperament.

'A stalking ghost'

Nevertheless, teaching was to be the Brontë sisters' profession. Charlotte as the eldest began the search for independence by taking up a post at Miss Wooler's school in July 1835, when she was 19, and where she stayed for a period of three years. Miss Wooler was an interesting person in her own right. Related to the

Allbutt family of Leeds, which produced distinguished physicians, she served as a model to Charlotte of what an independent unmarried woman could achieve. It was to her credit that she remained Charlotte's friend and saw her exceptional qualities, because Charlotte was almost certainly not a success as a teacher. Miss Wooler's loyalty to Charlotte and her dislike of publicity led her to express significant reservations about Mrs Gaskell's *Life*. Her nephew, Professor Sir Clifford Allbutt, of Cambridge, commented in his aunt's copy of *The Life of Charlotte Brontë*:

> The erasures of her name in this book were the doing of my aunt who, rather defiant of Mrs Gaskell's effusive interviewing – at that day a novelty among women, had stipulated that her own name should not be published, or no more of it than an occasional initial letter. A shrewd intellectual woman, with a keen sense of humour, Miss Wooler resented also the rather vapid amiability attributed to her by Mrs Gaskell. The life was therefore perused with some exasperation. My aunt, however, admitted that the life gave a true picture of Charlotte Brontë and her world.

Even at Miss Wooler's school, under a relatively liberal employer, Charlotte was desperately unhappy and homesick:

> I heard that she had gone as a teacher to Miss Wooler's. I went to see her, and asked how she could give so much for so little, when she could live without it. . . . She confessed it was not brilliant, but what could she do? . . . She seemed to have no interest or pleasure beyond the feeling of duty, and when she could get the opportunity, used to sit alone and 'make out'.
> (Mary Taylor quoted in *The Life of Charlotte Brontë*)

Her initial reason for taking the post was that Miss Wooler offered a free place at the school for one of her sisters. Emily accompanied Charlotte to Roe Head when she was only 17, and aside from her period at Cowan Bridge, when she was little more than a baby, had never been away from home. She could not bear the monotony, the rote learning and the schoolgirl games. She found herself separated from Haworth and from Anne, with little chance to see Charlotte, who was immersed in her teaching duties. The latter, not gifted with sympathy for the meagre talents of the girls in her charge, felt only impatience and scorn for her pupils, and had the added worry of seeing Emily pining away before her eyes. 'Liberty was the breath of Emily's nostrils. . . . I felt in my heart she would die, if she did not go home' (1850 Biographical Notice to *Wuthering Heights*). After a stay of only three months Emily was sent home, and Anne took her place at Roe Head in October 1835.

For Charlotte, the three years at Roe Head marked a major crisis in her life. It left her with a permanent tendency to nervous

28

The station at Luddenden Foot where Branwell Brontë worked between 1841 and 1842

depression. She began to have hallucinatory visions of her Angrian characters and eventually had to leave Miss Wooler's employment. She recalled this difficult period in a letter to Miss Wooler probably written late in 1852:

> concentrated anguish of certain insufferable moments and the heavy gloom of many long hours – besides a preternatural horror which seemed to clothe existence and Nature – and which made life a continual waking nightmare. . . . I could have been no better company to you than a stalking ghost – and I remember I felt my incapacity to *impart* pleasure fully as much as my powerlessness to receive it.

One result of the girls' separation from home was a shift in their allegiances. Hitherto Charlotte and Branwell had been companions, joint authors in the Angrian adventures, whereas Anne and Emily as the youngest devised their separate world of Gondal. Emily's return to Haworth in 1835 coincided with Branwell's unsuccessful expedition to London. Both came home suffering from a sense of failure, and from this period on Emily became Branwell's champion, as he gradually declined into drink and opium. On one memorable occasion, some years later, when in a drunken stupor he had set his bed on fire, she rescued him and put out the blaze. Emily seems to have seen Branwell as a quasi-Byronic figure, rejected by society. Her poetry in the two years that Charlotte and Anne were at Roe Head shows a preoccupation with guilt and failure, as for example her fragment, 'The Old Church Tower' (Oct. 1837):

> The old church tower and garden wall
> Are blank with autumn rain,
> And dreary winds forboding call
> The darkness down again
>
> I watched how evening took the place
> Of glad and glorious day,
> I watched a deeper gloom efface
> The evening's lingering ray.
>
> And as I gazed on the cheerless sky
> Sad thoughts rose in my mind . . .

By the end of Branwell's catastrophic decline, Charlotte had lost sympathy with him, as had Anne. Emily, however, remained his silent ally.

Both Emily and Branwell did make further attempts to find employment. In October 1836, Emily went to teach at Law Hill School near Halifax where she remained between six and eighteen months (the period is disputed by scholars), and it was then that she probably heard stories of local family feuds which she adapted when she wrote *Wuthering Heights*. Otherwise almost nothing is known of her time at Law Hill. But it is fair to say that none of the Brontë sisters throve as governesses. Emily held one post, Charlotte two brief posts as governess, in addition to her three-year period at Miss Wooler's; Anne held two posts. In the second, at the Robinsons, she appears to have gained the affection of her pupils, but said, 'I dislike the situation and wish to change it for another' (Anne's diary, 30 July 1841). One may feel some sympathy for their employers who must have found the sisters almost impossible to communicate with, so extreme was their shyness.

In the early 1840s Charlotte launched the plan of starting their own school at Haworth, in order that they might be genuinely independent, and above all, not be forced to live among strangers. She recognized that they needed more qualifications, particularly in foreign languages. Since there were no established teacher-training courses available at this period, they decided to seek further training abroad. We know that they could read French and that Emily taught herself German, but in order to offer a successful school curriculum they needed fluency in one or more foreign languages. Charlotte, with characteristic energy and determination, persuaded their Aunt Branwell to finance a stay for two of the sisters at a school in Brussels. It was decided that Charlotte and Emily should go, and on 8 February 1842 they set out for Brussels accompanied by their father and Mary Taylor's brother.

Brussels

Belgium in 1842 was a newly independent country. Part of the Austro-Hungarian Empire until the French Revolution, it fell under French rule during Napoleon's reign. After the battle of Waterloo in 1815, the victorious powers, Prussia, Britain, Russia and Austria, established a kingdom uniting the Netherlands and Belgium, to be ruled by the Dutch king, William I of Orange. The Belgians, however, resented their subservience to the Dutch, from whom they were separated both by language and religion. The Netherlands were largely Protestant, whereas Belgium was predominantly Catholic. The French Revolution of 1830 proved a spur to Belgian liberal nationalists, who rioted on 24 August, and in September, with the help of the working-class population of Brussels, barricaded themselves in the lower part of the town, where they fought off the Dutch troops for four days. William I was ultimately forced to accept Belgian independence. A new constitutional monarch, Leopold of Saxe-Coburg, a son-in-law of George IV of England, was chosen. The constitution which the

Richard Redgrave, 'The Governess', 1844

new king swore to defend was the most liberal in Europe, guaranteeing freedom of the press, freedom of assembly, of education and of religion.

In 1842, when the Brontës arrived, Brussels was a cosmopolitan city, still partly medieval in character. The upper town was largely eighteenth century and neo-classical, containing many 'hôtels particuliers', parks, and the Palais Royal; the lower town retained an imprint of Spanish style with narrow streets where traders and shopkeepers flourished. The heart of the city held a pauper population in timbered tenements. The school where Charlotte and Emily were to reside, the Pensionnat Heger, lay in the town's middle stratum, surrounded by prosperous middle-class houses and other scholastic establishments.

M. and Mme Heger, who ran the school, were an unusual couple. Zoë Heger, née Parent, came from French émigré stock and had followed in the footsteps of her aunt, a former nun, who had fled France during the revolution of 1789, in setting up a girls' school. She was probably also influenced in her choice of career by her friend, Zoë de Gammond, who campaigned vigorously for improved educational opportunities for Belgian women. Constantin Heger, her husband, a teacher in the neighbouring boys' school, had a somewhat romantic background. His father, who had been a wealthy jeweller, lost his fortune in middle life. Constantin, thrown on his own resources, went to Paris as a solicitor's clerk in the hope of making his fortune in the law. But as Balzac showed in *Le Père Goriot*, it was virtually impossible for a young man in Paris to rise in the law without private means. Constantin therefore returned to Brussels in 1829 and took up teaching, for which he appears to have been naturally gifted. In 1830 he married Marie-Joseph Noyer (the model for Justine-Marie in *Villette*). At the outbreak of the Belgian Revolution he fought with the nationalists in the bloody September battle against the Dutch, where his brother-in-law was killed. Shortly after independence, in September 1833, his wife and child were both wiped out in a cholera epidemic. Three years later, Constantin married Zoë Parent. When Charlotte and Emily arrived in 1842, the Hegers had been married for six years, had three children and were subsequently to have three more. This family atmosphere of the Pensionnat Heger contrasted sharply with the schools run by maiden ladies to which the Brontës had been accustomed in England.

Charlotte and Emily met with considerable kindness from the Hegers, who early recognized their exceptional abilities and coped imaginatively with teaching grown women in a school designed for adolescents. The Brussels sojourn was to have a profound effect on Charlotte; it became crucial to both her intellectual and emotional development. Concerning Emily, we know that she attained a good standard of written French, became proficient on the piano, giving music lessons at the pensionnat, and that Constantin Heger considered her to possess a remarkable and forceful mind. But the experience of life in a foreign country does not appear to have influenced her writing. Both sisters were plunged into an alien environment at an age when their characters had already formed. The combination of French language and a Catholic culture drove these two Protestant Englishwomen back on themselves. Charlotte spoke in the most contemptuous terms, in her letters, of the Belgians at the school:

> If the national character of the Belgians is to be measured by the character of most of the girls in this school, it is a character singularly cold, selfish, animal and inferior . . . their principles are rotten to the core.
>
> (Charlotte Brontë to Ellen Nussey, July 1842)

Such animadversions against Belgian youth seem more than a little harsh. The tone of intolerance and disdain was a curious response to a world in which Charlotte had longed to immerse herself. Both she and Emily seem to have repulsed any attempts at friendliness. They ignored or despised the other teachers and found visiting in the English community in Brussels an intolerable social effort. One family, the Jenkinses, who invited them out on Sundays, found them so unbearably shy that it was a penance to have them. Emily almost never spoke, and Charlotte would turn her back on her audience before she could bring herself to say a word. They were by this time 24 and 26 years of age and completely unused to society.

It is evident that Emily and Charlotte were not sympathetic travellers. Unlike Charlotte's friend, Mary Taylor, who emigrated to New Zealand, and who in her old age went on walking tours of Switzerland, they were not afflicted with wanderlust. We have no record of Emily's impressions of Brussels, either in her poems or in *Wuthering Heights*. Charlotte in her letters appears to have been largely intolerant and negative, yet paradoxically Brussels proved to be the experience which galvanized her imaginative energy. *The Professor* and *Villette* show considerable sensitivity and affection for Belgium. M. Heger, whom she idolized, provided her with an intellectual model she could respect and was an example of a committed Catholic who did not conform to her anti-Papist preconceptions. However Charlotte does not seem to have understood much about his patriotic radicalism, nor to have been interested in Belgian politics. She treated the country like a toy kingdom. She emphasized the Catholic character of Belgium to the exclusion of its political and religious liberalism. These limited views can partly be explained by the fact that Emily and Charlotte led very circumscribed lives in Brussels. They did not move in 'society', aside from their abortive efforts to visit English families. Their lack of cosmopolitan ease may have been an exaggeration of, but not a deviation from, the habits of their fellow countrymen. The Brontës' provincialism and shyness merely exacerbated their national insularity.

Nevertheless, much that was positive emerged from their year in Brussels. There was the experience of a foreign capital and they found genuine intellectual stimulation in the school environment. M. Heger, charged with the further education of two highly intelligent, if eccentric, young women, seemed to have understood their hunger for learning and to have been a gifted teacher. Their progress in French language and literature under his guidance was rapid. He taught them to write an excellent French by reading them passages from favourite authors and then asking them to write essays in imitation of their styles. Some of Emily and Charlotte's *devoirs* survive. These show unusual literary and linguistic ability. It seems evident that they saw their essays not merely as tools for learning a language but as a means of imaginative expression, a part of their literary apprenticeship. M. Heger recognized their talent, though he did not entirely approve of their literary ambitions. And for Charlotte especially, her studies with M. Heger were her first contact with a mature critical intelligence.

The sisters passed the summer holidays of 1842 in Brussels, visiting the painting exhibition of that year. However, September brought the first of a series of misfortunes. They received news that William Weightman, who by his humour and charm had lightened the generally sombre tone of parsonage life, had died at Haworth at the age of 28. Then, at the end of September, Martha Taylor, Mary's sister, who was also at school in Belgium, near the Brontës at Koehelberg, fell ill of cholera and died on 12 October. Charlotte was particularly struck by the pathos of Martha's burial in a foreign churchyard, an episode she later transcribed in the death of Jessy Yorke in *Shirley*:

> Do you know this place? No, you never saw it; but you recognise the nature of these trees, this foliage, – the cypress, the willow, the yew. Stone crosses like these are not unfamiliar to you, nor are these dim garlands of everlasting flowers. Here is the place; green sod and a grey marble headstone – Jessy sleeps below. . . . Her death was tranquil and happy in Rose's guardian arms . . . the dying and the watching English girls were at that hour alone in a foreign country, and the soil of that country gave Jessy a grave.
>
> (Ch. 9)

Then on 29 October, their Aunt Branwell died and the sisters immediately journeyed home. Although Miss Branwell seemed to have engaged little of her nieces' affection, they did respect her. It was she who had made possible the Brussels journey and who, by a small legacy to each of the girls, gave them a measure of financial security. Her strict and gloomy religious views probably contributed to the religious melancholia from which Anne and Charlotte both suffered. She was not a sympathetic figure, but she honourably devoted her life to caring for her dead sister's children in a cold and inhospitable part of the world, as she considered Yorkshire to be.

The death of Miss Branwell entailed a reorganization of the parsonage domestic life. Emily stepped into the vacant post of housekeeper. Charlotte, meanwhile, was eager to return to Brussels to continue her studies and received cordial letters of encouragement from M. and Mme Heger, who urged that at least one of the sisters return. Anne, whose health had been a source of some concern, seemed stronger, and in her capacity as governess to the Robinson family at Thorp Green Hall, at Little Ouseburn near York, she obtained a post for Branwell, in 1843, as tutor. Charlotte, to her great joy, could therefore justify a return to Brussels and continue her education.

Her second year at the Pensionnat Heger began auspiciously. She was warmly received by the Hegers and offered the use of their family sitting room. She gave English lessons to M. Heger and his brother-in-law, and was invited out by Mary Taylor's cousins, the Dixons. Charlotte's ostensible reason for returning to Brussels was to qualify herself both in French and in German. But the underlying reason, which she dared not admit to herself, lay almost certainly in her feelings of attachment for M. Heger. Charlotte's childhood and adolescence, with their dreams of Byronic heroes, had in a sense prepared her for just such an unhappy relationship. Though M. Heger, irascible and small of stature, was scarcely the Zamorna figure of her adolescent fiction, nevertheless, as a relatively young man in his early thirties, he possessed great charm and powers of intellect. Married, and therefore unobtainable, he became the object of Charlotte's intense if unacknowledged admiration. There is no question whatever of any impropriety in this master–pupil relationship, or that either M. Heger or Charlotte fully recognized her infatuation for him. One of the ironies of Charlotte's position at the pensionnat was that it was precisely her strong sense of duty and her rigid ethical principles which did not allow her to admit the nature of her feelings for M. Heger. However, Mme Zoë Heger, more clear-sighted than either Charlotte or her husband, appears to have detected evidence of Charlotte's passionate feelings, and in order to avoid scandal, curtailed contact between M. Heger and his English pupil. Without being able to acknowledge to herself the source of the problem, Charlotte felt her isolation bitterly and resented Mme Heger as its cause. Her fictionalized portraits of Mme Heger, in *Villette* and *The Professor*, as a Machiavellian schemer, have a partial truth about them, but are quite unfair. It was only in the painful and tortured letters she wrote M. Heger after leaving Brussels that the unmistakable nature of her infatuation became explicit:

> I tell you frankly that I have tried meanwhile to forget you, for the remembrance of a person whom one thinks never to see again and whom, nevertheless, one greatly esteems, frets too much the mind; and when one has suffered that kind of anxiety for a year or two, one is ready to do anything to find peace once more. I have done everything; I have sought occupations; I have denied myself absolutely the pleasure of speaking about you – even to Emily; but I have been able to conquer neither my regrets nor my impatience. That indeed is humiliating – to be unable to control one's own thoughts, to be the slave of a regret, of a memory, the slave of a fixed and dominant idea which lords it over the mind. . . . So long as I believe you are pleased with me, so long as I have hope of receiving news from you, I can be at rest and not too sad. But when a prolonged and gloomy silence seems to threaten me with estrangement of my master – when day by day I await a letter and when day by day disappointment comes to fling me back to overwhelming sorrow, and the sweet delight of seeing your handwriting and reading your counsel escapes me as a vision that is vain, then fever claims me – I lose appetite and sleep – I pine away.
>
> (Charlotte Brontë to M. Heger, 18 Nov. 1845)

M. Heger did not reply to this, the last of Charlotte's letters addressed to him. In after years, the Hegers and their school continued to prosper. Mme Zoë Heger, however, could not forgive Charlotte for her fictional portrait of her as Mme Beck in *Villette*, and refused to see Mrs Gaskell when she visited Brussels. M. Constantin Heger, however, did receive her and provided a valuable glimpse of the sisters during their Belgian sojourn.

In her second year in Brussels, without Emily to support her, Charlotte became increasingly isolated. Part of her loneliness was self-imposed (she continued to despise the other teachers and the pupils and to shun their company) and partly brought on by Mme Heger's surveillance. 'It is a curious position', she wrote Emily, 'to be so utterly solitary in the midst of numbers.' Charlotte was plunged into a state of depression, similar to, but more intense than, the nervous illness she had suffered when teaching at Miss Wooler's. She passed a lonely summer holiday in the empty school and was driven on one occasion to confess to a Catholic priest, presumably in the desperation of overwhelming loneliness. This act from the ultra-Protestant Charlotte gives one some indication of her mental disorientation at the time. Finally, by December 1843, she could bear her isolation, homesickness and unacknowledged passion for M. Heger no longer, and returned to Haworth.

Though Charlotte's Brussels experience caused her great pain, it also immeasurably enriched her life. Always more restless than Emily, she absorbed from her stay in Brussels a whole range of social, cultural and emotional stimuli. Her very disappointments in love gave her an experience of the real as opposed to the ideal world of romance she had formerly nourished herself upon. Her Protestantism was confronted with a Catholic culture which she affected to despise, but which undoubtedly broadened her religious awareness. From M. Heger, she gained an understanding of the revolutionary enthusiasm which Napoleon had inspired, a view to counterbalance her father's hero worship of Wellington. For two years she lived in a cosmopolitan capital, visited galleries, museums and the theatre, all great events for the daughter of a Yorkshire parson. Whereas Emily's creative genius seems to have found sufficient stimulus in Haworth, for Charlotte, the Brussels journey was a spur to her intellectual and artistic development.

Return to Haworth

Meanwhile Branwell, employed as tutor to the Robinson family at Thorp Green, where Anne also held the post of governess, had been reproducing Charlotte's unhappy experience by falling in love with a married person, his employer's wife, Mrs Robinson. Unlike Charlotte, he believed his feelings reciprocated and declared his passion. When eventually dismissed by the Reverend Mr Robinson in July 1845, he abandoned himself to total despair. Anne too was obliged to quit her post. She made her exit from Thorp Green a few weeks before Branwell, no doubt foreseeing the approaching catastrophe. Branwell's melodramatic behaviour stands in marked contrast to Charlotte's heroic efforts to overcome her feelings for M. Heger. Biographers differ as to whether Branwell was encouraged by Mrs Robinson, or merely deluded by his vanity into believing she loved him. His sisters considered Branwell the injured party, convinced that Mrs Robinson had led him on. However, after his dismissal from Thorp Green, he never received any further encouragement from her. The effect of his infatuation, on himself and his family, was catastrophic. He gave way completely to drink and drugs, and the parsonage became the unwilling theatre for his ravings:

I begin to fear that he [Branwell] has rendered himself incapable of filling any respectable station in life, besides, if money were at his disposal he would use it to his own injury – the faculty of self-government is, I fear, almost destroyed in him.

(Charlotte to Miss Wooler, 30 June 1846)

All attempts at social life had to be abandoned by the sisters. Charlotte commented to Miss Wooler, 'It seems grievous indeed that those who have not sinned should suffer so largely.'

After her return from Brussels, Charlotte found Haworth a melancholy place. But by mid-1845, with Anne also back in Haworth, the family was at least reunited. Anne and Emily, freed from the burden of living among strangers, seem to have experienced a period of relative contentment even in the midst of Branwell's terrible last illness. Another significant change at Haworth in this year, 1845, lay in the arrival of a new curate, the Reverend Arthur Bell Nicholls. Charlotte, it emerges in her letters, did not like him but by July 1846 was already having to deny rumours that she was going to marry him.

Anne and Emily left four memoranda, dating from a more tranquil period which give a glimpse into life at the parsonage and of the personality of the writers. In her diary papers, Emily, particularly, shows an ease, a humour and a zest for life that one finds reflected in *Wuthering Heights* and which contrasts markedly with the grim persona she displayed in public. Her scorn of social conventions, her indifference to fashion, her refusal to make the slightest social effort, render her an enigmatic figure in biographical terms. The diary papers, however, are like a window opening on the sisters' ordinary life:

> This morning Branwell went down to Mr Driver's and brought news that Sir Robert Peel was going to be invited to stand for Leeds. Anne and I have been peeling apples for Charlotte to make an apple pudding ... Charlotte said she made puddings perfectly and she is of a quick but limited intellect. Taby said just now, Come Anne pillopatate (i.e. pill a potato) Aunt has come into the kitchen just now and said Where are your feet Anne Anne answered On the floor Aunt. . . . The Gondals are discovering the interior of Gaaldine. Sally Mosley is washing in the back kitchen.

(Diary paper, 24 Nov. 1834)

Or again:

> It is Friday evening, near nine o'clock – wild rainy weather. I am seated in the dining-room alone, having just concluded tidying our desk boxes, writing this document. Papa is in the parlour – aunt upstairs in her room. She has been reading *Blackwood's Magazine* to papa. Victoria and Adelaide [two geese] are

ensconced in the peat-house. Keeper [the dog] is in the kitchen – Hero [a hawk] in his cage.

(Emily Jane Brontë, 30 July 1841)

Anne's diary paper also reveals a quality central to the Brontës' life, the seamless relationship, on the one hand, between the concrete reality of housework, their pets, life with their servant, Tabitha, and, on the other hand, their private imaginative world. 'The Gondals still flourish as bright as ever.' Indeed the two worlds did not appear to be in competition, but to function on planes of equal reality. Whereas Charlotte, by her late twenties, felt the need to exorcise Angria from her life because it represented a diversion from reality, Emily and Anne's diary papers suggest a much easier relationship between the claims of the real and the imaginary.

The sisters' plan, to found a school at Haworth in the parsonage, failed in spite of a well-organized effort to publish a prospectus and to approach sympathetic patrons. The practicality of the scheme must always have been in question given the isolation of the site and the parsonage's restricted accommodation. In addition, Branwell's deteriorating condition, his constant and painful drunken scenes, meant that Haworth parsonage could not welcome anyone outside the family, certainly not young children. It was at this low point in the Brontë sisters' fortunes, with no prospects of employment, and Branwell a 'hopeless being' in Emily's words, that the three sisters decided to publish their poems. This venture inaugurated their careers as authors, consolidating their determination to become novelists.

Early publications

With all hope in Branwell lost, Charlotte, Emily and Anne's future lay entirely in their own hands; authorship was their attempt to escape a life of increasing economic insecurity and loneliness. In September 1845, Charlotte, always the most ambitious of the three, discovered some of Emily's poems, and decided to print them at their own expense with a selection of her own and Anne's poetry. By February 1846, a manuscript had been sent to the publishers, Aylott and Jones. The sisters adopted the pseudonyms of Ellis, Acton and Currer Bell, in the belief that their work would be taken more seriously if they were thought to be male. In the event, the edition, which appeared in 1846, received a unanimous lack of critical acclaim; only two copies were ever sold. What is significant about this otherwise unsuccessful venture was Charlotte's conviction that Emily, in particular, showed genius as a poet and her unshakeable belief that they would all become recognized authors. Shortly after the publication of *The Poems of Currer, Ellis and Acton*

Bell, the sisters sent three novels the rounds of the publishers. *The Professor*, Charlotte's first mature novel, was rejected, but *Wuthering Heights* and *Agnes Grey* were accepted by the house of William Newby in July 1847, and appeared in print in December 1847. Though Newby seems to have been an unscrupulous and slovenly publisher, the Brontës nevertheless were launched.

Before the publication of Emily and Anne's novels, Patrick Brontë, whose vision had been growing increasingly impaired, had an operation in August 1846 for the removal of cataracts. The operation, performed without anaesthetic and stoically endured, was entirely successful. Charlotte attended her father throughout his ordeal, sitting with him in his darkened room during the period of his recovery. Patrick's operation is further memorable because in the five weeks he and Charlotte were obliged to remain in seclusion in Manchester, Charlotte wrote a major portion of *Jane Eyre*. She submitted the completed manuscript to the firm of London publishers, Smith, Elder and Co., who had in fact refused *The Professor* but with such encouraging criticisms that Charlotte felt able to send them *Jane Eyre* in August 1847. Smith and Elder accepted it, and it appeared on 16 October 1847, before either of her sisters' novels, though theirs had been accepted first. Remarkably, their first novels all appeared within a few months of one another.

Charlotte was fortunate in her publishers, with whom she maintained a close friendship and correspondence until her death. It was through George M. Smith and his reader, William Smith Williams, that she was able to meet many of the major literary figures of the day. Her publishers kept her liberally supplied with new books and, by their correspondence, did much to mitigate her solitude in 'the torpid retirement where we live like dormice', as Charlotte described life in Haworth (letter to W. S. Williams, December 1847).

The year 1848 was one of recognition and even fame for the sisters. The novels created a stir, partly of a scandalous nature, as their subjects were thought too coarse for polite literature. *Jane Eyre* received the most favourable notices. Thackeray praised it, to Charlotte's great delight. *Wuthering Heights* tended to shock critics by its brutality; 'disagreeable' and 'diabolical' were adjectives lavished on it. As Charlotte later said, 'the immature but very real powers revealed in *Wuthering Heights* were scarcely recognised ; its import and nature were misunderstood' (Biographical Notice to *Wuthering Heights*, 19 Sept. 1850). *Agnes Grey*, a deliberately understated tale about governess life, took no critic by storm. Because the Brontës, not wishing to be stigmatized as 'lady writers', wrote under male pseudonyms, there was immense speculation as to their identity and sex and as to whether they were one person or three.

It was generally assumed that *Jane Eyre* and *Wuthering Heights* were by the same author. Thackeray, however, thought that Currer Bell must be a woman who had received a classical education. Others felt sure that no woman could write about the passions as Currer Bell had done in *Jane Eyre*. Not only did the sisters publish under pseudonyms, but they kept their secret from their immediate circle. It is not certain whether Branwell knew about their success; he may have been incapable of understanding anything by the time their novels appeared. Patrick only learned about the novels when Charlotte presented him with a copy of *Jane Eyre* after publication. He pronounced it as 'better than likely'. Charlotte did not even tell Ellen Nussey, her best friend, that she was the author of *Jane Eyre*. When Ellen asked her opinion of the book, she prevaricated by saying that she could not comment, because she could not get hold of a copy. She did send one to Mary Taylor in New Zealand, however.

It was in the context of considerable public speculation about the true identity of the Bells that in June 1848 Newby published Anne Brontë's *The Tenant of Wildfell Hall*. Not averse to publicity, Newby realized that he could capitalize on the fame of *Jane Eyre*, and suggested to the New York agents that *The Tenant* was also by Currer Bell, or that Currer and Acton were the same person. At this juncture, Charlotte's publishers, Smith and Elder, who also were in the dark about the identity of their now famous author, wrote to her suggesting that they publish a denial respecting Newby's claims. Smith and Elder's letter arrived at Haworth on 7 July 1848; Charlotte and Anne immediately concluded that full disclosure of their identity was the only proper course. They decided to travel to London immediately and, although Emily refused to accompany them, being even more opposed to publicity than her retiring sisters, Anne and Charlotte packed up a few necessaries in a parcel, walked four miles to Keighley in a July hail-storm and caught a train to Leeds and thence to London.

When we remember Anne and Charlotte's physical frailty and their shyness, there is something particularly touching in the thought of their descent on the capital. Once arrived in London, they stayed in an inn known to their father, the Chapter Coffee House, frequented by clergymen but unaccustomed to housing provincial ladies. Early on the following morning, they set off to Smith, Elder and Co., knowing nothing about them, save what Charlotte called their 'gentlemanly dealings'. The head of the firm was George Smith, who had, in 1846, taken over the business after his father's death. Anne and Charlotte presented themselves before the startled Mr Smith and his reader, Mr Williams, who had first discerned promise in *The Professor*. They handed Smith a letter addressed to Currer Bell as evidence of their identity. George

Smith described them as 'two rather quaintly dressed little ladies, pale faced and anxious looking' (*Cornhill Magazine*, Dec. 1900).

Though he wrote the account half a century after the event, George Smith remembered the visit vividly:

> This was the only occasion on which I saw Anne Brontë. She was a gentle, quiet, rather subdued person, by no means pretty, yet of a pleasing appearance.

Of Charlotte, Smith had even stronger strictures about her lack of beauty:

> She was very small . . . her head seemed too large for her body. She had fine eyes, but her face was marred by the shape of the mouth and by the complexion. There was little feminine charm about her; and of this fact she herself was uneasily and perpetually conscious.

Well might the sisters be 'uneasily and perpetually conscious' of their lack of striking beauty, when they knew from experience, as the evidence of George Smith's comments shows, that first judgements on them as authors would be based on their feminine desirability or lack of it. Charlotte, in particular, was convinced throughout her life that she could not attract other people, men or women. She was aware of her lack of physical stature, reputedly four foot six, and probably the result of poor nourishment as a child. Yet most testimony points to her capacity to charm when she chose to. Though painfully reserved, she became fluent, and even brilliant, when she was able to forget herself. From her schooldays onwards, her friends testified to her personal magnetism. 'Her quick and clear intelligence was delightful,' George Smith comments. On the other hand, she had no stock of small talk, so that a Mrs Brookfield who met Charlotte in London and who 'was perfectly at home in any society' said that 'Charlotte Brontë was the most difficult woman to talk to she had ever met'. She was too intense, too observant, too intellectual and too sincere to deal in the small change of social life.

This first, and for Anne, last trip to London was fraught with social events. George Smith called on them with his elegant sisters, and took them to the opera to hear Rossini's *Barber of Seville*; they visited Mr Williams at home, and saw the Royal Academy and the National Gallery. Then, after only two days, they journeyed back to Haworth, utterly exhausted, but secure in the knowledge that their separate identities as authors had been established.

3 The deaths of Branwell, Emily and Anne

This London journey, in retrospect, was the only bright moment of the year. Branwell had been deteriorating steadily. He habitually cadged money from his family for drink, was often in danger of arrest for debt, wrote abject letters to his cronies begging them to bring him gin, and regularly terrorized his family with his drunken fits. He died suddenly on 24 September 1848. His emaciation had been extreme for some time but he continued to frequent the village until two days before the end. His final prostration was so like earlier symptoms that his death took the family by surprise. Patrick was at first inconsolable at the loss of the son for whom he had had such extravagant and ill-founded hopes.

Whatever Branwell's artistic and intellectual talents, and they were certainly not negligible, their over-estimation by his family, particularly by his father and Aunt Branwell, made his repeated failures more painful and humiliating both for him and for them. The sense of social shame the family was forced to undergo during the period of Branwell's all too public roisterings may account for a good deal of the defensive pride exhibited by Charlotte, especially in relation to her father's curate, the Reverend Arthur Bell Nicholls, and indeed for the wall of silence within which Emily increasingly encased herself. The most explicit testimony to Branwell's decline comes from Anne. In advance of Branwell's death, the quiet, gentle woman observed by George Smith had already written, in *The Tenant of Wildfell Hall*, an indictment of the frightful toll taken by an inadequate and egotistical personality on those around him.

Charlotte's letter to Mr Williams, 2 October 1848, provides a searing epitaph for Branwell:

> I do not weep from a sense of bereavement, there is no prop withdrawn, no consolation torn away, no dear companion lost – but for the wreck of talent, the ruin of promise, the untimely dreary extinction of what might have been a burning and shining light. My brother was a year my junior. I had aspirations and ambitions for him once, long ago – they have perished mournfully. Nothing remains of him but a memory of errors and sufferings. There is such a bitterness of pity for his life and death, such a yearning for the emptiness of his whole existence as I cannot describe.

Branwell Brontë, 'The Gun Group' – the Brontë family

Endowed with talent, like his sisters, but unlike them spoiled by his father and aunt, Branwell bore the burden of the family's hopes and ambitions. He was to have been, in Charlotte's phrase, 'a burning and a shining light'. His incapacity to fulfil their excessive expectations, coupled with his indulgent education, unfitted him for a lesser rôle. Branwell's abortive affair with Mrs Robinson was characteristic of his behaviour in adversity. Whether or not he had been encouraged by Mrs Robinson, as his sisters believed, he was entirely unable to accept the disappointment of rejection, rendered especially bitter when Mrs Robinson refused to have any contact with him after her husband's death. Until that point, Branwell may have believed that they were separated by fate; after that it was clear that Mrs Robinson wanted none of him. Branwell even claimed that a codicil existed in Mr Robinson's will forbidding his wife to marry him, but no such codicil was ever found.

In his poetry, Branwell brooded on death and his incapacity to deal with life. (A 1983 edition of his poems, edited by Tom Winnifrith, gives evidence of his considerable abilities.) A sonnet entitled 'On Peaceful Death and Painful Life' and published in the *Halifax Guardian* expresses his despair and the incipient atheism that so troubled his father:

Why doest thou sorrow for the happy dead?
For, if their life be lost, their toils are o'er,
And woe and want can trouble them no more;
Nor ever slept they in an earthly bed
So sound as now they sleep, while dreamless laid
In the dark chambers of the unknown shore,
Where Night and Silence guard each sealed door.
So, turn from such as these thy drooping head,
And mourn the *Dead Alive* – whose spirit flies –
Whose life departs, before his death has come;
Who knows no Heaven beneath Life's gloomy skies,
Who sees no Hope to brighten up that gloom, –
'Tis *He* who feels the worm that never dies, –
The *real* death and darkness of the tomb.

(14 May 1842)

In a family where the sibling ties were as claustrophobically close as with the Brontës, Branwell's deterioration had important consequences for them all. Quite apart from the paralyzing social embarrassment he must have caused (the roistering of the vicar's son could scarcely pass unnoticed in a village the size of Haworth), the sisters suffered a psychological dislocation. Emily, though always loyal, finally admitted he was 'a hopeless being'. Anne painted his fictional portrait as a tyrannical and querulous alcoholic in *The Tenant of Wildfell Hall*, and Charlotte, who had

Branwell Brontë, a pen and ink sketch of Death summoning Branwell Brontë to a fight. Note what appears to be Haworth Church in the background.

been his partner in the Angrian Saga for many years, lost not just a brother but a part of her imaginative faith and idealism.

Branwell's death also produced dramatic physical effects on the family. Charlotte was prostrated and could not attend the funeral. Emily, who did attend, caught a bad cold which refused to disappear. After Branwell's burial in the Haworth churchyard, she never again left the house. Mrs Gaskell relays a graphic account, from the Brontës' former servant, Martha Brown, of Emily's rapid deterioration:

> 'Yes!' said Martha, 'They were all well when Mr Branwell was buried; but Miss Emily broke down the next week. We saw she was ill, but she would never own it, never would have a doctor near her, never would breakfast in bed – the last morning she got up, and she dying all the time – the rattle in her throat while she would dress herself; and neither Miss Brontë nor I dared to offer to help her. She died just before Christmas – you'll see the date there – '
>
> (Mrs Gaskell to John Forster, Sept. 1853)

As Martha's testimony indicates, Emily's decline, into what proved to be consumption, was swift. She refused to discuss her physical symptoms or to see a doctor. Always taciturn, she spoke scarcely at all now. Her stoicism, and her refusal to give way to her disease or even to speak of it makes her death as much of an enigma as her life. She died at about two in the afternoon on 19 December 1848. On the morning of her death she insisted on dressing, coming downstairs and feeding the dogs before collapsing on the sofa. Charlotte had rushed out to find her a spray of heather. She returned just in time to see her sister die. Emily was 30 years old.

Emily has teased biographers ever since her death. Silent, strong-willed and physically courageous, she gave little away about her feelings and her motivations. Her poems and her novel are her two testaments. It is generally accepted that whereas an autobiographical element tends to colour Charlotte's novels, Emily in *Wuthering Heights* achieved a remarkable degree of impersonality. The largely unfavourable contemporary reception of the book did, according to Charlotte, wound her:

> But Emily – poor Emily – the pangs of disappointment as review after review came out about 'Wuthering Heights' were terrible. Miss B. said she had no recollection of pleasure or gladness about 'Jane Eyre', every such feeling was lost in seeing Emily's resolute endurance, yet knowing what she felt.
>
> (Mrs Gaskell to John Forster, Sept. 1853)

A surviving letter from her publisher, Newby, speaks of another novel, but whether this was only planned or had been written, we do not know. No further manuscript has yet been proved to survive.

When Charlotte wrote of their loss to Mr Williams on Christmas Day she betrayed considerable bitterness:

> So I will not ask why Emily was torn from us in the fulness of our attachment, rooted up in the prime of her own days, in the promise of her powers; why her existence now lies like a field of green corn trodden down, like a tree in full bearing struck at the root. I will only say, sweet is rest after labour and calm after tempest, and repeat again and again that Emily knows that now.

The blow brought by Emily's death was soon repeated. By January 1849, there were fears for Anne's health. She, unlike Emily, consented to see a specialist, who came on 5 January to conclude that Anne, too, had an incurable case of tuberculosis. Though Anne received careful medical treatment, she only survived until May. In a last desperate attempt to stave off the inevitable, Charlotte and Ellen Nussey accompanied her to Scarborough, on 24 May, in the hope that the sea air and the place she loved, which she had described movingly in *Agnes Grey*, would restore her. The journey from Haworth, by way of York, to Scarborough, with the increasingly frail invalid, must have been a nightmare. Anne collapsed soon after reaching their lodgings in Scarborough and on the following Monday, 28 May 1849, she died. Charlotte arranged for her to be buried in the churchyard overlooking the bay. She was 29 years old at her death.

In the space of nine months the Brontë family had been virtually wiped out, leaving only Charlotte and Patrick. The beings with whom Charlotte had enjoyed the closest ties had disappeared. She found herself a single woman of 33, living in a remote Yorkshire parish with an ageing and grief-stricken father, to whose care she felt bound to attend, and deprived of her sisters who had given her solitary life its meaning. Mary Taylor had long felt alarm at Charlotte's probable future:

> I told her very warmly that she ought not to stay at home; that to spend the next five years at home in solitude and weak health would ruin her; that she would never recover it. Such a dark shadow came over her face when I said 'Think what you'll be five years hence!' that I stopped, and said, 'Don't cry, Charlotte!' She did not cry, but went on walking up and down the room, and said in a little while, 'But I intend to stay, Polly.'
>
> (to Mrs Gaskell, Feb. 1854)

John Martin, 'The Destruction of Tyre', 1840. 'A heavy tempest lay upon us; all hope that we should be saved was taken away . . . the ship was lost, the crew perished.' (Villette, Ch. 4)

Mrs Gaskell, who met Charlotte in 1850, only a year after this catalogue of bereavements, and who visited her at Haworth, was struck by the silent household where Mr Brontë rarely spoke to his daughter and where he always dined alone. In addition, the memory of Branwell's violent behaviour remained. 'You do not know what she had to bear and what she had to hear,' Mrs Gaskell wrote to Charles Kingsley (6 June 1857) replying to criticism of her *Life*, and evidently feeling that she had erred on the side of discretion rather than of frankness in her portrayal of the Brontë family.

4   Charlotte's later novels and marriage

Charlotte was immensely devoted to her father; in her letters the concern for his welfare was a constant and often painful preoccupation, but their sympathetic intercourse was limited. Mr Brontë had led a retired life for decades; his family misfortunes had thrown him further upon himself, and he had developed an eccentric and forbidding disposition. Branwell had always been his favourite child, and Charlotte was aware that she could not be the first in his affections, a lack of parental preference that may partially explain her lack of self-esteem. She remarked sadly of her father's feelings for Branwell: 'My poor father naturally thought more of his only son than of his daughters' (Charlotte Brontë to William S. Williams, 2 Oct. 1848).

Charlotte found her return to Haworth, after burying Anne at Scarborough, a desolating experience:

> I felt that the house was all silent, the rooms were all empty. I remembered where the three were laid, – in what narrow dark dwelling – never more to reappear on earth. So the sense of desolation and bitterness took possession of me.
>
> (Charlotte Brontë to Ellen Nussey, 23 June 1849)

Yet the year 1848–49, which had seen the death of her brother and two sisters, also saw the publication of her second novel, *Shirley*. Charlotte's ability to tap the sources of her imaginative life may have enabled her to survive the losses she experienced. *Shirley*, published in October 1849, had been largely written in the previous calamitous year. The first volume was probably completed before Branwell's death, the latter two volumes punctuated by the loss of her sisters. The character of the eponymous heroine came increasingly to be identified with Emily and the novel was finished in the shadow of Anne's death, so that Caroline Helstone became, in the end, a loving portrait of this last sister. Though less structurally coherent than her other work, *Shirley* contains some of the most compelling social commentary of Charlotte Brontë's novels.

The next five years were for Charlotte a time of literary success and public recognition, though she found social occasions a great strain, especially when she was invited to meet the famous. Throughout her London visits, she was perpetually nervous of being viewed as a celebrity. Nevertheless, she made five separate

G. Richmond, Charlotte Brontë, 1850

trips to the capital where she met, among others, such eminent literary figures as Thackeray and George Henry Lewes. She heard Cardinal Wiseman preach and visited the Great Exhibition. On one occasion her publisher, George Smith, and his mother showed her Edinburgh. She visited, and was visited by, her friends Ellen Nussey and Miss Wooler, and she made the last major friendships of her life, those of Elizabeth Gaskell and Harriet Martineau.

Charlotte met Elizabeth Gaskell on a visit to the Lake District in August 1850, where she was the guest of Sir James and Lady Kay-Shuttleworth, large landowners who lived not far from Haworth and who had made earnest efforts to cultivate her. Charlotte, normally painfully slow to make friends, was immediately drawn to Mrs Gaskell. Their friendship survived a certain amount of literary competition and received its full tribute in Mrs Gaskell's *Life*. Charlotte was even able to overcome her self-mistrust and shyness sufficiently to visit Mrs Gaskell at her home in Manchester and to receive visits from her at Haworth.

Charlotte's relations with Harriet Martineau, the philanthropist, novelist, economist and free-thinker, were more chequered. She first met her in December 1849. Martineau invited Charlotte for a visit to her home at Ambleside in December 1850, an occasion which Charlotte described with gusto. She was much struck with Martineau's strength of character, the magnificent organization of her household, her moral fervour and her energy and appetite for work. She seemed to Charlotte to suffer from none of the nervous debility of which she herself was so conscious. However, she was deeply shocked by Martineau's advocacy of atheism. A belief in immortality was all that reconciled Charlotte to the early deaths of her brother and sisters. When Harriet Martineau made a public profession of her atheism, Charlotte broke with her.

In 1851, Mr Taylor, the business manager of Smith and Elder, whom Charlotte had known for a number of years, visited her at Haworth before setting off for an extended stay in India, and proposed marriage. Although Charlotte admired his intellectual qualities, she seems to have been physically repelled by him. In any event, she refused his proposal. This was her third offer of marriage: the first had been from a boorish Irish curate and the second from Helen Nussey's brother, Henry. Yet she continued to be convinced that she was unattractive to men and was destined to be an 'old maid'. A preoccupation with spinsterhood, and all it implied within Victorian society, allied to her fierce pride and a horror of 'husband seeking', emerges as one of the recurrent themes of her letters.

One of the most interesting aspects of Charlotte Brontë's short career as a major novelist was her capacity to impress her contemporaries with her intellectual powers in spite of an absence of social ease. Her letters to Ellen Nussey, to whom she could confide her self-doubt, chronicle her dread of social occasions. The letters dwell on her frequent bouts of sickness and migraine, referred to as 'bilious attacks', her fits of depression in the solitude of Haworth, and her refusal to find much alleviation by visiting the many friends who urged her to seek change and companionship. These conditions operating on a nervous, highly-strung woman committed to caring for her father, coupled with her dread of society, make her rapid development as a writer and as an intellectual the more remarkable. We are fortunate in having her correspondence, which deals not so much with the process of writings, as with her interests in a variety of contemporary topics; social, political and religious. Though Charlotte's physical and social development may have been stunted by a life of deprivation, she throve intellectually and culturally in the period from 1846 to 1855.

In 1851 Charlotte began what was to be her last novel, *Villette*, based on her Brussels experience. Here she succeeded in transposing the legacy of her passion for M. Heger into fictional form. In a review of the novel (*Daily News*, 3 Feb. 1853) Harriet Martineau spoke of a sense of the novel's 'pervading pain'. Given the personal desolation that afflicted Charlotte at this period, the pervading pain is less astonishing than the imaginative energy that emanates from the novel. *Villette* can, on one level, be considered a study of the corrosive effects of loneliness, which haunted Charlotte from the early conviction she developed that she would never marry, to the time of writing the novel in the now empty parsonage. *Villette's* introspective and morbid atmosphere may possibly also be based on Charlotte's even earlier perception of parental rejection in favour of Branwell. The novel's composition was constantly interrupted by bouts of severe depression and by illness. Her publishers became worried about her difficulties in finishing it. She eventually submitted *Villette* in November of the following year, 1852. Smith and Elder published it in January 1853.

In December 1852, while the manuscript of *Villette* was still with her publishers, her father's curate, the Reverend Arthur Bell Nicholls, made her a proposal of marriage. Nicholls, an Irishman like her father, had been his curate for the previous six years, and a sympathetic witness to the series of tragedies which pursued the family. Charlotte's earliest mention of Arthur Nicholls in a letter to Ellen Nussey was dismissive, and her portrait of the local curates in *Shirley*, for one of whom Nicholls was a model, was hilarious and disrespectful. Mr Nicholls is said to have laughed when he read *Shirley* out loud to Mr Brontë, deriving particular pleasure from the satire on the curates:

Mr Donne and his guests, as I have said, are at dinner; Mrs Gale waits on them, but a spark of the hot kitchen fire is in her eye. She considers that the privilege of inviting a friend to a meal occasionally, without additional charge, . . . has been quite sufficiently exercised of late. The present week is yet but at Thursday, and on Monday, Mr Malone, the curate of Briarfield, came to breakfast and stayed dinner; on Tuesday, Mr Malone and Mr Sweeting of Nunnely, came to tea, remained to supper, occupied the spare bed, and favoured her with their company to breakfast on Wednesday morning; now on Thursday, they are both here at dinner and she is almost certain they will stay all night. 'C'en est trop,' she would say, if she could speak French.

(*Shirley*, Ch. 1)

Arthur Bell Nicholls was a High Church clergyman, a Puseyite, unbending in his religious opinions, and not a man of particularly broad intellectual interests. On the other hand, he had shown great tact and sensitivity over the Brontës' difficulties. He had been a support from the time of Branwell's dismissal from Thorp Green; he had officiated at Emily's funeral, and had been a silent and devoted admirer of Charlotte's for years. But until he blurted out his proposal to her, one December evening, she apparently had little idea of the intensity of his attachment, his sense of certain rejection, nor of his misery. Mr Nicholls, stolid-looking as he was, bore many of the marks of internal suffering and loneliness undergone by Charlotte's own heroines. This discovery appears to have startled her and provoked her compassion. Charlotte, too, had known what it was to love without any hope.

Though Charlotte judged herself not in love with Mr Nicholls, she was spared the embarrassment of a refusal by her father's reaction. Patrick's response seemed excessive even by the dictatorial standards of the Victorian paterfamilias. When informed of Mr Nicholls' proposal, Mr Brontë, according to Charlotte, threw himself into a 'towering rage'. Although his daughter was 37, and sought for in marriage by a clergyman, Patrick behaved as though she were an unprotected minor wooed by a rake. Charlotte sent a dramatic account of this spectacular family row to Ellen:

Agitation and anger disproportionate to the occasion ensued. If I had loved Mr Nicholls and had heard such epithets applied to him as were used, it would have transported me past patience; as it was my blood boiled with a sense of injustice, but papa worked himself into such a state not to be trifled with, the veins of his temples started up like whipcord, and his eyes became suddenly bloodshot. I made haste to promise that Mr Nicholls should on the morrow have a distinct refusal.

(Charlotte Brontë to Ellen Nussey, 15 Dec. 1852)

Reverend Arthur Bell Nicholls (top) and a portrait presumed to be of Charlotte Brontë, c. 1854–55 (bottom)

By a stroke of irony, the effect of Mr Brontë's intemperate response led Charlotte to pity Mr Nicholls, who was suffering agonies through no fault of his own, and was being vilified by Mr Brontë, into the bargain, for having made an honest proposal. Neither Charlotte nor Mr Nicholls seems to have considered defying Mr Brontë, which gives one some indication of the power he exercised over his family. 'Conscience will not suffer me to take one step in opposition to papa's will,' Charlotte wrote, somewhat melodramatically to Ellen on 6 April 1853. Though she felt that her father was deeply unjust to Mr Nicholls, she did not consider the former's behaviour extraordinary. It was left to her sceptical friend, Mary Taylor, to refer to Mr Brontë in this context as 'that selfish old man'. Mr Brontë's anger made it impossible for Nicholls to remain as his curate at Haworth, and he therefore found another curacy, leaving Haworth in May 1853, not before, however, breaking down during a church service and sobbing bitterly when he took leave of Charlotte. Mrs Gaskell offers a telling version of this domestic drama:

> To hear her description of the conversation with her father when she quietly insisted on her right to see something more of Mr Nicholls was really fine. Her father thought that she had a chance of somebody higher or at least farther removed from poverty. She said 'Father, I am not a young girl, not a young woman even – I never was pretty. I now am ugly. At your death I shall have £300 besides the little I have earned myself – do you think there are many men who would serve seven years for me?. . . The sightless old man stood up and said solemnly 'Never. I will never have another man in this house', and stalked out of the room. For a week he never spoke to her. She had not made up her mind to accept Mr Nicholls and the worry on both sides made her ill – then the old servant interfered, and asked him, sitting blind and alone, 'if he wished to kill his daughter?', and went up to her and abused Mr Nicholls for not having 'more brass'.

(Mrs Gaskell to John Forster, 17 May 1854)

Events were to work in Mr Nicholls' favour. Mr Brontë, now very frail, partially sighted and consequently needing reliable help with his parish duties, was forced to take on a new, and as it transpired, unsatisfactory curate. Prodded by Charlotte, he almost began to regret Mr Nicholls' departure. In the meantime, Nicholls met secretly with Charlotte in January, and in April they obtained Mr Brontë's consent to their marriage. The latter's intransigence crumbled when he belatedly recognized Mr Nicholls' usefulness.

More surprising, perhaps, than Mr Brontë's consent was Charlotte's. Her feelings towards Arthur Nicholls throughout the period of their courtship continued to be ambivalent. All her Romantic models, dating from the Byronic figure of Zamorna in her juvenilia, made Mr Nicholls' stolidity and intellectual narrowness seem antipathetic. Yet she had become convinced of his overwhelming loyalty, devotion and moral worth. He was, for example, prepared to remain Mr Brontë's curate at a salary of £90 per annum rather than to take up an independent living of £200, offered by the Kay-Shuttleworths, in order to ensure that Mr Brontë, by his services, could retain his living throughout his life. By the expedient of her marriage, Charlotte gave her father financial security. Mr Nicholls did not meet Charlotte's Romantic criteria, nor was he as masterful as M. Heger, but in marrying Arthur Nicholls, she showed herself capable of shedding her old illusions about Romantic love. 'If ever I marry', Charlotte had written to Ellen Nussey in their early youth, 'it must be in that light of adoration that I will regard my husband' (12 March 1839). This youthful idealism had given way to a more just appreciation of Mr Nicholls' human qualities.

Ellen Nussey, indeed, rather disapproved of Charlotte's proposed match, considering, like Mr Brontë, that Charlotte should have made a more brilliant matrimonial choice. Mary Taylor, however, felt otherwise. She attacked Charlotte's excessive sense of duty to her father and the puritanical ethic which both she and Ellen cultivated on the subject of marriage:

> You talk wonderful nonsense about Charlotte Brontë in your letter. What do you mean about 'Bearing her position so long' and 'enduring to the end'? and still better, 'bearing our lot, whatever it is'? If it's Charlotte's lot to be married shouldn't she bear that too? or does your strange morality mean that she should refuse to ameliorate her lot when it is in her power? How would she be inconsistent with herself in marrying? Because she considers her own pleasure? If this is new for her to do, it is high time she began to make it more common. It is an outrageous exaction to expect her to give up her choice in a matter so important, and I think her to blame in having been hitherto so yielding that her friends can think of making such an impudent demand.

> (Mary Taylor to Ellen Nussey, 24 Feb. 1854)

Mary Taylor had always been impatient of the fatalism implicit in the Victorian ethos of duty as it applied to women.

The marriage took place on 29 June 1854, at 8 o'clock in the morning, to accommodate the wedding journey. Ellen Nussey and Miss Wooler were invited to Haworth as the only guests. At the last moment, Mr Brontë, who was due to give his daughter away, refused to attend the ceremony. It was his final protest. The situation was saved by Miss Wooler, who agreed to give away the bride. Immediately after the wedding breakfast, the couple set off for Wales and a tour of Ireland to visit Arthur's relations. There Charlotte was introduced to her new Irish family, who ran a school at Banagher and who had adopted their nephew, Arthur, as a boy. The school was housed in an elegant Palladian mansion. The whole tenor of life at Banagher was one of hospitality and ease. Charlotte, delighted with her surroundings and her new relations, began to realize her husband's modesty in rarely speaking of his quite distinguished background when among the Brontës' humble circumstances at Haworth:

> My dear husband too appears in a new light here in his own country. More than once I have had deep pleasure in hearing his praises on all sides. Some of the old servants and followers of the family tell me I am a most fortunate person 'for that I have got one of the best gentlemen in the country'.
>
> (to Miss Wooler, 10 July 1854)

Charlotte's married life was short and much of it passed in a state of severe illness. Nevertheless, in the first months of her marriage her health and spirits both improved; she began to make jokes in her letters and to show pride in, and affection for, her husband. Her time was now filled with family and parish matters. Yet her final illness and decline were as dramatic as those of her sisters. In November 1854, she fell prey to a cold caught during an adventurous but drenching walk. Then, towards the end of January, she began to suffer from violent and continuous sickness, and became terribly emaciated. On 17 February, their old servant, Tabitha Aykroyd, fell ill and died. Charlotte by this time was too weak to attend the funeral. She herself died on 31 March 1855, at the age of 39. Her death certificate gave phthisis, or tuberculosis, as the cause of death. Mrs Gaskell suggests pregnancy as a contributing cause.

An interesting discussion of Charlotte's last illness may be found in John Maynard's *Charlotte Brontë and Sexuality* in which he analyses all the evidence about her illness and submits it to medical interpretation. According to Maynard, there can be no certainty that Charlotte was pregnant, though she may have thought she was. Her death was probably caused by a wasting disease, such as tuberculosis, rather than by acute morning sickness, as has often been suggested. The very high incidence of tuberculosis in the nineteenth century, and the family predisposition to the disease, make this likely. Her illness has provoked a great deal of psychological interpretation by psychoanalytic and feminist critics in particular, though Emily and Anne have also been studied from this perspective. At its most extreme, varieties of such criticism have reduced the Brontës to a cluster of neurotic symptoms, within a repressive Victorian society, to be pitied for the limitations of their lives and their vision. Though the Brontës had their share of human suffering, they do not stand in need of critical patronage. There is even an implicitly anti-feminist tinge to the suggestion that had the Brontës been 'normal' women they would not have written novels. In particular the view that gained considerable currency since 1972 from an article by Dr Philip Rhodes ('A Medical Appraisal of the Brontës', *The Brontë Society Transactions*) that Charlotte's last illness was psychosomatic, was adduced as proof that Charlotte was severely neurotic and rejected marriage and children for death. Such an interpretation seems entirely perverse and unsustainable on medical or other grounds. Indeed, if we consider the evidence of Charlotte's letters alone, though they often speak of depression, hypochondria and bilious attacks, they also give the picture of a clear-minded woman, reflecting deeply on a multitude of topics, and by no means neurotically obsessed with herself. There is, in particular, a refreshing openness and common sense in her correspondence with Miss Wooler.

On a domestic level, Charlotte also derived considerable pleasure from the details of ordinary life; new curtains for the sitting room, wallpaper for her husband's study. It is pleasant to think that, though her father may have actually or psychologically played the rôle of the tyrant, as an adult, Charlotte was not unduly tyrannized over. Not only did she travel widely, write novels, mix in London society and form distinguished literary friendships, but at the parsonage, too, she actually broadened her territory. Before her marriage she paid, from her own earnings, to have alterations done to the house. She had the rooms she herself particularly used, her bedroom and the downstairs dining room, enlarged. A pragmatist might say these changes made the parsonage a pleasanter place. A psychologist could suggest that Charlotte was asserting her rights in the house dominated by her father, and formerly by her brother. Either interpretation allows one to suppose that Charlotte was not entirely downtrodden.

The privacy which the Brontës had maintained, both by choice and by force of circumstance, was invaded soon after Charlotte's death. Wild rumours about the sisters, particularly about Charlotte, began to circulate, and, largely to quell them, Mr Brontë decided to ask Mrs Gaskell to write an authorized life. The decision was opposed by Mr Nicholls, who had a fiercely protective attitude towards his wife's memory. Mrs Gaskell's biography, scrupulous in its research for its time (she visited all the places Charlotte had been, most notably Brussels, and met M. Heger), is a brilliant and moving portrait of her friend, though inevitably it has some distortions. We have noted Miss Wooler's irritation, coupled

Haworth Parsonage, c. 1860. 'The sitting room of the parsonage looks in to the church-yard filled with graves.' (Mrs Gaskell, 25 August 1850)

with an acknowledgement that Mrs Gaskell knew her subject admirably. Mr Brontë suffered perhaps unduly at her hands, and Emily emerged as a shadowy and unsympathetic figure. Mrs Gaskell's account of Branwell's imbroglio with the Robinson family, and her uncritical condemnation of Mrs Robinson as the sole author of Branwell's troubles, led to legal action by Mrs Robinson and the withdrawal of the first edition. Nevertheless, *The Life* is a remarkable work, evincing Mrs Gaskell's admiration for Charlotte's moral courage and for her capacity to endure both physical and psychological suffering.

Mr Brontë and Arthur Bell Nicholls lived on in the parsonage for six more years. There is a certain irony in Mr Brontë, who had worried obsessively about his health, who ate alone because he did not wish his digestion troubled by childish noise, and who wore an elaborate stock wound round his throat to ward off bronchitis, living to the ripe age of 84, whereas his wife and children all died before the age of 40. After Mr Brontë's death, 7 June 1861, Mr Nicholls was refused the living at Haworth. He accordingly returned to Ireland where he remarried and settled down as a farmer, preserving Charlotte Brontë's portrait by Richmond, many letters and the juvenilia. Even during Mr Brontë's lifetime, the family passed into legend. The peculiar strangeness and appeal of the Brontës' experience vindicates Mrs Gaskell's initial reaction that we noted at the beginning of the Introduction: 'Such a life as Miss Brontë's I never heard of before.'

Part Two
Contextual Background

5   History and politics

The Brontës were born into the post-Napoleonic era in the after-
math of Waterloo. Europeans living after 1815 inherited a world
where rapid social change and the ever-present possibility of
revolution coexisted within a climate of political reaction. In their
juvenilia, the Brontës celebrated the glorious exploits of the Napoleonic Wars from both the French and English sides; they
worshipped Wellington and shared their father's hatred of social
unrest. Their political and historical consciousness was deeply
conservative. Yet their father, Patrick Brontë, who held unbending
Tory principles, was himself a living contradiction to a static and
traditionalist view of society, having risen from the humblest
circumstances to relative comfort and gentility as Rector of
Haworth. In that sense, he was an advertisement for the possibility
of rising through merit in defiance of humble birth, like the
dreaded Napoleon himself. The idea of meritocracy and a defence
of individual worth, regardless of birth, informs all the Brontë
novels, in spite of their political conservatism, though it is most
striking perhaps in *Jane Eyre*, which was attacked by contemporary
critics for its subversive and egalitarian implications. The Toryism
the Brontë children imbibed from Patrick Brontë involved, among
other things, a belief in the right of the new manufacturing mill-
owning classes to rule their labour-force as the landed gentry had
traditionally ruled their agricultural workers. But these ideas of
authority, obedience and resistance to social change were often
contradicted in their own experience. Assertion of equality is a
feature of their novels in an age when 'equality' and 'democracy'
were thought of as dangerous words. As Robert Moore, the mill
owner, argues in *Shirley*:

> I know so well that human nature is human nature everywhere,
> whether under tile or thatch, and that in every specimen of
> human nature that breathes, vice and virtue are ever found
> blended, in smaller or greater proportions, and that the propor-
> tion is not determined by station.
>
> (Ch. 5)

Haworth, though rural, was relatively close to the newly
expanding manufacturing centres of Leeds and Bradford. Avid
readers of the local newspapers, the Brontës were in touch with the
major class and industrial conflicts of the day and, as they grew
up, observed a society undergoing transformation both industrially
and agriculturally. Though the hill farmers around Haworth were

not typical of large-scale British agriculture, the poverty of most of the common people was a central fact of life there as elsewhere. Haworth had a high infant and adult mortality rate, thanks in a large part to its lack of a proper water supply. Outlying farmers refused to pay rates to supply a village water system from which they themselves would not benefit. It was left to Mrs Gaskell in 1858 to send £100 to Mr Nicholls from the profits of *The Life of Charlotte Brontë* for a well in the village: 'I should like a village pump; they are terribly off for water' (to George Smith, 29 Dec. 1856).

The seeming rural stagnation around Haworth was deceptive; here, as in most of Britain, agricultural life was in transition at the turn of the century. In the previous decade, during the Napoleonic blockade of British ships, British farmers had enjoyed a boom, thanks to the enforced lack of foreign competition. Peace brought with it the fear of a slump in agricultural prices as cheaper imports flooded into Britain. The landed interest, massively over-represented in Parliament before the 1832 Reform Bill, succeeded in passing the Corn Laws in 1815. These effectively protected the farming lobby by prohibiting imports of corn, with the result that prices remained high. Low agricultural wages, coupled with the enclosure of common land, in progress since the mid-eighteenth century and largely completed by 1815, meant that farm labourers could no longer supplement their wages by farming on common land. Formerly, rural poverty had been compensated for to some extent by poor relief, paid from the rates, under the so-called 'Speenhamland system', named after a Berkshire village where in 1795 magistrates had first attempted to relieve the 'industrious poor' according to family size and the prevailing price of corn. After 1815, the conjunction of the Corn Laws and the Speenhamland system meant that farmers were effectively subsidized twice. Poor relief paid part of their wage bills from the rates and the Corn Laws kept prices high. Agricultural poverty and unemployment increased remorselessly, at the same time as land use became more efficient, requiring fewer labourers. The migration of landless labourers from the country to the cities, which, like Leeds and Bradford, seemed to mushroom overnight, fed the revolution in industrial practice then under way. In part, the industrial revolution in manufacturing, and the growth of the factory system were made possible by the economic pressures leading to rural depopulation.

The Brontës were unusual in writing about their rural environment without nostalgia. Their novels do not sentimentalize the countryside or rural life. *Wuthering Heights*, in particular, which was judged so 'coarse' when it was first published, shows a somewhat Hobbesian view of country manners where life is likely to be nasty and brutish. None of the Brontës could have imagined a cosy pastoral in their Yorkshire community. The facts of hill farming life were often harsh: isolated farmsteads, rigorous weather conditions and a rural populace struggling to survive.

The agricultural interest, which triumphed during the Napoleonic Wars, militated not only against the poor but also against the new industries, especially in cotton manufacture. Prices were kept high at home. Other countries refused to buy British manufactured goods because Britain practised protectionism in food imports. The Free Trade movement launched by industrialists for repeal of the Corn Laws finally achieved its aim in 1847. Opening British markets to imports meant that corn-producing countries, enriched by exports to Britain, would buy British products. But the divergence in interest between landowners and the new manufacturing sector was a major feature of political life in the early part of the nineteenth century. One theme of *Shirley* is the struggle to reconcile the landed and the manufacturing interest, a solution not very plausibly achieved in the context of the novel. However, Robert Moore, who attempts to develop a modern manufacturing system for his cloth mill, epitomizes the difficulties which industrialists faced prior to the repeal of the Corn Laws:

> his aim had been to effect a radical reform, which he had executed as fast as his very limited capital would allow; and the narrowness of that capital, and consequent check on his progress, was a restraint which galled his spirit sorely.
>
> (Ch. 2)

In manufacturing, conflict also grew between the mine and mill owners, anxious to gain maximum profits, and the workers in those industries whose wages and terms of employment were subject to no kind of regulation. At a time of high unemployment, employers could dictate their own terms. They paid minimum wages and had few qualms in laying off workers when business was poor. Unlike the landed gentry, who at least in theory had had some feeling of obligation for the welfare of their agricultural workforce, the manufacturers and industrialists recognized no bond except what Carlyle termed 'the cash nexus'. Robert Moore is again an example of such a manufacturer:

> Not being a native, nor for any length of time a resident of the neighbourhood, he did not sufficiently care when the new inventions threw the old work-people out of employ: he never asked himself where those to whom he no longer paid weekly wages found daily bread; and in this negligence he only resembled thousands besides, on whom the starving poor of Yorkshire seemed to have a closer claim.
>
> (Ch. 2)

Though *Shirley* is set during the Napoleonic Wars, it chronicles the general problems of industrial reorganization and unemployment characteristic of much of the century. Ultimately, the combination of low wages and a large pool of unemployed created the conditions for both industrial expansion and political unrest in the nineteenth century.

Patrick Brontë had first-hand experience of such unrest when he was minister at Hartshead, Yorkshire, in 1812, before his marriage. His ministry at Hartshead coincided with the period of the Luddite riots, involving extensive sabotage of the new mill machinery which, it was realized, would throw thousands out of work by replacing hand-loom weavers with mechanical looms. The new machines and the mill owners became the focus of bitter hostility from a threatened labour force. Outbreaks of violence occurred in 1811 in Nottingham and spread to Leicestershire, Derbyshire and Lancashire. Parliament introduced a bill making frame breaking (that is, the destruction of the new looms), a crime punishable by death. The clergy, Patrick among them, who saw themselves as upholding the interests of the state, denounced frame breaking from the pulpit.

The most important mill near Hartshead, at Rawfolds, was owned by a manufacturer named William Cartwright, who became the focus for local discontent. He decided to stock his mill with the new machinery and brought in a small number of troops to help guard it. In the event, he was able to ward off an attack by some one hundred rioters with a force of ten well-armed soldiers. Cartwright's aim was to pre-empt an attack and defeat Luddite resistance in the region. He was largely successful. In the attack on his mill, two badly wounded rioters were captured and subsequently died. Others unknown, who managed to flee, later died and were secretly buried. It was at this juncture that Patrick Brontë came into contact with the rioters. He witnessed a clandestine burial in his own churchyard at Hartshead but forbore to inform on those involved. In this he showed an almost uncharacteristic compassion for the sufferings of the rebels, as he would have considered them. He may also have been influenced by a perception of how his flock would regard him should he turn informer. Though his previous sermons had denounced violence, they had at the same time expressed some sympathy for the poor; poverty was something that he knew at first hand from his boyhood in Ireland. Patrick was far less extreme in his Toryism than his neighbour, the preacher Hammond Roberson, who declaimed violently against the rioters. Mary Taylor remarked that 'old Roberson said he would wade to the knees in blood rather than that the then state of things should be altered'. Patrick Brontë and Roberson were jointly transformed by Charlotte into the figure of

Mathewson Helstone in *Shirley*, who is shown as absolutely rigid in response to a situation of social crisis. The story, of the attack on Cartwright's Mill, which Patrick told and retold to his children, until it became a family legend, emerges as the central dramatic incident of *Shirley*. (Ch. 2)

The significance of this family anecdote lies in Charlotte's response to it; she understood that the conflicts expressed in a local battle were typical of those thrown up by the Industrial Revolution. *Shirley* conflates the past of the Luddite riots of 1812 with contemporary social unrest in the 1840s. Class conflict, which Charlotte feared, but which is also shown as having justice on the side of the poor, is at the core of the novel's sense of struggle.

Low wages, unemployment and the growth of a displaced class of landless poor posed a continual threat of insurrection and of revolution in the early years of the century. The Peterloo Massacre of 1819, when a crowd of some 60,000 people listening to the Radical orator, Hunt, were charged by mounted soldiers, killing 11 people and wounding 400, was one index of the repressive climate of the period. Though the Brontës' political sympathies lay with the ruling class, the novels also show evidence of other feelings. *Shirley* conveys an ambivalent message; for all her sympathy with working-class poverty, Charlotte could not alter her Tory, middle-class outlook. But she represented the legitimacy of other views. In the attack on the mill, the rioters are described from the perspective of the genteel reader, as terrifying but not despised:

A crash-smash-shiver-stopped their whispers. A simultaneously-hurled volley of stones had saluted the broad front of the mill, with all its windows; and now every pane of every lattice lay in shattered and pounded fragments. A yell followed this demonstration – a rioters' yell – a North-of-England – a Yorkshire – a West Riding – a West Riding-clothing-district-of-Yorkshire rioters' yell. You never heard that sound, perhaps, reader? So much the better for your ears – perhaps for your heart; since, if it rends the air in hate to yourself, or to the men or principles you approve, the interests to which you wish well, Wrath wakens to the cry of Hate: the Lion shakes his mane, and rises to the howl of the Hyena: Caste stands up, ireful, against Caste; and the indignant, wronged spirit of the Middle Rank bears down in zeal and scorn on the famished and furious mass of the Operative Class. It is difficult to be tolerant – difficult to be just – in such moments. (Ch. 19)

In spite of the post-Napoleonic spirit of reaction, Britain underwent a series of gradual reforms in the nineteenth century. The claims of the new middle-class manufacturing interest, depicted in

Shirley, were the first to be answered. Parliamentary reform, allowing the new manufacturing areas of the Midlands and the North to be represented in Parliament, was achieved by the Reform Bill of 1832. Though the bill had a property qualification and excluded women, it was the beginning of more democratic parliamentary representation. The young Brontës, as good Tories, were opposed to the passage of the Reform Bill. Charlotte, aged 15, wrote solemnly to Branwell about the 1831 Bill, which had been defeated in the Lords, before being reintroduced and successfully passed in the following year:

> Lately I had begun to think that I had lost all the interest which I used formerly to take in politics, but the extreme pleasure I felt at the news of the Reform Bill's being thrown out by the House of Lords, and the expulsion or resignation of Earl Grey . . . convinced me that I have not as yet lost *all* my penchant for politics.   (Roe Head, 17 May 1831)

Mary Taylor also records that, as a schoolgirl, Charlotte's sympathies were conservative as opposed to her own radical views:

> We used to be furious politicians as one could hardly help being in 1832. She [Charlotte] knew the names of the two Ministers; the one that resigned, and the one that succeeded and passed the Reform Bill. She worshipped the Duke of Wellington, but said that Sir Robert Peel was not to be trusted; he did not act from principle, like the rest, but from expediency. I, being of the furious Radical party told her, 'How could any of them trust one another? They were all of them rascals.' Then she would launch out in praises of the Duke of Wellington. . . . She said she had taken an interest in politics ever since she was five years old. She did not get her opinions from her father – that is, not directly – but from the papers, etc., he preferred.

A second major reform occurred in the field of religious toleration. The Roman Catholic Relief Act of 1829 finally annulled the civil disabilities against Roman Catholics dating from the English Revolution. Thirdly, as mentioned above, the repeal of the Corn Laws in 1847 allowed expansion of British trade to foreign markets. However, the problems of working-class conditions were not so easily answered. The Chartist movement arose out of working-class disappointments over the Reform Bill. It called for secret ballots, equal suffrage, removal of property qualifications for MPs, equal electoral districts and annual general elections. Although the Chartists failed in their immediate aims, in the end all but one of their points (annual general elections) were achieved. In the short term, they helped to unite and to radicalize the working class. It was these debates which the Brontës not only followed with interest but responded to in their novels by conveying some of the sense of division, anger and energy arising from the social and political climate of early nineteenth-century England. Although *Shirley* is the only Brontë novel dealing explicitly with working-class unrest, *Wuthering Heights*, *Agnes Grey* and *Jane Eyre* all examine the conflicts generated by class divisions and new money. One further notes the scathing portraits of the *nouveaux riches* in *Agnes Grey* and *Villette*.

Apart from the explicit political and social conflicts which are treated in their novels, the Brontës' lives also encapsulated the conflict experienced between the Romantic imagination and the demands of the new industrial, market-oriented economy. Branwell was the clearest example of the wholly negative effects of this conflict. His was a largely 'Romantic' education in which the imagination was given free play. He was not sent to school but taught at home. His artistic training befitted someone of independent means, or of unusual genius, but was quite inappropriate to a moderately endowed young man expected to 'capitalize' on his talents and to be the support of his three sisters. His self-absorption, melancholia and despair were all genuine Romantic attitudes, but catastrophic as strategies to negotiate a career in which his painting must function not as a diversion but as a business. Branwell's tragic absurdities can be interpreted as the consequence of a Romantic education that ensured his inadaptability for industrial England.

Emily, Charlotte and Anne, less favoured thanks to their sex, were also less burdened with illusions of success. Their Evangelical training had included ideas of independence and self-help, yet they were simultaneously imbued with a nostalgia for the lady-like and the genteel, and a somewhat aristocratic distaste for contemporary life. The ambiguities of their social position, genteel but poor, allowed them to internalize some of the most complex and irresolvable issues of the day. The fact that, unlike Branwell, they were able to turn their experience to creative account, suggests that to the degree that they were less indulged than Branwell by their father and aunt, they escaped the self-destructive egocentricity characteristic of the Romantic temperament.

A consideration of the Brontës' novels as 'historical' does not merely involve an assessment of whether particular events mentioned have their basis in fact, or whether the fabric of social life is drawn accurately (dress, customs, incomes, manners and so on), but whether they are historical in the sense of conveying a sense of how life was experienced at a given period, both for particular individuals and in a way characteristic of that time. A historical perspective on the Brontës suggests that their particular, even eccentric, experience attained a high degree of historical universality.

6 Religion

One cannot overestimate the influence of religion in the Brontës' experience; its effects are visible both in their novels and their poetry. The difficulty lies in identifying exactly what their own complex, and even shifting, religious positions were. The extent of their orthodoxy, or lack of it, has been a vexed question. But even to discuss religion under a separate heading may obscure the degree to which it formed the bed-rock of their lives. Debates on Church doctrine and Church politics were the commonplaces of Brontë family conversation as they would have been for many people at this period. A central preoccupation of orthodox Christians was the concern with death, salvation and the fear of forfeiting it. Imbuing children with a healthy respect for hell fire, as evinced in Mr Brontë's sermons, was standard nineteenth-century religious practice. In any case, the children had death always before them. The high mortality rate of the period (between 1838 and 1849, for example, 41.6 per cent of the Haworth population died before the age of six) would have been graphically illustrated by the burials constantly taking place before their eyes in the churchyard next to the parsonage. The fear of hell, struggling against the hope of salvation, troubled their adolescence and emerges powerfully as a theme in their works. Each of the sisters seems to have evolved a personal form of religion. Significantly, one of the first reactions to the Brontës' novels, in an age sensitive to doctrinal issues, was a recognition of their religious individualism in the form of criticism of their religious orthodoxy. This section will examine the limits of orthodoxy in the Victorian period and the extent to which the Brontës exceeded them.

The Evangelical movement and the Established Church

We know that, as a theological student at Cambridge, Patrick Brontë had come under the influence of the Evangelical wing of the Anglican Church. The Evangelical movement was a religious revival launched by John Wesley and Whitefield in the late eighteenth century within the Church of England, leading ultimately to the formation of the Methodist Church but also deeply affecting Anglicanism in what is referred to as the Evangelical revival. It called for personal regeneration through faith, what is now known as being born again, and looked for the experience of conversion as evidence of faith. Methodists stressed God's love and the idea that Christ died for all and not for a few of the elect. In this respect they were anti-Calvinist. In the strict Calvinist view, God's omnipotent power and knowledge meant that he had already, before the creation, predestined the salvation of individuals. John Wesley, the father of Methodism, believed, on the contrary, that if Christ died for all men, then individual regeneration was always possible. Hence he stressed the widest possibility of sanctification or perfection. The onus was on the individual to treat each act and thought of his, or her, life as a determining step towards salvation or damnation. This view was movingly expressed by John Wesley's brother, Charles, in the verse 'Free Grace':

> And can it be, that I should gain
> An interest in the Saviour's blood?
> Died He for me, who caused His pain –
> For me, who Him to death pursued?
> Amazing love! how can it be
> That Thou, my God, shouldst die for me?

Methodism can also be interpreted as a reaction against the deistic rationalism characteristic of much of the eighteenth-century Anglican Church, which was suspicious of religious enthusiasm in personal terms, and which conceived of a universe controlled by a rational God who had no direct involvement with the individual destinies of human beings. Methodism, by contrast, stressed the need for intense communion of the individual with God. Failure to communicate effectively with God was taken as evidence of personal unworthiness. Thus William Wilberforce, the philanthropist, anti-slavery campaigner and member of the Clapham sect, a group of Evangelical social reformers, wrote in his Journal of 1785:

> Was very fervent in prayer this morning, and thought these warm impressions would never go off. Yet in vain endeavoured in the evening to rouse myself. God grant it may not all prove vain; oh if it does, how will my punishment be deservedly increased! The only way I find of moving myself, is by thinking of my great transgressions, weakness, blindness, and of God's having promised to supply these defects. But though I firmly believe them, yet I read of future judgement, and think of God's wrath against sinners, with no great emotions. What can so strongly show the stony heart? O God, give me a heart of flesh!

This fear of a 'stony heart', and a sense of sin, obsessed Charlotte as a schoolgirl at Miss Wooler's. She and Anne both suffered adolescent crises which took the form of a belief in their own sinfulness. The Puritan conscience common to Anglicans, Evangelicals and dissenters left conscientious individuals grappling with a sense of personal unworthiness. A morbid conviction of sin afflicted some of the most high-minded people of the age. Harriet Martineau described the sense of freedom and relief she felt when she cast off religious belief, a tribute to the weight of fear under which many devout believers laboured and from which she felt she had been delivered. To those who, like the Brontës, retained religious belief, the experience of divine grace was felt to be necessary to assure the believer of salvation. Charlotte's despairing letters from Roe Head indicate that she received no such illumination. The ecstatic visions which she did experience were of Angria, not of heaven:

> I *do* wish to be better than I am. I pray fervently sometimes to be made so. I have stings of conscience, visitings of remorse, glimpses of holy, of inexpressible things, which formerly I used to be a stranger to; it may all die away, and I may be in utter midnight, but I implore a merciful Redeemer, that, if this be the dawn of the gospel, it may still brighten to perfect day. . . . Oh! I am no better than ever I was. I am in that state of horrid, gloomy uncertainty that, at this moment, I would submit to be old, grey-haired, to have passed all my youthful days of enjoyment, and to be settling on the verge of the grave, if I could thereby ensure the prospect of reconciliation to God, and redemption through his Son's merits.
>
> (to Ellen Nussey, 1836)

In a further letter Charlotte reveals the degree to which the Calvinism imbued from their Aunt Branwell still informed her religious sensibility. She speaks of:

> the melancholic state I now live in, uncertain that I ever felt true contrition, wandering in thought and deed, longing for holiness, which I shall *never*, *never* obtain, smitten at times to the heart with the conviction that ghastly Calvinistic doctrines are true – darkened, in short, by the very shadows of spiritual death.
>
> (to Ellen Nussey, 1837)

These 'ghastly Calvinistic doctrines' – namely, the fear that God had predestined all to salvation or damnation – were ultimately rejected by Charlotte and Anne. Branwell claimed to believe himself damned, though to what extent this was a piece of self-dramatization it is difficult to say. Of Emily we only know that she satirized Calvinism in the figure of Joseph, in *Wuthering Heights*, as well as in the sermon of Jabes Branderham. However, Joseph does have a certain integrity, grumbling away like the bad fairy at the princess's christening. But from Cathy's and Heathcliff's gesture of throwing away the improving tracts given them to read by Joseph ('The Helmet of Salvation' and 'The Broad Way to Destruction'), to Joseph's gloating over Heathcliff's corpse ('"Th' divil's harried off his soul", he cried, "and he muh hev his carcass intuh t'bargain, for ow't Aw care" . . . and the old sinner grinned in mockery'), Emily Brontë rejects the self-righteousness of those who considered themselves the elect. Heathcliff's words to Nelly before he dies suggest that the Christian heaven may have seemed an irrelevant goal: 'I tell you, I have nearly attained *my* heaven; and that of others is altogether unvalued, and uncoveted by me' (Ch. 34).

Traditionally, the Church of England occupied an ambiguous position between its rôle as an arm of the state and its religious mission. Bishops were appointed by the state and sat in the House of Lords, where they had considerable political influence. One objection commonly levelled against the Church concerned the alleged worldliness of its clergy and the vast material wealth it possessed. Many of the higher clergy (deans, archdeacons and bishops) lived in aristocratic style. Lower clergy were often extremely poor. Vicars tended to be drawn from the upper classes and to take on more than one parish to supplement their incomes. The practice of plural benefices was extremely widespread, with the result that many parishes scarcely saw their vicar and made do with the services of a badly paid curate. As late as 1827, of 10,533 benefices surveyed, only 4,413 had resident incumbents. Haworth was more fortunate than the majority of English parishes in having a resident vicar. Lockwood describes a deserted rural church or chapel in his dream of Jabes Branderham:

> We came to the chapel – I have passed it really in my walks, twice or thrice . . . . The roof has been kept whole hitherto, but, as the clergyman's stipend is only twenty pounds per annum, and a house with two rooms, threatening speedily to determine into one, no clergyman will undertake the duties of pastor, especially as it is currently reported that his flock would rather let him starve than increase the living by one penny from their own pockets.   (Ch. 3, *Wuthering Heights*)

It was common for infants in an age of high infant mortality to go unbaptized through lack of attendance of clergy. The popular image of the eighteenth- and early nineteenth-century English clergyman was of a well-living country squire who engaged in occasional ecclesiastical duties, an unspiritual member of an unspiritual establishment. Voltaire in his *English Letters* of 1734 caught the tone associated with the Anglican clergy by remarking that they had no major vice save avarice.

The Evangelical revival addressed itself, therefore, to the perceived absenteeism and worldliness of the Church of England and to the fact that the poor had little access to religious instruc-tion. John Wesley, its guiding spirit, remained an Anglican, though founding the Methodists, but Evangelicalism permeated all denominations. Mr Brontë, as an Evangelical Anglican in Yorkshire, was representative of a significant section of Church opinion. Evangelicalism was not a sect but an attitude of personal commitment towards religion. In the nineteenth century the Evangelical movement was responsible for the conversion of the labouring poor and for the great missionary movements. St John Rivers in *Jane Eyre*, departing to teach Christianity in India, was characteristic of this Evangelical strain. His speech to Jane, announcing his intention to embark for the East, captures the language of Evangelical enthusiasm:

> 'Humility, Jane,' said he, 'is the groundwork of Christian virtues: you say right that you are not fit for the work. Who is fit for it? Or who, that ever was truly called, believed himself worthy of the summons? I, for instance, am but dust and ashes. With St Paul, I acknowledge myself the chiefest of sinners; but I do not suffer this sense of my personal vileness to daunt me. I know my Leader: that He is just as well as mighty; and while He has chosen a feeble instrument to perform a great task, He will, from the boundless stores of His providence, supply the inadequacy of the means to the end. Think like me, Jane – trust like me. It is the Rock of Ages I ask you to lean on: do not doubt but it will bear the weight of your human weakness.'

(Ch. 34)

Paradoxically, though politically conservative, the Evangelical movement, by educating the poor and revitalizing their religion, paved the way for working-class reform. The Established Church, on the other hand, was firmly identified with the status quo and with the landed interest, playing a significant rôle in the defeat of the first Reform Bill by the crucial vote of the bishops in the House of Lords. It was no accident that a mob burned down the palace of the Bishop of Bristol during the public disorders that preceded the passage of the Reform Bill of 1832. The bishops had become symbols to the lower classes of political reaction.

The Evangelical movement, as I have suggested, took firm root within Anglicanism itself. Patrick Brontë, whose studies at Cambridge had brought him under the influence of Charles Simeon (1759–1836), a leading Evangelical, was a good example of an Evangelical or 'Low Church' Anglican. He appears to have been a zealous performer of his parish duties, and preached regularly in church in an extempore manner, delivering plain-spoken if uncompromising sermons. Haworth, however, lay in the midst of a nonconformist, or dissenting, community like much of the industrial North of England. Most parish churches were maintained by a tithe, or church rate, levied on property-owners, a tax not finally abolished until 1868. In Haworth, as in many such parishes at that period, the church rate became a source of friction, as local ratepayers, who were dissenters, declined to support a church which they did not attend. Charlotte's letters contain several references to fierce sermons preached by Mr Brontë's curates to persuade their flock to pay the church rate. She shows some sympathy with the dissenters, coupled with dislike of the curates' pomposity, though her Toryism and Anglicanism made her unsympathetic to dissent in general.

Another of the anomalies of the Church of England in this period may be seen in a certain popular confusion on doctrine. Thus one could be an Anglican Evangelical and a Calvinist simultaneously, as Miss Branwell seems to have been: that is to say, believing in personal salvation and also in predestination. Aunt Branwell was even more Low Church than Mr Brontë, and subscribed, as we know, to the *Methodist Magazine*. Alternatively, one could be an Anglican-Arminian, opposed to the strict views on predestination, stressing free will and the possibility of salvation for all, through Christ. This would appear to have been Anne's and Charlotte's position. Such overlap of beliefs were also evident in the dissenting communities among Baptists, Methodists, Quakers and Unitarians. To some extent, these sects were divided less by theology than by social class. Though theologically speaking the Church of England was broad enough to encompass most Christian doctrines, socially it represented the middle classes and rural England. Dissenters on the whole flourished in the newer industrial centres.

The Oxford movement

The politico-religious conflicts of the day produced a shift of doctrinal emphasis in the Church of England itself and led to the other major renewal in the nineteenth-century Church, the Oxford movement. At the beginning of the nineteenth century, the Church of England still considered itself a largely Protestant and national Church, dating from the English Reformation in the sixteenth century when, in 1534, Henry VIII ended Papal power with the Act of Supremacy. The Thirty-Nine Articles of the Church of England, promulgated in 1571, set out its official doctrinal position. Among the major differences with Roman Catholicism were the reduction of the sacraments from seven to two (baptism and communion), and an emphasis on faith, rather than works, as evidence of salvation. Later, under Oliver Cromwell, the English Commonwealth (1649–60) enshrined anti-Catholic legislation in the Constitution. This legislation remained in force for nearly three centuries. It was not until 1829 that the Catholic Emancipation Act abolished most civil restrictions on Catholics. As a result, the

1830s brought some increase in the political power of Irish Catholic MPs, while simultaneously the English Catholics began to engage more in public life. The Oxford movement arose, both as a response to a perceived threat from a renascent English Roman Catholic Church, and as an attempt to counter Evangelical influence within the Church of England.

Also referred to as Tractarian (so called because of the series of *Tracts for the Times* issued by Newman and others between 1833 and 1841), High Church or Puseyite, the Oxford movement was led by a group of Anglican divines; Hurrell Froude, Newman, Keble and Pusey from Oxford University. In their view, the Church of England, far from being a fundamentally Protestant Church, was the true descendant of the Church of Rome, the genuine Catholic Church. Anglicans, they pointed out, had a Catholic liturgy. The Tractarians placed emphasis on ritual and on the sacraments, all of which certainly had existed in the Church structure, but which had not been stressed in their 'Catholic' context. Puseyites fought for the doctrine of apostolic succession and for the integrity of the Prayer Book. They wanted to establish the Church of England, not as a national Protestant Church arising out of historical circumstance (Henry VIII's quarrels with the Pope), but as a Church with a sound theological and therefore Roman Catholic foundation, the true descendant of the early Christian Church. It was in 1845 when Newman could no longer believe in the claim of the Church of England to be the 'true' Catholic Church, that he became a convert to Roman Catholicism. Many others, however, remained within the Anglican Church and sought to make its observances conform to Roman Catholic practice.

The influence of the Oxford movement and the awakened interest in Roman Catholicism impinged on the Brontës' lives in significant ways. Mr Brontë, almost certainly against his own inclinations, acquired a series of High Church curates at Haworth. From Charlotte's letters we learn that they fitted badly into the Yorkshire Evangelical setting, and that they were intolerant in their attitudes to Evangelical and dissenting groups. Charlotte was repelled by their arrogance. 'I consider them bigoted, intolerant and wholly unjustifiable on the grounds of common sense' (to Ellen Nussey, 7 April 1840). In *Shirley* she satirized three curates as a mixture of social crassness and complacency. The novel's opening damns the new type of clergy with faint praise:

Of late years, an abundant shower of curates has fallen upon the north of England: they lie very thick on the hills; every parish has one or more of them; they are young enough to be very active, and ought to be doing a great deal of good.

(Ch. 1)

One notes the implication of frenetic but useless activity, and the 'ought' suggesting that little good is being done. In a letter to Miss Wooler (17 Feb. 1850) defending *Shirley* against hostile criticism, Charlotte remarked: 'I confess the work has one prevailing fault – that of too tenderly and partially veiling the errors of the curates.'

An equally striking satire on High Church manners and doctrine emerges in Anne's first novel, *Agnes Grey*. Here we find two contrasting clergymen; Mr Hatfield, the vicar; and Mr Weston, his curate. The former can be identified as High Church by his authoritarianism, dandyism and snobbery. He visits the poor only to hector them, refuses to discuss Nancy Brown's religious crisis with her (she is an old, poor and ailing parishioner) and is personally vain. He takes a traditionalist and dogmatic view of the nature of belief:

Mr Hatfield would come sailing up the aisle, or rather sweeping along like a whirlwind, with his rich silk gown flying behind him and rustling against the pew doors, mount the pulpit like a conqueror ascending his triumphal car; then, sinking on the velvet cushion in an attitude of studied grace, remain in silent prostration for a certain time; then mutter over a Collect, and gabble through the Lord's Prayer, rise, draw off one bright lavender glove, to give the congregation the benefit of his sparkling rings, lightly pass his fingers through his well-curled hair, flourish a cambric handkerchief, recite a very short passage, or perhaps, a mere phrase of Scripture, as a headpiece to his discourse, and, finally, deliver a composition which, as a composition, might be considered good, though far too studied and too artificial to be pleasing to me. . . . His favourite subjects were Church discipline, rites and ceremonies, apostolical succession, the duty of reverence and obedience to the clergy, the atrocious criminality of dissent, the absolute necessity of observing all forms of godliness . . . the necessity of deferential obedience from the poor to the rich.

(Ch. 10)

Mr Weston, his curate, on the other hand, is represented as a model of Evangelical rectitude and charity. His sermons strike Agnes immediately:

I did hear him preach, and was decidedly pleased with the evangelical truth of his doctrine, as well as the earnest simplicity of his manner, and the clearness and force of his style. It was truly refreshing to hear such a sermon, after being so long accustomed to the dry, prosy discourses of the former curate, and the still less edifying harangues of the rector.

(Ch. 10)

In addition to his virtues as a preacher, Mr Weston visits the poor, helps resolve their religious doubts and performs quiet acts of practical charity. In *Agnes Grey*, Evangelicalism, as practised by Mr Weston and Agnes, functions as a mark of sincerity and true belief. The High Church vicar represents, within the context of the novel, an attitude of hypocrisy and social and personal vanity. He is the bad shepherd. To a marked extent, both *Agnes Grey* and *Shirley* reflect doctrinal issues as they impinged on the ordinary parishes of England and give one an idea of the kinds of resentment generated by the differing religious currents.

Though Charlotte, in particular, was staunchly Protestant, by her mid-thirties her religious sympathies and interests had widened. However, she retained a vigorous anti-Catholic prejudice, probably attributable to her father's Irish Protestant origins. Charlotte's strictures against Catholicism emerge only too vividly in *Villette*. Phrases like 'Babylonish furnace', 'popish superstition' (Ch. 15), 'Moloch Church', 'mitred aspirants for this world's kingdoms' (Ch. 36), come readily to her pen, in spite of the fact that she had both lived in a Catholic country and admired sincere Catholics like M. Heger. Conversely, she showed some capacity for religious tolerance, demonstrated by the fact that she had friends in the dissenting community – notably, the Gaskells and Harriet Martineau. As Unitarians, who did not believe in the Trinity or the Divinity of Christ, they were problematic friends for the daughter of an Anglican vicar. Mary Taylor stressed Charlotte's breadth of religious sympathy:

> She had a larger religious toleration than a person would have who had never questioned, and her manner of recommending religion was always that of offering comfort, not fiercely enforcing a duty.
>
> (18 Jan. 1856)

Charlotte's attitude towards Roman Catholicism was particularly complex. It is evident that her reaction to living in the Catholic milieu of Brussels was negative and prejudiced. In *Villette* the passages on the Belgian/Catholic character are a blemish from a writer of her intellectual distinction. She certainly was aware that the archetypal 'no-Popery' views expressed in *Villette* were considered extreme. In her review Harriet Martineau noted:

> 'Currer Bell' . . . goes out of her way to express a passionate hatred of Romanism. . . . We do not exactly see the moral necessity for this (there is no artificial necessity) and we are rather sorry for it occurring as it does at a time when Catholics and Protestants hate each other quite sufficiently.
>
> (*Daily News*, 3 Feb. 1853)

In a letter to Miss Wooler, Charlotte invoked 'Conscience and Reason' in defence of her attitude. 'Miss Martineau' (who though a free-thinker was prepared to see some virtues in every system and was in any case committed to toleration), 'accuses me of attacking Popery with virulence – and of going out of my way to assault it passionately' (to Miss Wooler, 13 April 1853). But excessive hostility to Roman Catholicism, even by the standards of her own age, probably revealed the converse, a certain attraction to it. We know that in a period of severe depression, Charlotte confessed to a priest in Brussels. And Lucy Snowe, enacting a similar confessional scene, admits that she might have been tempted to enter a convent. Catholicism with its ritual and poetry does appear to have been a temptation that Charlotte was anxious to exorcise by the very violence of her reaction. Nor was she alone in her ambivalent feelings towards Roman Catholicism. Florence Nightingale, too, was attracted to the conventual life, which offered a satisfying career of service, an opportunity lacking for middle-class women in Protestant Britain. As Nightingale wrote to Cardinal Manning in 1852:

> If you knew what a home the Catholic Church would be to me! All I want I should find in her. All my difficulties should be removed. I have laboriously to pick up, here and there, crumbs by which to live. She would give me daily bread. The daughters of St Vincent would open their arms to me. . . . My work already laid out for me instead of seeking it to and fro and finding none; my home sympathy, human and divine. You do not know, with all its faults, what a Home the Catholic Church is. And yet what is she to you, compared to what she would be to me? No one can tell, no man can tell what she is to woman. . . . What training is there (in the Church of England) compared to that of the Catholic nun?

A similar note is struck, albeit with complex irony, by George Eliot's comparison between the Spanish nun, St Teresa, who found a vocation and a purpose in life, and her own heroine, Dorothea Brooke, shown as lacking a 'coherent social faith and order' within which to shape her life. Charlotte's interest in, and antipathy towards, Roman Catholicism can be linked to central preoccupations of the Victorian age.

Charlotte remained engaged in doctrinal questions throughout her life. On her London visit of 1851, she visited a Friends' Meeting House, heard the French Protestant D'Aubigné preach and went, twice, to hear Cardinal Wiseman, the recently appointed Roman Catholic Cardinal of Westminster. The English Roman Catholic Church had been fully reinstated by the Pope the previous year and Cardinal Wiseman was the first English cardinal appointed to England since the Commonwealth. Charlotte's description of him to her father stressing his 'treble and quadruple chin', his 'large mouth with oily lips', 'the picture of a sleek hypocrite' (to Patrick Brontë, 17 June 1851), pandered to her father's anti-Catholic prejudices, as well as reflecting renewed anti-Catholic hostility in the country at large. What is more significant, and ambiguous, is that she should have twice been to hear the despised cardinal preach.

Religious ideas in the novels

As far as the Brontës' novels and poetry are concerned, the most important religious theme to emerge was that of salvation. *Jane Eyre* and *Shirley* were accused of being unorthodox and of promoting a doctrine of universal salvation – the view that anyone, no matter how wicked, can be saved by God's grace. 'I am sorry', wrote Charlotte to Miss Wooler (14 Feb. 1850), sounding entirely unrepentant, 'that the Clergy do not like the doctrine of Universal Salvation; I think it is a great pity for their sakes, but surely they are not so unreasonable as to expect me to deny or suppress what I believe to be the truth!' Charlotte's need to believe in a generous vision of redemption, something wider than the rigours of either Calvinism or Methodism allowed, was strengthened by the deaths of her brother and sisters. It seemed to her intolerable, particularly in the cases of Anne and Emily, that their lives might have been for nothing.

As already suggested, the fear of hell would have been a natural part of most Christians' lives. Mr Brontë's sermons, describing the infernal horrors and the need for Christian submission and suffering in this world, were not exceptionally gloomy or unusual for the period. The Calvinist emphasis on predestination affected Anne and Branwell strongly, the former to moral rectitude, the latter to revolt. Both Anne and Charlotte underwent severe religious crises in adolescence. Charlotte's anguished letters from Roe Head in 1836–37, quoted above, complaining of her moral unworthiness, coincide with the period of the temptation of Angria. The sexually charged nature of many of the Angrian fantasies would have given her guilty pause, since in the moral theology of the time the 'sinful' thought was considered equivalent to the deed.

Like Charlotte's, Anne's religious crisis also involved a sense of hopelessness and personal unworthiness. But her novels, especially *The Tenant of Wildfell Hall*, affirm the redemptive power of suffering, the effective struggle of the will to overcome evil, and because didactic, are anything but despairing. Didacticism itself argues a belief in the effectiveness of persuasion to bring about change. One also needs to take into account the rôle of Branwell's decline in the

Brontë sisters' religious development. Without restricting *The Tenant of Wildfell Hall* to a biographical interpretation, it is the case that the sinner, Arthur Huntingdon, though not assured of salvation in the novel, is not seen as irremediably damned either:

> How could I endure to think that that poor trembling soul was hurried away to everlasting torment? it would drive me mad! But, thank God, I have hope – not only from a vague dependence on the possibility that penitence and pardon might have reached him at the last, but from the blessed confidence that, through whatever purging fires the erring spirit may be doomed to pass – whatever fate awaits it, still, it is not lost, and God, who hateth nothing that He hath made, *will* bless it in the end.
> (Ch. 49)

But Arthur Huntingdon is not given an edifying death; rather, he dies in a state of panic, aware of the likelihood of damnation. A more conventional, and indeed genuinely didactic, writer would have engineered a death-bed repentance which assured salvation. Anne Brontë's account, from a religious perspective, retains the dreadful sense of uncertainty about the after-life that she believed to face everyone, but holds out the image of God's mercy predominating over his justice. For Anne and Charlotte, the doctrine of universal salvation appeared to offer religious hope while other doctrines induced despair. A God 'who hateth nothing that He hath made' was Anne's consolation. Charlotte also believed that Branwell's sufferings and the suffering that they had all endured on his behalf could be understood as having a redemptive function.

The influence of Methodism, or of religious enthusiasm, on the Brontës was arguably less doctrinal than temperamental. Charlotte feared 'enthusiasm' in her own nature and tried to control it by appeals to Duty and Reason, a tendency particularly marked in *Villette*. However, the anxieties generated by the fear of damnation, and the importance of personal feeling in religious response derived from Methodism, produced a creative tension demonstrated most clearly in Emily's writing. On one level, *Wuthering Heights* can be interpreted as a struggle between good and evil, not in an orthodox religious sense, in which good, if not triumphant emerges as at least morally vindicated, but as an amoral struggle between opposing cosmic forces. The world is conceived as one of necessary suffering but also of joy. Heaven, lacking the dimension of struggle, is not a place in which one would necessarily be happy. Cathy's account of her dream of heaven illustrates this point:

> I was only going to say that heaven did not seem to be my home; and I broke my heart with weeping to come back to earth; and the angels were so angry that they flung me out, into the middle

of the heath on the top of Wuthering Heights, where I woke sobbing for joy.

(Ch. 9)

'Heaven did not seem to be my home' suggests a sensibility which lacked the assurance of divine election. *Wuthering Heights* could be said to celebrate the true home, the landscape in which Emily lived and died.

Emily and Charlotte both attacked religious fanaticism. The figure of Joseph in *Wuthering Heights*, with his dour Old Testament morality and glee at prescribing eternal damnation for anyone of whom he disapproves, as well as Lockwood's dream, with its hell-fire sermon, ridicule the narrowness and fanaticism of religious enthusiasm. Similarly Charlotte mocks the dreary Methodist teaching of Mr Brocklehurst in *Jane Eyre* and Methodist literature in *Shirley* (the library at Briarfield). The arrogance associated with the certainty of a religious vocation emerges powerfully in the figure of St John Rivers in *Jane Eyre*, morally admirable and emotionally frozen.

From Emily we have only one explicit comment about religion. Mary Taylor tells how, on a visit to Haworth, she had remarked that her religious beliefs were 'between God and me'. Emily is reported to have exclaimed, 'That's right!'. As was her enigmatic way, she added nothing more. Emily shielded her privacy with regard to her exact religious beliefs as in everything else. Though few of her characters show overtly religious enthusiasm, and this is usually a negative quality, they all show a certain fanaticism, a capacity to follow ideas or impulses to the bitter end. In Emily, religious zeal was transformed into the amoral energy of *Wuthering Heights*.

Without minimizing the strictures and privations of their religious education, one can plausibly argue that the Brontës' religious training, from their early immersion in the Bible to the dreary didactic stories in the *Methodist Magazine*, provided a major imaginative and emotional impetus for their lives as creative artists. Far from crushing and disciplining their imaginations, religion acted as a creative spur. The Brontës struggled to follow the religious impulse to transcendence and freedom, while undergoing the imperatives of a narrow moral/religious orthodoxy. Anne and Charlotte remained closely bound to the moral ethos of their religious upbringing but manifested a strong sense of conflict. Emily, freer than either of her sisters of social opinion, revelled in the very conflicts engendered between the desire for transcendence and conventional morality.

7   Reading and literary influences

As children, the Brontës read voraciously and precociously in both serious and popular literature, devouring any reading matter they could get their hands on. Books and magazines were a luxury in the Haworth parsonage, eagerly sought and highly valued. Whether by accident or design, Mr Brontë appears to have given his children free rein in their reading. The only known instance of parental censorship was suffered by Charlotte, who was forbidden to read *The Ladies' Magazine*, a purveyor of what Mr Brontë considered salacious romantic tales. In every other respect, Mr Brontë seems to have encouraged his children's taste for reading and for reading aloud. When still very young, they were enchanted by Aesop's *Fables* and by *The Arabian Nights*. The latter, particularly, informs the juvenilia in its sense of the marvellous, and the attraction of the supernatural, themes which eventually emerged in the Brontës' adult fiction.

The Brontës were fortunate in having access to a number of periodicals, a consequence of Mr Brontë's passion for politics. They received two newspapers, the *Leeds Intelligencer* and the *Leeds Mercury*. Aunt Branwell subscribed to *Fraser's Magazine* and to the *Methodist Magazine*. But their great periodical resource was *Blackwood's*. This monthly journal, loaned to Mr Brontë by the local doctor from 1825 onwards, contained a diverse and stimulating range of articles, poems and serialized novels. The first acquisition of *Blackwood's* coincided with the deaths of Maria and Elizabeth and the return of Emily and Charlotte to Haworth. It was advanced reading matter for young children. In 1825, Charlotte was nine, Branwell eight, Emily seven, and Anne five. Branwell, with characteristic rhodomontade, writing to the magazine's editor in 1835, when he was 18, described the effect *Blackwood's* had on him as a child:

> I cannot express, though you can understand, the heavenliness of associations connected with such articles as Professor Wilson's, read and re-read while a little child, with all their poetry of language and divine flights into that visionary region of imagination which one very young would believe reality, and which one entering into manhood would look back on as a glorious dream. I speak so, sir, because as a child *Blackwood's* formed my chief delight.
>
> (Mrs Oliphant, *Annals of a Publishing House*, vol. 2, p. 178)

Branwell's telling phrase, 'which one very young would believe reality', conveys the Brontës' response to the vicarious experience of reading. *Blackwood's*, this source of 'poetry of language and divine flights of imagination' to which Branwell refers, was, more soberly considered, a periodical that combined articles on history, current events, literary criticism, theology and politics, in addition to serialized novels. The young Brontës would have been kept well informed of contemporary cultural and political issues, and these they often transposed, almost wholesale, into their juvenilia. *Blackwood's* yearly bound volume of 1826, for example, carries a defence of the character of Lord Byron, a poet very much the object of Charlotte's admiration, and an article and map on the geography of Central Africa, grist to the mill of the Glass Town authors (see p. 101). The value of *Blackwood's* for the Brontës lay in its wide coverage. It carried translations of Schiller's plays, for example, and extended articles on foreign literature. While perhaps not possessing the 'divine flights' Branwell attributed to it, *Blackwood's* enlarged their mental horizons and ambitions. It made them feel they had real links with the world of letters. The direct imitations of *Blackwood's* magazine format in the early juvenilia are evidence of its crucial influence on their development.

In an age when books were still expensive and access often limited, the question of where the Brontë children came by the books they read is of some interest. There was first of all their father's library, which, though largely composed of theological works, also included a good selection of standard authors. The Bible, not surprisingly, formed the theological and linguistic bedrock of their minds; the cadences of its language are evident in their adult fiction. The Book of Revelations, full of splendid and fabulous visions, almost certainly coloured the juvenilia, and Charlotte, in particular, retained its visionary sense in her mature work (see, for example, the fête in *Villette*). Patrick Brontë's library further contained the works of Homer, Virgil, Bunyan, Milton, Dr Johnson, the Romantic poets, Scott, and novels such as *Evelina* and *Clarissa*. He also owned a *Description of London*, with plates of classical buildings that served the children as models for Glass Town. His Goldsmith's *Grammar of General Geography* was dramatized by the children into the fictional islands and kingdoms of their juvenilia. Goldsmith's *History of Rome*, Hume's *History of England*, and Scott's *Life of Napoleon Bonaparte* were similarly works in their father's library reflected in the children's writing. They educated themselves unawares by absorbing history, politics and geography in order to incorporate it into their early fiction.

Much of the evidence for the Brontës' reading is derived from internal evidence in the novels. However, it is known that Mr Brontë subscribed to the Keighley Mechanics' Institute Library as soon as it was founded in 1825. This was relatively poor in new fiction but otherwise was a good source of books. The other library to which they may have had access is the Heaton family's Ponden House Library near Haworth. This was the local manor house, and Mr Brontë, as vicar, was on good terms with the Heatons. However, we have no evidence of social intercourse with the Heatons from Charlotte's letters, nor accounts of visits to their library. On the other hand, Charlotte, we know, had a wide knowledge of Jacobean and Elizabethan literature which it is difficult to see how she could have acquired from any other source than the Heaton collection.

As regards new fiction, the Brontës seem to have read relatively little besides novels serialized in magazines such as *Blackwood's* and *Fraser's*. Instead, they read many eighteenth-century novels, including the works of Fielding, Richardson, Smollett and Goldsmith. Not having access to a circulating library and insulated from the excessive proprieties of newer nineteenth-century fiction, the sisters were genuinely surprised by unfavourable critical response after the publication of *Wuthering Heights*, *Jane Eyre* and *The Tenant of Wildfell Hall*, which accused them of being 'coarse'. However, their reading of racy eighteenth-century novels was offset by the Evangelical strictness of the Methodist literature which they absorbed via their aunt. Novel reading, itself, was often regarded as a suspect pleasure in an Evangelical age. Charlotte showed a distinctly equivocal attitude towards novels. To Ellen Nussey she cited Scott as the only novelist worth reading:

> If you like poetry let it be first-rate; Milton, Shakespeare, Thomson, Goldsmith, Pope (if you will, though I don't admire him), Scott, Byron, Campbell, Wordsworth and Southey. Now don't be startled at the names of Shakespeare and Byron. Both these were great men, and their works are like themselves. . . . Omit the comedies of Shakespeare and the *Don Juan*, perhaps the *Cain* of Byron, though the latter is a magnificent poem and read the rest fearlessly. . . . For fiction, read Scott alone; all novels after his are worthless.
>
> (4 July 1834)

The influence of Scott was certainly a major one in the Brontës' writing; for example, Emily probably drew on Scott's *The Bride of Lammermoor* for the plot of *Wuthering Heights*. The above-quoted letter to Ellen Nussey is less interesting in revealing Charlotte's literary preferences than in showing her concern that one's reading should contribute to one's moral improvement. While displaying a becoming concern for the proprieties, in her reply to Ellen (who had worried that reading about wickedness in Shakespeare, for example, might tend to make one wicked), Charlotte, entirely at variance with her own advice, read widely in areas which she would not have approved of for Ellen. 'Got another bale of French books from Gomersal – they are like the rest, clever, wicked, sophisticated and immoral' (1840). Nevertheless she read them, and with relish. Not only did Charlotte, and presumably her sisters, enjoy fiction which they were aware was not considered 'suitable', they were also busy composing such fiction themselves in the form of the sensationalist and steamy works of the juvenilia. The following example from Charlotte's 'Hartford and Mina Laury' (1838) illustrates this point:

> Her beauty . . . struck through him – maddening sensation whetted to acuter power by a feeling like despair.
> 'You shall love me!' he exclaimed desperately; 'Do I not adore you? Would I not die for you? And must I in return receive only the cold regard of friendship? I am no Platonist, Miss Laury – I am not your friend. I am, hear me, madam, your declared lover! Nay, you shall not leave me; by heaven! I am stronger than you are'. . . . He thought she meant to withdraw, and determined not to be so balked, he clasped her at once in both his arms and kissed her furiously rather than fondly.

This is scarcely the kind of text that Charlotte could have recommended to the slightly priggish Ellen Nussey. One may smile at the stock phrases and situation, but this passage almost certainly reflects part of the literary diet on which the Brontës nourished themselves.

The Gothic

Catherine Morland, the heroine of *Northanger Abbey*, Jane Austen's satire on Gothic fiction, exclaims to her friend Isabella, in anticipation of a glut of as yet unread Gothic novels, 'Are they all horrid, are you sure they are all horrid?' (Ch. 6). Her happiest moments are those spent at home reading Mrs Radcliffe's extravaganza, *The Mysteries of Udolpho* (1794). Catherine is the fictional representation of the untutored but enthusiastic readers who devoured Gothic novels at the turn of the eighteenth century. The invented titles that Austen provides give us some idea of the attractions of the genre: *Castle of Wolfenbach*, *Clermont*, *Mysterious Warnings*, *Necromancer of the Black Forest*, *Midnight Bell*, *Orphan of the Rhine* and *Horrid Mysteries*. The Gothic and its vogue has very considerable historical and literary importance and relevance to our understanding of the Brontës' fiction.

The Gothic was a late-eighteenth-century offshoot of the cult of sensibility which arose in reaction to the predominant Enlightenment values of balance, reason and control. The cult of feeling and of nature, exemplified especially by the philosopher Rousseau, had its adherents in England in a turning to sentimental themes (Mackenzie's *The Man of Feeling*, 1771) and the popularity of the sublime and the picturesque in nature (Thomson's 'The Seasons', 1726–30, and Gilpin's *Tours in the Mountains and Lakes of Cumberland and Westmorland*, 1789). Unlike Rousseau's cult of nature, the Gothic attempted to move the sensibilities, not so much in the contemplation of the sublime as in the evocation of terror. Pleasure and pain were perceived as inextricably united. The late eighteenth century saw the development of an aesthetic theory of the Horrid and the Terrible, exemplified in the title of an anonymous essay, 'Enquiry into those kinds of Distress which excite agreeable sensations' (1773). 'The Horrid' became part of the Romantic, and eventually the Decadent, aesthetic and can be traced in Byron, Shelley, Keats, Novalis, Baudelaire and Huysmans. It left a strong imprint on the Brontës, who availed themselves of the convention in remarkably original ways.

Ann Radcliffe, the doyenne of Gothic novelists, whose *Udolpho* so thrilled Catherine Morland, developed the formulas on which the genre depended. The heroine, an individual of spotless purity and high moral and intellectual culture, is pursued by a satanic and remorseless villain. The novel's setting was of crucial importance: exotic travels through the Pyrenees, or through Italy, as the heroine fled her tormentor, and time spent in dilapidated castles or monasteries was obligatory. Haunted ruins, guilty secrets and an ultimately happy ending where the pursuing villain was foiled by the somewhat tardy pursuit of the hero, all contributed to the heady atmosphere. What horror films represent to the twentieth century, the Gothic novel offered to the eighteenth and early nineteenth centuries. Other well-known examples of the Gothic include Horace Walpole's *The Castle of Otranto* (1764), Beckford's *Vathek* (1782) and M. G. Lewis's *The Monk* (1796). Elements of the supernatural and a touch of vampirism and/or necrophilia (the love of dead bodies) were also part of the stock-in-trade of such novels. In the nineteenth century the Gothic villain merged into the Byronic hero (see pp. 92–4 below). Byron's Manfred comes out of a well-established Gothic tradition of hero-villains.

However, as Jane Austen points out, the Gothic novel was more than a subject of mockery and producer of cheap thrills; it was, she said, a source of 'unaffected pleasure'. Indeed, the Gothic in its cultivation of the 'horrid', drawing as it did on a psychological realm of dread and terror, appealed to those areas of the mind ignored by Enlightenment rationalism. In *Northanger Abbey*, Austen composed an anti-Gothic novel which is a tribute to the fascination of the genre. If Catherine Morland is originally not able to distinguish, in her *naïveté*, between the reality of life in provincial England and Gothic fantasy, the Brontës might be said in their youth to have suffered from a similar difficulty.

The Brontës' mature novels show strong traces of the creative adaptation of Gothic elements. One notices first of all a certain amount of Gothic 'furniture'. Heathcliff and Rochester both take the rôle of pursuers. The former has more than a touch of Satan about him. *Jane Eyre* has the most Gothic setting, with Thornfield functioning as the Gothic castle haunted, not by a ghost, but by the demonic Bertha Mason. Anne Brontë's Wildfell Hall is another Gothic, half-ruined castle, but domesticated and emptied of the supernatural. At the same time, in all the Brontë novels, there is a consistent strain of the anti-Gothic. The recourse to the supernatural occurs in *Jane Eyre* and *Wuthering Heights*, but in each case the emphasis is on recuperating the supernatural within a natural framework. In *Villette* the supernatural apparition of the nun is ultimately unmasked as nothing but a bundle of old clothes. The nun's function is to show Lucy's morbid psychological state. Similarly in *Wuthering Heights*, Heathcliff may be 'haunted' by Cathy, but this is as explicable on the level of a mental obsession as on that of the supernatural. Though both Charlotte and Emily successfully evoke the atmosphere of the ghost story (Bertha Mason's fearful laugh excites a *frisson* worthy of Mrs Radcliffe), finally, the novels' events are grounded in the real and have psychological credibility.

Emile Montégut, a nineteenth-century French critic, remarked of Charlotte Brontë:

> She excels in the natural depiction of the feelings born of spiritual terrors, the superstitions of solitude and the hallucinations of despair; she brings infinite art to the rendering of these intense and irresistible emotions.
>
> (quoted by M. Allott, in *Charlotte Brontë, a Casebook*, p. 136).

Charlotte handles the Gothic in two major ways; on one level she undercuts it; the sinister Grace Poole in *Jane Eyre* is a 'plain person' who drinks porter; Jane's rescue of Mr Rochester from his burning bed, a dramatic incident, has a comic twist, as she soaks him in water. On another level, however, the Gothic has symbolic significance, so that even the much-criticized recourse to the supernatural, when Jane 'hears' Mr Rochester calling her from Ferndean, can be interpreted psychologically, as indicating that Jane is finally independent enough to listen to her own inner promptings. But the fact that Rochester also 'hears' Jane suggests that Charlotte was still imbued with the charm of the Gothic and had not abandoned the supernatural. In *Villette*, by contrast, all mystery is revealed to have a natural origin. Yet here too, Charlotte avails herself of the conventions of the Gothic (for example, the plots enmeshing the heroine) to express complex levels of perception.

Emily also revitalized the Gothic. On one reading of her novel, Wuthering Heights can be seen as a haunted castle presided over by its Gothic ogre, Heathcliff. But at the same time, it is merely a Yorkshire farmhouse inhabited by unpleasant or eccentric rural characters. We do not, as readers, 'see' Cathy's ghost; she is visible only to Heathcliff, or Lockwood in his dream. Similarly, the Gothic contrivance of abducting the second Cathy to marry Linton is rendered largely plausible by the isolated rural setting. In Emily's novel there is no need to search for exoticism in the Pyrenees or Italy in the quest for human savagery. It has been located in the heart of rural England and established not just as socially, but as psychologically, credible. In a sense, the Gothic conventions of *Wuthering Heights* make it less rather than more strange: we find a point of conventional literary reference via the Gothic, in an otherwise uncharted psychological territory. Like Mary Shelley in *Frankenstein*, Emily appropriates in the Gothic a language that allows her to explore a virtually unknown inner world.

For both Charlotte and Emily, the Gothic helped to dramatize states of feeling not directly expressible thanks to their sexual or ambiguous nature. Charlotte's heroines are shown fighting continuous battles between duty and passion. What shocked a critic like Elizabeth Rigby, who said that Charlotte's work showed 'such genuine power with such horrid taste' (*Quarterly Review*, Dec. 1848), was that Charlotte revealed what her heroines felt, not what they were conventionally supposed to feel. Emily went further in traducing the virtuous Gothic heroine; Cathy does not even entertain the notion of duty, a concept left to her conventionally minded foster-sister, Nelly. Although such heroines are anti-Gothic in one sense, they are only too Gothic in exploiting the range of emotion available within the Gothic convention.

Byron

Possibly the single greatest literary influence on the Brontës was that of the poet George Gordon, Lord Byron. Byron and Byronism pervade the juvenilia and the adult fiction. In particular, the Byronic conception of love, the notion of fatal, guilt-ridden passions, is much in evidence in the Brontës' poetry and, in a destructive sense, in Branwell's life. Yet it is not only the Brontës' male protagonists who are Byronic (Heathcliff, Rochester, Huntingdon); their heroines often represent the transposition of the Byronic hero in a female form. This application of Byronic qualities to female characters had some curious consequences. Whereas the Gothic/Byronic hero could wallow in misery to his heart's content, for a heroine to do so was seen as somewhat blameworthy. Thus the overwhelming importance of love for Jane Eyre, Lucy Snowe or Cathy Earnshaw was seen by some Victorian critics as being in poor taste. Harriet Martineau complained when she reviewed *Villette* in 1853:

> Currer Bell here afflicts us with an amount of subjective misery which we may fairly remonstrate against, and she allows us no respite. . . . An atmosphere of pain hangs about the whole.

Martineau went on to argue that 'all the female characters are full of . . . one thought – love'. What in Byron's 'Don Juan' or 'The Giaour' would have formed a hero of fascination was felt to be unbecoming in a heroine. If Martineau was exercising a double standard of literary judgement, she correctly identified the powerful feelings raised by Lucy's character. The Brontë heroines, Cathy, Jane, Lucy and Helen Huntingdon, are passionate and rebellious. Their Byronism is arguably even more striking than that of Heathcliff or Rochester.

Given the scandals associated with Byron's life (his reputed liaison with his half-sister, Augusta Leigh, his spectacular separation from his wife, Annabella Milbanke, with its consequent exposure of brutality) and even his political radicalism and avowed sympathy for Napoleon, it is perhaps surprising that Mr Brontë, a stern moralist and Tory clergyman, should have bought the 1833 edition of Byron's *Life and Works*, edited by T. Moore. The children immediately absorbed his poetry. Charlotte's letter to Ellen Nussey, quoted above, shows this clearly. Already in the juvenilia of 1834, when Charlotte was 18, we can see her debt to Byron, both in her heroes (the fateful and fascinating Zamorna) and her heroines, who in the manner in which they hurl themselves at the feet of their lovers, are reminiscent both of the women in Byron's life and in his poetry.

What Byronic themes emerge in the Brontës' published works? The most striking is clearly that of the Byronic hero, such as Manfred, a descendant of Milton's Satan, characterized by a pale, high forehead and piercing eyes behind which seethe terrible passions. Possessing a fatal charm for women, he carries with him a burden of secret guilt and shows a demonic ruthlessness and drive for power. The Byronic hero was conceived of as an outcast, suffering partly from the stupidity of society, and partly from his own morbid impulses. In love, he destroyed what he adored, and fascinated his victims by his satanic traces of fallen beauty. Heathcliff, of mysterious origins, aspiring to the almost demonic possession of Cathy, and carrying out an endless revenge, provides a prototype of the fated Byronic hero.

Like Heathcliff, Rochester simultaneously both is and is not

Byronic. In him the high brow is not a sign of beauty; if anything, Jane describes him as rather ugly. However, in the Byronic tradition Rochester nourishes a guilty secret and, like Byron's Manfred ('I loved her and destroyed her'), attempts to harm his beloved. However, the most enduring legacy of Byronism on Charlotte can be found in her belief, noted by Martineau, that love alone could give meaning to life, a theme that pervades all her novels.

The Tenant of Wildfell Hall, on the other hand, seems to strike a strongly anti-Byronic note. The novel can be read as a dialogue between didacticism and Byronic libertinism. It is sometimes argued that Anne Brontë, influenced by Aunt Branwell's Methodism and living more in the world than her sisters, was the only Brontë not to be overwhelmed by Byronism. Yet it could be suggested that *The Tenant* is as Byronic a work as *Wuthering Heights* or *Jane Eyre*. Thanks to Charlotte's disapproval of the novel, based on her belief that it chronicled too closely Branwell's decline, it has often been read as Branwell's story, although it is admitted that Branwell's characteristics are divided between Arthur Huntingdon and Lord Lowborough. However, it is possible to overemphasize the novel's autobiographical basis. An equally probable model was Lord Byron's disastrous marriage to Annabella Milbanke, the details of which Anne would have known from Moore's *Life*. Helen Huntingdon's probity, her status as an heiress and her hope of reforming her husband, parallel Lady Byron's situation, character and unfortunate excursion into matrimony. Helen is captivated by Arthur Huntingdon's Byronic rakishness, and discovers, like Annabella Milbanke after her marriage, that he despises her moral idealism.

Charlotte, Branwell, Emily and Anne were outstandingly bookish children even in a bookish age. Their reading provided models for their writing and extended the range of their social and emotional perceptions. Books were their link with the world beyond Haworth. Whereas their early writing and much of their poetry bear the imprint of direct imitation and barely reworked cliché, we see in the published novels how the Brontës transformed and revitalized their literary experience. As Branwell said, 'I cannot express . . . the heavenliness of associations connected with such articles read and re-read while a little child.' His letter shows the passion of those whose real world lies between the covers of books.

94

8   The juvenilia

One of the problems endemic to Brontë studies, the blurring of distinctions between biographical fact and their published fictions, may be said to have bedevilled the Brontës themselves, since in their childhood writings they virtually lived their fictions as facts. In the juvenilia we can trace not only certain themes that emerge in their adult fiction, but also see, from this literary apprenticeship, how they conceived the rôle of writing in their lives.

Origins

In March 1895, the Brontë scholar Clement Shorter visited Mr Nicholls in Ireland and bought from him a parcel of manuscripts which included a collection of minute volumes in microscopic writing, the childhood output of Charlotte and Branwell Brontë. Mrs Gaskell, who had seen a selection of the tiny books in 1856, when she wrote her *Life*, considered the juvenilia to be evidence of the Brontës' precocious genius and literary apprenticeship, but she did not attempt the mammoth task of deciphering the manuscripts. Scholars who have subsequently analysed and transcribed the juvenilia, notably Fanny Ratchford and Christine Alexander (see Further Reading, p. 219), have shown the importance of the juvenilia for an understanding of the Brontës' lives and work. In their early writing, we have clear evidence that the Brontës' childhood was productive and imaginatively stimulating. To a great extent, their fictions compensated for the family's material and social limitations; indeed, these fictions were so glorious that they found it difficult to abandon them for the drabber conditions of adult life. Their gorgeous tales of fantasy, set in the warm climate of Africa or in the more bracing winds of the North Pacific and peopled by swashbuckling, powerful, amoral heroes and beautiful, suffering, adventurous and equally amoral heroines, created a world that gave these young authors god-like powers. Angria and Gondal, their imaginary kingdoms, were what Balzac described his *Human Comedy* as being, 'The world improved'.

The juvenilia also provide an illuminating psychological glimpse into the Brontës' lives, making credible the bold attempt to break into print and to publish poetry in 1845:

> We had very early cherished the dream of one day becoming authors. The highest stimulus, as well as the liveliest pleasure we had known from childhood upwards, lay in attempts at

literary composition; formerly we used to show each other what we wrote.

(Biographical Notice of Ellis, Acton and Currer Bell, 19 Sept. 1850)

Since childhood, the Brontës had considered themselves novelists and poets who enjoyed an appreciative public in one another. Formal publication meant expanding that public beyond their four selves and encountering for the first time the chill wind of criticism. The juvenilia, by contrast, was a shared and enclosed world, a secret paradise.

The juvenilia first date from 1826, when Charlotte was ten, Branwell nine, Emily eight and Anne six, but composition extended into adulthood. Charlotte wrote her Angrian romances until she was 23, when she renounced them. Emily and Anne referred familiarly to the Gondalians in their diary paper of 30 July 1841, when Emily was 23 and Anne 21. 'I wonder whether The Gondalians will still be flourishing [four years hence] and what will be their condition,' wrote Anne. 'I am now engaged in writing the fourth volume of Solala Vernon's *Life*.' This laconic reference is all we know of Solala Vernon, or her *Life*, whereas extensive prose works remain of the Angrian saga. No entire manuscripts of Gondal survive, and nothing in prose. All that is known of Anne's and Emily's juvenilia has been pieced together from references in their poetry.

The origins of the sagas will be found in a game the children devised with a set of toy soldiers that Mr Brontë brought Branwell from Leeds on 5 June 1826. Each child adopted a soldier as his or her own character, Branwell christening a soldier 'Buonaparte', Charlotte, 'Wellington', Emily, 'Gravey', and Anne, 'Waiting Boy'. Their games originally took the form of battles as befitted the participants, but then developed into a series of co-operative plays, in which the authors appear to have worked out the plots together and then to have written, individually, aspects of the complex civilization of Glass Town (subsequently and more grandly named 'Verreopolis', then 'Verdopolis') and finally, Gondal and Angria. There developed a sequence of three 'plays': the 'Young Men's Play', 'Our Fellows Play', and 'The Islanders Play'. By 1829, the children were writing miniature books about these adventures to correspond in scale with the toy soldiers' size. The tiny 'books' (see picture opposite) had their format modelled on *Blackwood's Magazine*. What is even more remarkable is that they kept the tiny writing into adolescence and early maturity, long after they had all outgrown the toy soldiers that inspired the stories. One supposes that since the later stories expressed the Brontës' adolescent fantasies, the small scale was, in part, a strategy of

Little books, Charlotte Brontë, 1824 and 1830

concealment. Patrick Brontë with his failing eyesight was unlikely to decipher them and hence to disapprove of his children's writing. But in the early stages, the juvenilia reflect the children's notion of how the adult world appeared from the Lilliputian perspective of a toy soldier.

The Glass Town Saga

The juvenilia fall into three stages. The earliest, in 1826, involved three 'plays'. These rapidly merged into the Glass Town Saga (1826–31), to which all four children contributed and which they acted out as a game. Eventually, between 1829 and 1830 they began to produce written versions of these games. In the third stage, beginning in 1831, Charlotte and Branwell developed their kingdom of Angria whereas Emily and Anne went their own way to chronicle the history of Gondal. Angrian literature was 'published' in their imitation of *Blackwood's* which they called 'The Young Men's Magazine'.

There is almost certainly significance in the fact that the Glass Town Saga was first launched in 1826, a year after the deaths of Maria and Elizabeth. The children imagined themselves as four genii with stupendous powers, able even to bring the dead back to life. Daily events and childish rages were transformed into epic battles in which the genii meted out fearful punishments to those who displeased them. As genii, the children could shape the world entirely to their own desires.

The early characters of the Glass Town Saga were sometimes rogues and pirates, but more frequently drawn from current events or recent history, the visible effect of Mr Brontë's interest in politics and of the periodicals to which he subscribed. Thus the Peninsular Wars and the names of Buonaparte and Arthur Wellesley, 1st Duke of Wellington, become central to the plots. Glass Town, set in deserts studded with oases and surrounded by mountains, had a lush, fairy-tale setting. At the same time, it was an industrial town, like nearby Leeds or Halifax. Eventually, imaginary young aristocrats began to predominate over the purely historical characters, as the authors' individual preferences began to shape the different tales. Branwell was initially fascinated in enumerating not only battles but populations, trades and so on, providing a kind of economic and social history; Charlotte early began to concentrate on psychological analysis and Romantic fantasy. Her Romanticism and Branwell's sanguinary battles did not, apparently, appeal to the younger Emily and Anne. Their early heroes, Parry and Ross, were Yorkshiremen, whose lack of polish formed a marked contrast to the otherwise aristocratic flavour of Verdopolis. 'Gravey' and 'Waiting Boy', the names

Emily and Anne chose for their original soldiers, contrast prosaically with Branwell's Buonaparte and Charlotte's Wellington. Evidently, the older children were entering their heroic phase. The works of these early juvenilia also show considerable humour. Charlotte, for example, mocked Branwell's artistic pretensions in the persona of Soult the Rhymer, a bombastic and hyper-enthusiastic poet. One of the characteristics of the early works is the good-natured raillery that shines through them.

We can get a sense of the interplay between the children's fictional creations from an article written by Charlotte for the 'Young Men's Magazine' of October 1830 under the pseudonym of Lord Charles Wellesley (son of the Duke of Wellington) which gives an account of a visit to Genius Emily's Kingdom, or Sir Edward Barry's Land. This piece offers evidence of the bent of Anne and Emily's fiction, altogether more realistic and based on their everyday world, with factories 'breathing thick columns of almost tangible smoke!'. The narrator of this sketch finds the inhabitants (namely, characters from Emily and Anne's stories) speaking in an uncouth Northern accent, and eating a mundane diet of roast beef, Yorkshire pudding, mashed potatoes and apple pie. In Charlotte's lampoon, one sees the two teams of children moving in different directions; Anne and Emily concentrating on local details of ordinary life, though also influenced by Byronic models, and Charlotte and Branwell already gripped by the Romantic, heroic and extravagant.

Two other themes to emerge in the juvenilia at this juncture are a fascination with France, stimulated by Branwell's hero-worship of Napoleon, and an interest in the supernatural. It is not known how Charlotte first learned French, which she seems to have read prior to going to Roe Head, but in 1830 she translated Book I of Voltaire's epic, *L'Henriade*. As a girl, she nourished an ambition to go to Paris, for which her eventual journey to Brussels was a partial substitute. With regard to the supernatural, Charlotte wrote an article in 'The Young Men's Magazine' about 'the truth of supernatural interference with the affairs of men'. This was also a question debated in *Blackwood's* (for example, in the issue of June 1826). It is possible to trace common preoccupations in the young Brontës' writing, which for many years remained largely collaborative. Developments by one influenced the others. When Branwell decided to kill off Zamorna's long-suffering wife, for example, Charlotte, then at school, felt bereaved and resurrected her. If Anne or Emily showed an early tendency to 'realism', they were by no means immune from the aristocratic ethos of Charlotte's Verdopolis or unacquainted with the supernatural; they were simply filling in another aspect of a joint fantasy world.

In spite of European characters and occasional reminiscences of the Yorkshire moors, most of Charlotte's and Branwell's stories took place in a mythical Africa. This setting reflects contemporary interest in African exploration which the Brontës would have read about in *Blackwood's Magazine*. The Africa they imagined was a luxuriant and exotic world, in every respect unlike the harsh climate and scanty vegetation around Haworth. A manuscript of 1830 describing Glass Town shows a curious mixture of Palladian palaces and African flora. As the 14-year-old Charlotte expressed it in a hackneyed but precocious vocabulary:

> Here the tufted olive, the fragrant myrtle, the stately palm-tree, the graceful almond, the rich vine and the queenly rose mingled in sweet odorous shadiness, and bordered the high banks of a clear and murmuring river over whose waters a fresh breeze swept which cooled delightfully the burning air of the desert which surrounded it.

In this land of lush vegetation surrounded by burning deserts lived characters of an enviable sophistication, reflecting young Charlotte's ideas of high life.

Angria

The intense phase of her juvenile writing obsessed Charlotte, particularly at Roe Head, where her imaginary world was so visibly in conflict with school routine. Angria was a secret kingdom to which she retreated mentally from an uncongenial reality. She did not reveal its existence to Ellen Nussey (to whom she confided almost nothing about her artistic ambitions) but did tell Mary Taylor something about it:

> She [Charlotte] had a habit of writing in italics, and she said she had learnt it by writing in their magazine. They brought out a 'magazine' once a month, and wished it to look as like print as possible. She told us a tale out of it. No one wrote in it, and no one read it, but herself, her brother and two sisters. She promised to show me some of these magazines, but retracted it afterwards, and would never be persuaded to do so. This habit of 'making out' interests for themselves, that most children get who have none in actual life, was very strong in her. The whole family used to 'make out' histories and invent characters and events.
>
> (Mary Taylor, 18 Jan. 1856)

Mary was struck by the inward-looking quality of these Angrian fantasies and, in a characteristically homely metaphor, told Charlotte that 'they were like growing potatoes in a cellar'.

Charlotte's most powerful character, with whom she strongly

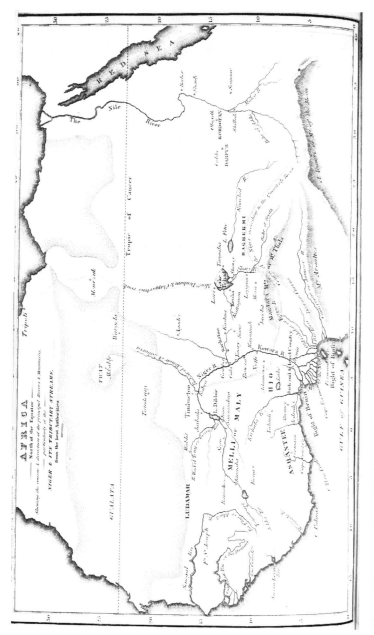

Map of Northern Africa, Blackwood's Magazine, 1826, a possible inspiration for Glass Town's geography

identified, the Duke of Zamorna, was a masterful aristocrat, imbued, in the Byronic manner, with a fatal charm over women. Her 'nether world' as she came to refer to it with Branwell, was a source of growing conflict, coming between her and familial/religious duties. Though the Angrian vision which she experienced with a hallucinatory intensity became something to be shunned, it nevertheless was an overwhelming reality for her. As she recorded in her Roe Head journal:

> Never shall I, Charlotte Brontë, forget what a voice of wild and wailing music now came thrillingly to my mind's, almost my body's ear, nor how distinctly I, sitting in the schoolroom at Roe Head, saw the Duke of Zamorna leaning against that obelisk. . . . I was quite gone. I had really, utterly forgot where I was and all the gloom and cheerlessness of my situation. I felt myself breathing quick and short as I beheld the Duke lifting up his sable crest, which undulated as the plume of a hearse waves to the wind, and knew that music which sprang as mournfully triumphant as the scriptural verse, O Grave, where is thy sting? O Death where is thy Victory? was exciting him and quickening his ever-rapid pulse. 'Miss Brontë, what are you thinking about?' said a voice that dissipated all the charm, and Miss Lister thrust her little rough black head into my face.

The vision is both seen and heard, a drug-like dream, yet what is most characteristic of her later work in this passage is the ironic perception of the chasm between visionary power and the mundane world, intruding in the unwelcome form of Miss Lister. Even in her Journal, Charlotte is, as it were, composing the drama of her own perceptions.

Charlotte's juvenilia are entertaining to read in their unabashed recourse to melodrama. One of the basic plots involves the rivalry of Northangerland and Zamorna for power and influence in Verdopolis. This male rivalry is paralleled by female rivalry for the divine Zamorna's attentions. Mary, his wife, the daughter of Northangerland, shares his affections with a mistress, Mina Laury. Similarly, an earlier tale recounts the passion of Mariane Hume for the Marquis of Douro, nearly wrecked by the jealous machinations of Zenobia, Lady Ellrington. A description of Zamorna will convey some notion of Charlotte's literary style at this period, as well as of his charms:

> He seemed to be in the full bloom of youth; his figure was toweringly, overbearingly lofty, moulded in statuelike perfection, and invested with something which I cannot describe; something superb, impetuous, resistless; something, in short, no single word can altogether express. His hair was intensely black, curled

'Zamorna', drawing by Charlotte Brontë, c. 1831

luxuriantly, but the forehead underneath, instead of having the swarthy tinge proper to such Italian locks, looked white and smooth as ivory. His eyebrows were black and broad, but his long eyelashes and large clear eyes were deep sepia brown. The wreaths on his temples were brought so low as to meet the profusely curled raven whiskers and mustachios, which hid his mouth and chin, and shadowed his fair-complexioned cheeks. I thought these symbols of manhood much too strong and abundant for his evident juvenility. When he smiled, lips and teeth appeared such as any lady might have envied, coral-red and pearl-white. The upper lip was very short – Grecian – and had a haughty curl which I knew well. At the first glance I discerned him to be a military man.

('My Angria and the Angrians')

In effect, this description is a prose version of Byron's Conrad, in *The Corsair*. The curls, in particular, are telling:

> Sun-burnt his cheek, his forehead high and pale
> The sable curls in wild profusion veil;
> And oft perforce his rising lip reveals
> The haughtier thought it curbs, but scarce conceals.

(Canto I, Section IX)

If Zamorna is haughty with a Grecian profile, raven whiskers and mustachios, the Angrian beauties are a similar amalgam of ideal qualities, reminiscent of the figures in ladies' annuals that Charlotte, Anne and Emily loved to copy. Zenobia, who reminds us of the Ingram ladies in *Jane Eyre*, is described in exclamatory terms:

> What eyes! What raven hair! What an imposing contour of form and countenance! She is perfectly grand in her velvet robes, dark plume, and crown-like turban. . . . There is fire in her eyes, and command on her brow; and some touch of a pride that would spurn restraint in the curl of her rich lip. But all is so tempered with womanly dignity that it would seem as if neither fire nor pride nor imperiousness could awaken the towering fits of ungoverned and frantic rage that often deform her beauty.

('Mary')

The 'towering fits of ungoverned and frantic rage that often deform her beauty', while more than faintly comic in the context of Zenobia's supposed grandeur, suggest the menacing character of Bertha Mason in *Jane Eyre*.

The ideal and gentle heroine Mariane Hume is the opposite in character and physique. Here one sees the type of Polly Home (even to the similarity in names), developed in *Villette*:

The other form was that of a very young and slender girl, whose complexion was delicately, almost transparently, fair. Her cheeks were tinted with rich, soft, crimson, her features moulded in the utmost perfection of loveliness; while the clear light of her brilliant hazel eyes, and the soft waving of her auburn ringlets, gave additional charms to what seemed already infinitely too beautiful for this earth.

('The Bridal')

Nor does Charlotte neglect more earth-bound types. In the later juvenilia she introduces Elizabeth, a governess, whose father lives in a remote country parish, and whose brother has been disgraced and forced to flee society. In the stories about Elizabeth, Charlotte was experimenting with themes closer to home. The figure of the cad and the disgraced brother, Henry Hastings, reflects early and well-founded anxieties about Branwell.

Gondal

From the evidence of their diary papers, it does not appear that Emily and Anne felt the same qualms about their Gondalian world as Charlotte experienced with regard to Angria. For example, in 1845, while the family was undergoing Branwell's appalling scenes in the wake of his dismissal from Thorp Green, Emily's and Anne's birthday notes contain matter-of-fact news of Gondal as well as details of daily life in Haworth. The two are mentioned in the same linguistic register, quite unselfconsciously, as could only occur in a private document, and reveal the closely shared nature of the Gondalian experience. Emily's description of a trip she and Anne took to York indicates the extent to which they 'lived' in Gondal:

Anne and I went on our first long journey by ourselves together, leaving home on the 30th of June, Monday, sleeping at York, returning to Keighley Tuesday evening, sleeping there and walking home on Wednesday morning. . . . And during our excursion we were, Roland Macalgin, Henry Angora, Juliet Angusteena, Isabella Esmaldan, Ella and Julian Egremont, Catharine Navarre, and Cordilia Fitzaphnold, escaping from the palace of instruction to join the Royalists who are hard driven at present by the victorious Republicans. The Gondals still flourish bright as ever. I am at present writing a work on the First Wars. Anne has been writing some articles on this, and a book by Henry Sophona. We intend sticking firm by the rascals as long as they delight us, which I am glad to say they do at present.

An interesting omission in this diary paper is of any description of the actual journey. Emily provides us with no details of York and its antiquities; rather, the trip is a holiday into Gondal. Having escaped the parsonage, they could indulge in the wider and wilder world of their fantasies. It is pleasant to think of these two shy vicar's daughters, outwardly unremarkable on their journey to York, ranging over the most astonishing if not lurid adventures in their imaginations. Though the works in which the above-named characters appeared do not survive, this passage suggests some key qualities of Gondal. The names are redolent, like Charlotte's and Branwell's, of a high life, so different from the meagre setting of the Haworth parsonage with its stone floors, curtainless windows and limited social resources. It is a curious but pleasing contradiction that the taciturn Emily, now in her late twenties and despising social norms in dress and behaviour, should have vicariously enjoyed richly extravagant society in her Gondalian life and that the self-effacing Anne should have done the same.

Emily Brontë's poems and the juvenilia

Emily's poetry will be considered in Part Three. It is raised here only it in its Gondal/Gaaldine context. Gondal was an island in the North Pacific, a land of lakes and mountains, with a harsh and blustering climate reminiscent of Yorkshire. Its people were characterized by their passionate temperaments and were intensely patriotic. Gondal was organized politically into a confederation of provinces each governed by a hereditary ruling family, a situation giving scope for endless feuds and wars. There existed, for example, a deadly rivalry between the House of Brensaida, in the Kingdom of Angora, and the House of Exina. Gaaldine, on the other hand, was a large tropical island in the South Pacific, discovered and colonized by Gondalian mariners. The feuds of Gondal were transposed intact to Gaaldine where the rival houses contested their new empire. The prose literature of Gondal/Gaaldine, which appears to have been extensive, does not survive.

Emily's poetry has been notoriously resistant to interpretation. The majority of the 200-odd poems can be understood as commemorating events in the Gondalian Saga, whose protagonist is Queen Augusta Geraldine Almeda. The efforts of readers to find a consistent pattern of development of theme and character have been foiled by the often contradictory evidence deduced from the poems. It is likely that the assumptions about critical intelligibility and coherence, upon which we traditionally operate as readers, did not trouble Emily. The saga was a collection of accounts of, or meditations on, the world of Gondal and Gaaldine. But Emily does not offer one unified perspective from which to piece it together.

This device of plural perspectives could be seen as anticipating the narrative technique of *Wuthering Heights*.

It is, however, possible to build up a narrative sequence for the poems, though not in a chronological order. The same incident may be commemorated at a distance of several years and from the viewpoints of different characters. This confirms the sense, gathered from the diary papers, that Emily and Anne thought of Gondal not merely as their fiction, but as an autonomous world on whose history different characters within that world could comment. Queen Augusta Geraldine Almeda, for example, undergoes an astonishing series of adventures and shifts in character: she is originally a 'being whose very presence blessed, like gladsome summer day'. She subsequently loses her lover, Alexander, Lord of Elbe, in Gaaldine, is imprisoned in a dungeon, escapes, and becomes in further adventures an unscrupulous destroyer of men. She is the equivalent to the Byronic hero, a female Zamorna, indulging in a stunning series of unconventional passions for improbably named lovers, one of whom commits suicide. To say that Gondalian plots are melodramatic is an understatement. As far as Emily's poetry is concerned, they have the advantage of allowing the expression of heightened feeling and extravagant passion. Gondal/Gaaldine characters, from the evidence of the poetry, lived in a world of extraordinary intensity, in this respect resembling the characters in the otherwise more realistically rooted world of *Wuthering Heights*.

With the exception of Emily's poetry, the Brontë juvenilia has little strictly literary value. The juvenile writings have been anathematized by Queenie Leavis as 'vulgar', and, in the sense that they are largely self-indulgent fantasy, they do fall into a tradition of juvenile vulgarity which can also be found recorded in writers as diverse as Flaubert and Sartre. Though often banal and melodramatic, the juvenilia are, nevertheless, fascinating, even if they seem to verge on the pathological. In the Brontës' case it was the habit of writing itself that was to prove important. Like most children who enjoy writing, they wrote parodies of what they read. If we look at the derivative Byronic style, the sententious bombast of battles and high life, we see not great literary works in embryo but a delight in fantasy, in the manipulation of language and a sense of power and freedom that the exercise of their imaginations and intelligence gave them. They absorbed not only the actual world around them but everything they could find to read about. They were fortunate in having one another as readers and as critics. But as Charlotte discovered in her twenties, the indulgence of fantasy, to the exclusion of reality, was a state very close to madness. It is possible that it was partly the shared nature of the juvenilia that saved the Brontës from a complete mental retreat from the world.

In addition, the juvenilia, along with the *devoirs* that Charlotte and Emily wrote in French for M. Heger, are valuable evidence of apprenticeship in writing. The sheer volume of what they wrote is astonishing as well as its diminutive format. Their productivity seems to have been limitless. Significantly, it was only after Branwell's, Emily's and Anne's deaths that Charlotte experienced difficulty in writing, as the painful agonizing over *Villette* shows. She no longer had around her those beings, so close as to be extensions of herself, for whom she could write with unalloyed pleasure and unselfconsciousness.

The juvenilia thus form a fascinating parallel to the biographical history of the Brontës. In their case, the life of the imagination came close to swamping the life of external reality. Branwell, in the end, could not reconcile the pleasures of fantasy and the limitations of the real world. Emily seems to have enjoyed most unproblematically the experience of Gondalian freedom, and to have evinced the least conflict. But the balance for all the Brontës must have been precarious. Charlotte's lines, 'We wove a web in childhood, a web of sunny air', convey the ambiguous attraction of Gondal and Angria. The web was both a symbol of fragility and entrapment. It was their adult fiction which showed that they were able to escape from the spell of the genii. Because the Brontë children effectively created their own heaven in their writings, fantasy seemed to them to operate in opposition to the voice of religion. Angria and Gondal offer one clue to the dialectical structure of the novels. 'Heaven did not seem to be my home,' says Cathy. Their heaven lay in the shared mythology recorded in the juvenilia.

9 The Brontës and the visual arts

When Mr Brontë engaged a painting master, William Robinson of Leeds, for Branwell in 1835, Emily, Anne and Charlotte were allowed to share the lessons. Sketching or water-colour painting, especially of landscapes or of flowers, were considered part of a genteel girl's education. Branwell, unlike his sisters, was to train as a professional painter; for them, a career in the fine arts would not have been thought possible. However, nourishing, perhaps, secret ambitions of artistic success, the girls, in addition, taught themselves drawing by copying engravings from periodicals. Lucy Snowe is shown engaged in this form of painstaking transcription:

> I sat bent over my desk, drawing – that is, copying an elaborate line engraving, tediously working up my copy to the finish of the original, for that was my practical notion of art; and, strange to say, I took extreme pleasure in the labour, and could even produce curiously finical Chinese facsimilies of steel and mezzotint plates – things about as valuable as so many achievements in worsted-work, but I thought pretty well of them in those days.
>
> (*Villette*, Ch. 35)

Thomas Bewick

More significant for their imaginative development than the above method of producing 'finical Chinese facsimilies of steel and mezzotint plates', the Brontës were exposed to two artists, Thomas Bewick and John Martin, who became the inspiration for some of their most powerful images. Bewick was a wood engraver and naturalist, Martin, a nineteenth-century painter of enormous, visionary canvases. Bewick with his lovingly detailed sketches of rural life, a sort of homely pastoral, and Martin with his dramatic extravaganzas in colour, illustrating biblical scenes that the Brontës knew so well from Bunyan, Milton and the Bible itself, provided a Romantic avenue of escape through the visual imagination.

The most striking link between painting and the novels can be found in *Jane Eyre*, where Bewick's 1804 edition of *The History of British Birds*, owned by Mr Brontë and profusely illustrated in black and white woodcuts, appears in the opening chapter and informs the novel throughout in its imagery. *The History of British Birds* comprises a series of illustrated descriptions of the principal birds of the British Isles. At the end of each entry Bewick included smaller woodcuts unrelated to the text, showing either a vignette of country life (a fowler, a fisherman, a harvester) or some humorous, melancholic or supernatural scene. The introductions to the two volumes, written by the Reverend Cotes of Bedlington, near Newcastle, who collaborated with Bewick, were theoretical and philosophic: in them were stressed the astonishing variety and richness of the living world, and the interdependence of species. In the spectacle of nature, the reader was encouraged to discern the workings of a meaningful Providence in the seeming waste and struggle of life within the created world:

> It is a melancholy reflection, that, from man, downwards, to the smallest living creature, all are found to prey upon and devour each other. The philosophic mind, however, sees this waste of animal life again and again repaired by fresh stores, ever ready to supply the void, and the great work of generation and destruction perpetually going on, and to this dispensation of an all-wise Providence, so interesting to humanity, bows in awful silence.
>
> (Introduction, vol. 2, p. xv)

Both Bewick's drawings and the accompanying prose descriptions lingered in Charlotte's imagination. In 1832, when she was 16, she wrote some 'Lines on Bewick', demonstrating her admiration and describing certain vignettes that were later to appear in *Jane Eyre*:

> There rises some lone rock all wet with surge
> And dashing billows glimmering in the light
> Of a wan moon, whose silent rays emerge
> From clouds that veil their lustre, cold and bright.
>
> And there 'mongst reeds upon a river's side
> A wild bird sits, and brooding o'er her nest
> Still guards the priceless gems, her joy and pride,
> Now ripening 'neath her hope-enlivened breast.
>
> (lines 45–52)

All the children copied Bewick's drawings and may initially have been attracted to the vignettes because of their small size. They were almost ready-made illustrations for the diminutive Angrian and Gondal epics, appealing to the young Brontës much as comic books do to twentieth-century children, by offering visual examples of dramatic incidents.

Bewick further functions as an important anticipatory device in *Jane Eyre*. When Jane goes to Thornfield, she takes with her a portfolio of paintings whose subjects are reminiscent of scenes from both Bewick and John Martin. In Chapter 13 she describes three of her pictures at length; they are watercolours, macabre in conception. One is of a wreck, on which sits a cormorant, 'Sinking below the bird and mast, a drowned corpse glanced through the green water'; the second is personification of the evening star; the third 'showed the pinnacle of an iceberg piercing a polar winter sky', in the foreground 'a colossal head ... an eye hollow and fixed, blank of meaning but for the glassiness of despair'. Though these paintings are more allegorical than most of Bewick's vignettes, the wreck, the iceberg and the cormorant are certainly inspired by Bewick. More striking even than these 'paintings' is the opening of *Jane Eyre*, which begins with an account of Jane reading Bewick's description of the arctic region. She sits in the window-seat of the drawing room at Gateshead, screened from her unfriendly cousins by closed crimson curtains, enthralled by Bewick's description of the northern habitats of birds:

I returned to my book – Bewick's *History of British Birds*: the letter-press thereof I cared little for, generally speaking; and yet there were certain introductory pages that, child as I was, I could not pass quite as a blank. They were those which treat of the haunts of the sea-fowl; of 'the solitary rocks and promontories' by them only inhabited; of the coast of Norway, studded with isles from its southern extremity, the Lindeness, or Naze to the North Cape –

Where the Northern Ocean in vast whirls,
Boils round the naked, melancholy isles
Of farthest Thule; and the Atlantic surge
Pours in among the stormy Hebrides.

Nor could I pass unnoticed the suggestion of the bleak shores of Lapland, Siberia, Spitzbergen, Nova Zembla, Iceland, Greenland, with 'the vast sweep of the Arctic Zone, and those forlorn regions of dreary space – that reservoir of frost and snow, where firm fields of ice, the accumulation of centuries of winters, glazed in Alpine heights above heights, surround the pole, and concentre the multiplied rigours of extreme cold'. Of these death-white realms I formed an idea of my own: shadowy, like all the half-comprehended notions that float dim through children's brains, but strangely impressive. The words in these introductory pages connected themselves with the succeeding vignettes, and gave significance to the rock standing up alone in a sea of billow and spray; to the broken boat stranded on a desolate coast; to the cold and ghastly moon glancing through bars of cloud at a wreck just sinking.

(Ch. 1)

Thomas Bewick, British Birds
'*Two ships becalmed on a torpid sea*' (p. 112, top)
'*Churchyard*' (p. 112, bottom)
'*The Fiend pinning down the Thief's Pack*' (p. 113, top)
'*Devil and the Gallows*' (p. 113, bottom)

113

Bewick's evocation of Arctic snow and the frozen oceans provides a powerful symbol of desolation for the orphaned Jane. Throughout the novel, cold is associated with exclusion and love-lessness. For example, when Mr Rochester's attempted bigamy has been exposed (Chapter 26), Jane sits alone in her room trying to understand her feelings of loss; the imagery is of a desolate Arctic winter, like those Bewick described, overpowering what seemed an Angrian Paradise:

> A Christmas frost had come at midsummer; a white December storm had whirled over June . . . and the woods, which twelve hours since waved leafy and fragrant as groves between the tropics, now spread waste, wild and white as pine forests in wintry Norway.

(Ch. 26)

The polarity of heat and cold extends to description of characters. Fire and warmth are consistently associated with Rochester (even to the burning down of his house), winter and ice with the blood-less St John Rivers, who is as 'cold as an iceberg'.

There is another literal rendering of Bewick in *Jane Eyre*. The Arctic passage in Chapter 1 goes on to detail seven vignette drawings which can be identified from Bewick's second volume (see pp. 112–13). Bewick's vignettes typically show some small drama of rural life; a scene from which imaginative readers, like the Brontë children, might construct a whole romance. Rather than his more typical decorative, or comic, pictures of rural life, all the vignettes that Jane remembers concern fearsome or supernatural subjects: a shipwreck, marine phantoms, a deserted churchyard and a gibbet with a man hanging on it watched from afar by a devil-hobgoblin figure. Though these morbid or comic sketches are by no means characteristic of the majority of Bewick's decorative drawings, they are the ones that Charlotte isolated to project the feelings of Jane as a nervous and lonely child. The macabre and the supernatural, incidental to Bewick, are central to *Jane Eyre*. What begins as a visual image in the novel's opening chapter is transformed into a major theme, emerging in dreams and presentiments, first orchestrated in Bewick's graphic vignettes. The influence of natural history reading on Charlotte seems to have inculcated not so much an analytic and scientific view of the world as to have formed a mind furnished with images of isolation, grandeur and terror that paralleled inner states of being.

John Martin

The other painter who inspired the Brontës was John Martin (1789–1854). 'Inspired' is, perhaps, too weak a word. Martin's paintings, which to twentieth-century taste may appear, to say the least, melodramatic, fed the Brontës' appetite for dramatic situations and exotic settings. His paintings were like visual equivalents of Gondal and Angria. The huge canvases, often showing the clash of the human and divine, the overpowering of gigantic cities by the Deluge, for example, remind one of the clash of irreconcilable emotional forces in *Wuthering Heights*. The excitement of the apocalypse is characteristic of Martin's work. In turn, the apocalyptic imagination, nourished on its biblical sources and the real disasters that afflicted them, is a feature of the Brontës' work. The parsonage contained at least four of his engravings or mezzotints; 'Joshua Arresting the Sun', 'The Deluge', 'The Passage of the Red Sea' and 'Belshazzar's Feast', and the Brontës saw copies of many more in annuals such as *The Keepsake* or *Friendship's Offering*. 'Belshazzar's Feast' was clearly in Charlotte's mind in writing her 'Biographical Notice to *Wuthering Heights* of 1850':

> Too often do reviewers remind us of the mob of Astrologers, Chaldeans, and Soothsayers gathered before the 'writing on the wall,' and unable to read the characters or make known the interpretation. We have a right to rejoice when a true seer comes at last, some man in whom is an excellent spirit, to whom have been given light, wisdom and understanding; who can accurately read the 'Mene, Tekel, Upharsin' of an original mind.

This reference to the writing on the wall, a text which few can interpret but which is an omen for the future, has pictorial rather than merely biblical resonances for Charlotte. The terrified throng, contemplating the divine message in Martin's 'Belshazzar's Feast', (see cover) suggests the visionary power that the Brontës brought to their writing. The Brontës were by no means alone in admiring 'Belshazzar's Feast'; it was Martin's most famous painting and enjoyed enormous popularity. Instead of the traditional neoclassical depiction of the biblical scene, Martin created a vast, architectural geometry suggesting Babylonian grandeur, the whole on a red ground in which human figures were dwarfed.

Glass Town, as I have suggested, was heavily indebted to Martin's art. His vast architectural perspectives of the ancient world were visual equivalents of Romantic feeling. Combined with the legacy of Byronism, Martin's painting offered the Brontës an unlimited imaginative terrain. He recorded biblical moments of high drama, often set in architecturally magnificent cities, improbably combining elements of Babylon, Egypt and Greece. He can be compared with Piranesi in his architectural fantasies and with Gustave Doré and the Belgian painter James Ensor for conveying a sense of urban dream architecture. Martin also painted a series of immense canvases on the subjects of the Last Judgement and

Paradise Lost. Contemporary admiration was epitomized by the *Art Journal* of 1853 which characterized 'The Last Judgement' as 'of a character too awful to be made themes of the painter's art'. The sense of insignificance and vulnerability of the human figure was a remarkable property of Martin's paintings. The shipwreck and drowned figure in *Jane Eyre* partake of this quality. Another Martin painting, 'The Assuaging of the Waters' (1840), shows a raven attacking a snake as the Deluge recedes and a shell-like structure in the water which one might imagine to be a drowned corpse. It is reminiscent of Jane's painting of the cormorant. One suspects an amalgam of Bewick's cormorant and Martin's deluge in Jane's eerie composition (see p. 117).

Both the grandeur of the architectural vision and the frail yet indomitable human figure are themes echoed visually and metaphorically in the Brontës' novels. The satanic defiance of Heathcliff or Rochester, the isolation and iron reserve of Jane Eyre or Lucy Snowe evoke the biblical illustrations in which Martin depicts one figure, such as Samson or Joshua, in which the universe is ranged against the solitary subject. Similarly, Heathcliff's defiance of heaven and hell, when he begs to be haunted by Cathy's ghost, can be interpreted as a verbal equivalent of Martin's tormented visionaries:

> You said I killed you – haunt me then! The murdered *do* haunt their murderers I believe – I know that ghosts *have* wandered on earth. Be with me always – take any form – drive me mad! only *do* not leave me in this abyss, where I cannot find you!
>
> (*Wuthering Heights*, Ch. 16)

It was the hallucinatory quality of Martin's work which arguably had the greatest impact on the Brontës' imagination. We see it transposed in Charlotte's dream-like evocation of Brussels in *Villette*:

> . . . and where was I? In a land of enchantment, a garden most gorgeous, a plain sprinkled with coloured meteors, a forest with sparks of purple and ruby and golden fire gemming the foliage; a region, not of trees and shadow, but of strangest architectural wealth – of altar and of temple, of pyramid, obelisk, and sphinx; incredible to say, the wonders and symbols of Egypt teemed throughout the park of Villette.
>
> (Ch. 38)

Finally, one may remember that Anne's heroine, Helen Huntingdon, in *The Tenant of Wildfell Hall*, earns her living by painting landscapes. Her artistic talent both allows her to escape from an unhappy marriage and is a means of 'free' expression for one whose life is otherwise lived under conditions of great self-

John Martin, 'The Assuaging of the Waters', 1840

restraint. From Jane Eyre's unearthly drawings to Helen Huntingdon's canvases, painting functions in the novels as an important metaphor for revealing artistic ambition and suppressed personality.

Branwell's artistic career was not negligible, though he was never able to live from his portraits. As we know, he failed to enrol in the Royal Academy and returned home, having squandered his money on drink. However, he did continue to study and had a number of portraits of family, friends and local worthies to his credit. He painted Emily in profile and a family group with himself carrying a gun (see p. 45). The most striking and famous of Branwell's paintings, however, is the family grouping of Emily, Anne and Charlotte in which he originally included himself and subsequently blotted out his own likeness, leaving only a pillar. This group portrait was found folded in a drawer among Mr Nicholls' effects; its creases are still visible in the painting (see Frontispiece). The sisters' stark dresses, the dark backcloth and their sombre expressions convey the atmosphere of their lives as young adults. The very stiffness of the portrait, with its rather amateur execution, does not invalidate the individuality captured in each one of the three subjects. Branwell's eerie self-annihilation in this painting indicates, in all probability, how he saw himself in relation to his sisters, as better invisible. We may imagine Branwell performing a symbolic suicide. His pen and ink self-portrait as a corpse (p. 47) offers further evidence of his mixture of bravura and morbidity. But posterity can be grateful to him for preserving these visual images of his sisters, otherwise so elusive to us.

10   The condition of women question

Man to command and woman to obey;
All else confusion.

(Tennyson, 'The Princess', 1847)

Education and employment for women in the nineteenth century

The Brontë sisters were curiously placed with regard to the nineteenth-century struggle for women's emancipation. Politically and
socially conservative, neither Charlotte, Emily nor Anne overtly
rebelled against women's legal or psychological subordination;
nevertheless, they challenged many traditional assumptions about
women's position. Early critics of the Brontës were quick to
recognize a sexually and politically subversive quality in their
work. *Jane Eyre*, especially, came under attack in this regard. Lady
Eastlake, in 1848, accused its author of fomenting the spirit of
revolution and Chartism. It would be misleading to suggest,
however, that the Brontës in any sense campaigned as feminists
or that they rejected the Victorian feminine ideal. Rather, it will
be argued, one impulse behind their novels was their dreams of
feminine power, not attainable to them in reality, or only attainable through the medium of art.

If we remind ourselves of women's legal and social position in
early nineteenth-century Britain, we can appreciate how the
Brontës' novels seemed to their contemporary critics to challenge
traditional sexual attitudes. At the beginning of the century, for
example, women could not vote, a married woman could not own
property nor sue her husband for divorce, though he could divorce
her; and she had no rights of custody over their children, no legal
share in the house in which she lived and no control over the
money she herself might inherit or earn. As Charlotte put it
despairingly in a letter to Miss Wooler, after reading an article on
'the condition of woman question' by Harriet Taylor, these were
'evils . . . which no efforts of ours can touch; of which we cannot
complain; of which it is advisable not too often to think'. Improved
social and legal conditions for women arose partly as a consequence
of demands for greater equality and parliamentary representation
among other social groups. Such reform occurred slowly and
against great opposition. In 1839 the Infants Custody Bill, which

allowed women custody of their children in cases of separation or divorce, was passed after a five-year battle. In 1869 the Municipal Franchise Act gave single women property holders the right to vote in local elections; in 1870, the Married Woman's Property Act awarded women control over their own property; in 1875 women were allowed to sit on school boards and in 1894 on parish and district councils. Full suffrage did not occur until after protracted struggles and was only finally granted in the wake of the First World War, in 1918.

Employment prospects for women were poor and reflected class divisions as well as sexual prejudice. Where women were allowed to work, in factories and domestic service, for example, they earned much less than men. Whereas, thanks to industrialization and the growth of the servant class, more working-class women than ever before worked outside the home, nineteenth-century middle-class women, who symbolized their husbands' or fathers' affluence, were allowed no economically productive rôles. Middle-class girls, unlike their brothers, could not go to university, engage in business or enter the learned professions. The battles of women like Elizabeth Garrett Anderson to train as medical doctors were a significant aspect of broadly feminist activity to find useful employment for women. It is an understatement to say that the Victorians displayed a deep ambiguity with regard to the work ethic for women, when many thousands were employed at hard labour and the right to work was denied to others.

Thanks to the new affluence achieved through industrialization, the Victorian middle classes expanded the formerly aristocratic idea of leisure and applied it as a moral concept to women. Women were depicted as ethereal beings, too pure to aspire to male ambitions, only virtuous as long as they remained isolated from the world of paid labour and professional advancement. On a practical level, the ideal of leisure meant that women were excluded from virtually all useful, remunerative and interesting occupations. Worse, this ideal bore very little resemblance to reality. Most households did not have three or four servants and a parasitic mistress of the house lounging on a sofa, like Jane Austen's Lady Bertram in *Mansfield Park*. In the majority of middle-class homes the housewife employed one maid-of-all-work and herself organized, and performed, the bulk of household and child-care duties. Those women with ambitions beyond the domestic sphere found few outlets for their talents.

The Victorian feminine ideal was damaging not solely because it limited women's human potential, but also because it failed to correspond to their economic and social needs. Able women were denied the use of their talents: those not economically fortunate through inheritance, or marriage, had no effective means of earning a living. Not all middle-class women, no matter how virtuous, could hope to find husbands, or male relations, to provide for them. The Brontë sisters fell into the significant category of poor but genteel women who, being unlikely to marry, having no dowry to attract suitors, and without independent means, had to find work. Teaching was the one socially acceptable form of paid employment. However, whether in schools or as governesses, teaching was badly paid, low in status and socially isolating. The price of gentility was to be, as Charlotte phrased it, 'a prisoner in solitary confinement'.

Mary Taylor, Charlotte's outspoken school friend and a passionate advocate of women's right, and duty, to work wrote:

> There are no means for a woman to live in England but by teaching, sewing or washing. The last is best. The best paid, the least unhealthy and the most free. But it is not paid well enough to live by.

(19 Feb. 1849)

Despairing of life in England, Mary Taylor emigrated to Wellington, New Zealand, where she opened a shop and pursued a successful business career, an option not open to her at home if she wished to preserve any shred of self-respect. In England, entrepreneurial activity, the ideal for men, implied for women a serious loss of status. Mary repeatedly attempted to persuade Charlotte to join her in New Zealand. Not surprisingly, she was unsuccessful. One cannot imagine any of the introverted Brontës embracing the risks and culture shock of emigration. Another eminent Victorian writer, Harriet Martineau, thrown on her own resources when her father died, supported herself and her mother, for a short time, by sewing (the second activity listed by Mary Taylor). She then turned to writing, with phenomenal success. However, her example was the exception which confirmed the rule. Many thousands of Victorian middle-class women passed their lives in poverty as prisoners to the genteel tradition.

Educational work

> The prisoner in solitary confinement, the toad in the block of marble, all in time shape themselves to their lot.
> (Charlotte Brontë, Letter to W. S. Williams, 26 July 1849)

Yet it is true that women could support themselves as school-teachers or governesses. Teaching, however, was not a profession in the sense of having formal standards of training. It was badly paid and poorly regarded. Teachers were perceived by their employers as being little more than educated servants. Timetables were heavy and free time almost unknown. Employers frequently patronized and bullied their governesses. In many families governesses had longer hours, and poorer wages, than mill workers and, above all, they suffered from social isolation. Anne Brontë's descriptions of governessing in *Agnes Grey* offer an indictment of domineering and thoughtless employers. In fiction, the governess/teacher theme was by no means unique to the Brontës. Jane Fairfax in Jane Austen's *Emma* sees her destined career as a governess as equivalent to a living death. Ruth Pinch in Dickens's *Martin Chuzzlewit* is another portrait of the exploited governess. Minor novelists like Lady Blessington (*The Governess*, 1839) and Elizabeth Sewell (*Amy Herbert*, 1844) also drew attention to the exploitation of the governess. The Brontës' contribution was to illuminate both the inner tensions and the emotional vulnerability of the governesses' position.

The fact that the fate of governesses smote the Victorian conscience was partly due to the effect produced by novels in which the reality of governess work was exposed. The number of governesses was not statistically large, 25,000 in England in 1851, compared with 750,000 domestic servants; nor were governesses as exploited as servants or industrial workers. Nevertheless the 'plight' of the governess raised a great deal of public concern, leading, for example, to the founding of the Governesses' Benevolent Institution, in 1843, and of Queen's College, London, in 1848, for the training of governesses. It is likely that the publicity given to governesses arose, in part, because members of the middle class could identify with their situation, as they could not, save with difficulty, identify with working-class hardship. Finally, the position of the governess dramatized the precarious nature of middle-class women's status, depending, as it did, entirely on the support of men. When Anne and Charlotte wrote about the education of their heroines, or of their lives as teachers, they touched on more than personal experience; they illuminated an important contemporary problem. Charlotte was fully aware of the wider dimensions of women's education and economic dependency, as she indicated with blunt frankness in a letter to W. S. Williams, discussing his daughters' employment prospects:

> Come what may afterwards, an education secured is an advantage gained – a priceless advantage. Come what may, it is a step towards independency, and one great curse of a single female life is its dependency. . . . Believe me, teachers may be hard-worked, ill-paid, and despised, but the girl who stays at home doing nothing is worse off than the hardest-wrought and worst paid drudge of a school.

(3 July 1849)

Rebecca Solomon, 'The Governess'. 'Ye too, the friendless, yet
dependent, that find not home nor lover,/Sad imprisoned hearts,
captive to the net of circumstance.' (Martin Tupper, *Proverbial
Philosophy*)

What did girls learn at school? Middle-class girls were taught history, edifying literature, geography, French and possibly Italian. Unless taught by their fathers at home, they were unlikely to study Latin or Greek. Anne Brontë, we know, was unusual in being sufficiently proficient in Latin to offer it as a teaching subject. Charlotte, Emily and Mary Taylor studied German in Brussels, but they would not have found it in an ordinary school curriculum. A whole range of lady-like activities, such as music, drawing and fancy needlework, were also taught, depending on the aspirations and incomes of the parents. No pursuit of knowledge for its own sake was encouraged. Middle-class girls were primarily educated to attract husbands.

Charlotte was keenly aware of the different educational expectations for boys and girls, and of some of their untoward consequences:

> You ask me if I do not think that men are strange beings – I do indeed, I have often thought so and I think too that the mode of bringing them up is strange, they are not half sufficiently guarded from temptation – girls are protected as if they were something very frail and silly indeed while boys are turned loose on the world as if they – of all beings in existence, were the wisest and least liable to be led astray.
>
> (to Miss Wooler, 30 Jan. 1846)

The Brontës' experiences at Cowan Bridge and at Roe Head, both as pupils and as teachers, and their periods as governesses, shed light both on girls' schools and on the teaching profession. Cowan Bridge, as we know, was founded to train the daughters of the clergy for a career in teaching and emphasized the necessity of self-denial in after life. As Charlotte remarked, in a letter to Emily, while working as a governess in the Sidgwick family:

> I see now more clearly than I have ever done before, that a private governess has no existence, is not considered as a living and rational being except as connected with the wearisome duties she has to fill.   (8 June 1839)

Similarly, as a teacher at Roe Head School her hours were long, the work exhausting and the pay too poor to allow her to save money. Though very little is known about Emily's period of teaching in Halifax, or of Anne's various posts, it is clear that they wished above all to leave governessing. It must be said that Emily and Charlotte in particular could never have been suited to teaching under the best conditions. Their solitary upbringing had given them no experience of ordinary children, and modern educationists might shudder at Anne's account of educational discipline in *Agnes Grey*:

The task of instruction was as arduous for the body as the mind. I had to run after my pupils to catch them, to carry or drag them to the table, and often forcibly to hold them there till the lesson was done. Tom I frequently put into a corner, seating myself before him in a chair, with a book which contained the little task that must be said or read, before he was released, in my hand. He was not strong enough to push both me and the chair away, so he would stand twisting his body and face into the most grotesque and singular contortions – laughable, no doubt, to an unconcerned spectator, but not to me – and uttering loud yells and doleful outcries, intended to represent weeping, but wholly without the accompaniment of tears.

(Ch. 3)

His sister Mary Ann is even more difficult, and Agnes fails utterly to impart rote learning to her little mind:

Often she would stubbornly refuse to pronounce some particular word in her lesson; and now I regret the lost labour I have had in striving to conquer her obstinacy .... but I thought it my absolute duty to crush this vicious tendency in the bud.

(Ch. 3)

Life in the schoolroom for the Brontës, and for their pupils, must have been genuinely miserable.

Authorship: constraints on female authors

Authorship offered the best route by which a few talented Victorian women could escape from a dependent position. But writing, like other forms of paid work, carried anomalies with it. Charlotte's attempts to launch herself in a writing career provides a good illustration of the Victorian double standard for male and female authors. In December 1836, she wrote to Robert Southey telling him of her literary ambitions and sending him a selection of her poems. In his reply (March 1837), Southey gave Charlotte well-meaning advice which illuminates some of the paradoxes facing nineteenth-century women writers. Warning her against indulging in day-dreams which would unfit her for real life, Southey remarked:

Literature cannot be the business of a woman's life and it ought not to be. The more she is engaged in her proper duties, the less leisure will she have for it, even as an accomplishment and a recreation.

If literature 'cannot be the business of a woman's life', then the moral gloss 'and it ought not to be' is unnecessary and only shows

Southey's unease, whether conscious or unconscious, in making the comment. He would not have replied to Charlotte unless he had thought she showed talent, but having seen evidence of it, he felt obliged to warn her against becoming a writer. As J. S. Mill argued in his *The Subjection of Women*, in 1869, 'What women by nature cannot do, it is quite superfluous to forbid them from doing.' Southey did mention one acceptable form of women's writing, that engaged in as 'an accomplishment and a recreation'. This reflects the view that the entirely professional woman writer, or woman intellectual, was likely to be considered 'unwomanly'. Harriet Martineau offers telling anecdotal evidence on this question, when describing her youth in Norwich in the 1820s:

> When I was young, it was not thought proper for young ladies to study very conspicuously; and especially with pen in hand. Young ladies (at least in provincial towns) were expected to sit down in the parlour to sew, – during which reading aloud was permitted, – or to practise their music; but so as to be fit to receive callers, without any sign of blue-stockingism which could be reported abroad. Jane Austen herself, the Queen of novelists, was compelled by the feelings of her family to cover up her manuscripts with a large piece of muslin work, kept on the table for the purpose, whenever any genteel people came in. So it was with other young ladies, for some time after Jane Austen was in her grave.
>
> (Autobiography, 1877, vol. I)

Women writers, even if successful, faced another disability. Their work was judged by standards thought appropriate to a lady. Any departure in a woman author from supposed lady-like qualities brought condemnation. In part, this reflected a confessional view of writing, in which an author was conceived of as revealing his, or her, self in art. This legacy of Romantic subjectivism, applied to canons of realist fiction, meant that authors who wrote about low life, for example, were often charged with immorality. In the nineteenth-century English climate of ever-increasing prudery, even male authors found their freedom of expression circumscribed. For women the problem was more acute because their range of subjects was already limited to the 'womanly' and the decorous. Some twentieth-century critical theory, which avoids insistence on authorial point of view, may find the nineteenth-century preoccupation with authorial intention naïve. But the fact that women writers knew that their works would be read in a confessional manner was undoubtedly a major constraint on many authors, including the Brontës.

To avoid some of these difficulties, a number of women novelists of the period published either anonymously or under male pseudonyms. Most notable were George Sand in France, and George Eliot and the ambiguous 'Bell brothers' in England. In choosing their pseudonyms, Ellis, Acton and Currer Bell, the Brontës indicated that they refused the sexual double standard of literary judgement. Charlotte, in her 1850 biographical notice to the new edition of *Wuthering Heights*, was explicit on this point:

> ... we did not like to declare ourselves women, because – without at that time suspecting that our mode of writing and thinking was not what is called 'feminine' – we had a vague impression that authoresses are liable to be looked on with prejudice; we had noticed how critics sometimes used for their chastisement the weapon of personality, and for their reward, a flattery, which is not true praise.

The Brontës wished to be judged on what they wrote, not on who they were or on what it was thought appropriate for a particular category of writer to produce. In the event, the uncertainty over the Bells' sexual identity induced considerable anxiety in reviewers. In reply to a critic in the *North British Review* who wrote, 'If *Jane Eyre* be the production of a woman, she must be a woman unsexed', Charlotte remarked ironically and defiantly:

> I am reminded of *The Economist*. The literary critic of that paper praised the book if written by a man, and pronounced it 'odious' if the work of a woman. To such critics I would say, 'To you I am neither man nor woman – I come before you as an author only. It is the sole standard by which you have the right to judge me – the sole ground on which I accept your judgment.'
>
> (to W. S. Williams, 16 Aug. 1849)

Mrs Gaskell emphasized Charlotte's dislike of critical patronage towards women, a feeling fully shared by Anne and Emily:

> She [Charlotte] especially disliked the lowering of standards by which to judge a work of fiction, if it proceeded from a feminine pen; and praise mingled with pseudo-gallant allusions to her sex, mortified her far more than actual blame.
>
> (*The Life of Charlotte Brontë*, vol. 2, ch. 4)

Speaking, no doubt, as much for herself as for Charlotte, Mrs Gaskell analysed the problems raised by the woman writer's divided existence:

> When a man becomes an author, it is probably merely a change of employment to him. He takes a portion of that time which has hitherto been devoted to some other study or pursuit; he gives up something of the legal or medical profession ... or relinquishes part of the trade or business by which he has been

striving to gain a livelihood. . . . But no other can take up the quiet, regular duties of the daughter, the wife, or the mother, as well as she whom God has appointed to fill that particular place: a woman's principal work in life is hardly left to her own choice; nor can she drop the domestic charges devolving on her as an individual, for the exercise of the most splendid talents that were ever bestowed. And yet she must not shrink from the extra responsibility implied by the very fact of her possessing such talents.

(The Life of Charlotte Brontë, vol. 2, ch. 2)

Like Charlotte, Mrs Gaskell did not challenge women's 'natural' place in the domestic sphere ('she whom God has appointed to fill that particular place'), but she did invoke a moral responsibility to exercise one's talents, that implicitly argued for a much wider range of women's experience.

A further problem that particularly troubled Charlotte was that of spinsterhood. Independence for a woman had to be weighed against the need for love and the fear of loneliness. In addition, the position of the Victorian spinster was one that attracted facile ridicule. Charlotte keenly felt the plight of poor and single women. Not only did unmarried women lack economic security unless they inherited independent incomes, they also lacked status, since as single women they were not defined by their relations to men. And though women were expected to marry, husband-hunting was considered despicable. For Charlotte, many 'old maids' lacked 'a hope and a motive'(to W. S. Williams, 3 July 1849). Yet she could also be more positive on the subject, as in a letter to Miss Wooler:

> it seems that even 'a lone woman' can be happy, as well as cherished wives and proud mothers – I am glad of that – I speculate much on the existence of unmarried and never-to-be married women nowadays and I have already got to the point of considering that there is no more respectable character on this earth than an unmarried woman who makes her own way through life quietly, perseveringly – without support of husband or brother and who has attained the age of 45 or upwards – retains in her possession a well regulated mind – a disposition to enjoy simple pleasures – fortitude to support inevitable pains, sympathy with the sufferings of others and willingness to relieve want as far as her means extend.

(30 Jan. 1846)

But a single and financially dependent woman lacked both financial security and emotional enrichment. It was the spectre of loneliness as much as of poverty that tortured Charlotte and which she described with poignancy in *Villette*.

The 'condition of woman question' was a concrete, not an abstract problem for the Brontës, and was explored by them in some form in all their novels. Only Agnes Grey and Caroline Helstone resemble, superficially at least, the archetypal dutiful Victorian heroine; Cathy Earnshaw, Lucy Snowe, Helen Huntingdon and Jane Eyre all rebel against their lot. They appeared radical in suggesting a certain independence for women. Ultimately, in Charlotte's novels, the problem of female identity is solved via love and subservience, most noticeably in the conclusion to *Shirley*. Charlotte's conservatism made her wary of practical solutions to women's subordination. As she wrote to Miss Wooler, 'One can see where the evil lies, but who can point out the remedy?' Yet all the Brontës' novels concern the struggles of women to be free, or at least self-respecting, individuals in a world where women are not readily granted autonomy. None of the novels offers a solution to 'the condition of woman question': rather, they dramatize it.

Two feminist interpretations: Jane Eyre *and* Shirley

JANE EYRE   It seems appropriate in this context to illustrate how the Brontës' novels have lent themselves to twentieth-century feminist interpretations. To some extent, current feminist interpretations remind one of hostile nineteenth-century critical observations. It could be suggested, for example, that contemporary critics of *Jane Eyre*, who saw political and sexual radicalism in the novel, were essentially correct. On one level, the novel poses the question: 'What would happen if social and sexual inferiors asserted that they were the equals of their superiors?' As Mrs Oliphant remarked (*Blackwood's*, May 1855), 'here is your true revolution. France [scene of the first great European Revolution] is but one of the Western Powers – woman is half of the world.' Mrs Oliphant had grasped the point that the Jane/Rochester relationship represented a radical attack on traditional authority based on class and sex. Jane, a woman, and a nobody in social terms, demands, and is accorded, equality. She even takes the sexual initiative, being the one who, contrary to all notions of Victorian decorum, declares her love for Rochester before he declares his love for her. She cuts across class barriers, by insisting that she, not the rich but shallow Blanche Ingram, is Rochester's equal. Rochester, too, stresses his equality and kinship with Jane. '"My bride is here", he said, again drawing me to him, "because my equal is here, and my likeness"' (Ch. 23).

Not only is Jane a dangerous egalitarian, her appearance also is a radical departure from the feminine ideal of the period and allows the reader to see how far Charlotte had developed her ideas from the conventional beauties of the juvenilia. The portraits of the Angrian women, Mina Laury or Julia Vernon, show a feminine type derived from Charlotte's reading of Byron, Scott and ladies' annuals which incorporated white hands, drooping curls, and a graceful neck adorned with jewels. In *Jane Eyre*, Blanche Ingram and Rosamund Oliver represent this physical ideal, but though Jane envies their beauty, they are seen as trivial beings. Jane, by contrast, is physically small and plain, does not have a brilliant complexion and refuses ornament. Her value lies in spiritual and intellectual qualities. Nevertheless, Jane experiences a deep ambivalence on the score of her personal worth; on the one hand, she feels herself superior to merely beautiful women; on the other, she bitterly resents her physical inferiority which, she believes, cannot make her attractive to men:

> I sometimes regretted that I was not handsomer: I sometimes wished to have rosy cheeks, a straight nose, and small cherry mouth: I desired to be tall, stately and finely developed in figure; I felt it a misfortune that I was so little, so pale and had features so irregular and so marked. (Ch. 11)

Early in the novel, Jane connects her vague yearnings for wider horizons with the social restrictions felt by women in general; she links her lot to that of all women:

> Millions are condemned to a stiller doom than mine, and millions are in silent revolt against their lot. Nobody knows how many rebellions besides political rebellions ferment in the masses of life which people earth. Women are supposed to be very calm generally: but women feel just as men feel; . . . . they suffer from too rigid a restraint, too absolute a stagnation, precisely as men would suffer; and it is narrow-minded in their more privileged fellow-creatures to say that they ought to confine themselves to making puddings and knitting stockings, to playing the piano and embroidering bags. It is thoughtless to condemn them, or laugh at them, if they seek to do more or learn more than custom has pronounced necessary for their sex. (Ch. 12)

The evocation of restraint and stagnation, the list of traditional feminine activities – making puddings, knitting, playing the piano, embroidering bags – and the sense of masculine scorn for those women who express discontent, reveal how Jane regards traditional female employments. It is significant that she links her feelings to the language of political rebellion: 'silent revolt', 'how many rebellions'. It is not so much poverty that irks her as solitude, inaction and incarceration.

Another figure in *Jane Eyre* who plausibly sustains a feminist interpretation is that of Bertha Mason, Rochester's first wife. An example of such a view can be found in Gubar and Gilbert's *The Mad Woman in the Attic*, where it is suggested that Bertha's madness permits her to throw off the submissive functions thought appropriate to her sex. Certainly, she is strong and physically violent; knives, teeth and fire are her weapons. She is depicted as a woman without any traces of civilization, a she-savage. However, Bertha is not so mad as not to know what she hates. In fact, her cunning suggests planned malevolence against an enemy (either Rochester himself or all men), rather than the confusion of mental alienation. According to Rochester, her madness is hereditary, and particularly loathsome because it leads her into sexual profligacy. This view is in accordance with prevailing nineteenth-century psychiatric theory, which considered mental illness to be either inherited or the product of a degenerative disease, often of a sexual origin. Rochester's self-justification to Jane is a good literary example of the sexual double standard, comparable to Angel Clare's response to Tess's confession in Hardy's *Tess of the d'Urbervilles*. Rochester is, of course, himself a sexual profligate, telling Jane about his former mistresses, and preparing to marry her bigamously. Yet from the masculine perspective, he cannot see any parallel between Bertha and himself. His wife's sexuality is a sign of degeneracy and madness; his own a venial weakness.

Bertha's physical violence, and her confinement, also remind us of Jane's situation in the Reed household at the beginning of the novel. There, Jane was considered an unnatural and wicked child; she flew into passions; she was locked up in the Red Room, had hysterics and was eventually sent off to Mr Brocklehurst's school to learn submission and obedience. Jane's defence of Bertha to Mr Rochester could apply equally to a defence of herself as a child: '"Sir", I interrupted him, "you are inexorable for that unfortunate lady: you speak of her with hate – with vindictive antipathy. It is cruel – she cannot help being mad"' (Ch. 27). But if Jane, the child, resembled Bertha, the mad adult, she also differed crucially from her; by eventually learning self-control, she gained a weapon over herself and others. It is possible, then, to see in Bertha Mason more than a Gothic ornament; she represents an expression, or objectification, of the anger felt by the orphaned Jane – anger at a loveless world and at the man whom she loves yet who attempts to transform her into another of his many possessions.

The rage that consumes Bertha Mason, and which literally burns down Thornfield, may reflect a split view of the female experience. In Bertha, pure feeling is shown to be self-destructive. Yet paradoxically, imprisoned though she is, she has also attained a form of freedom. Bertha Mason, it could be suggested, represents

Jane's secret self. As Dickens in *Great Expectations* provides another self for Pip in the character of Orlick, a violent and brutal contrast to Pip's newly acquired gentlemanly veneer, so Charlotte Brontë in *Jane Eyre* juxtaposes civilized and elemental images of Jane's being. When Jane sees Bertha's face in the mirror, it is as though her livid features were those of her childish self locked in the Red Room at Gateshead so long ago.

SHIRLEY *Shirley*, Charlotte's second novel, is more explicitly concerned with social and political themes than *Jane Eyre*. Uneven in structure and tone, it betrays the misery which engulfed Charlotte in the dreadful period 1848–49, when she witnessed the deaths of her brother and sisters. Though generally conservative in its depiction of working-class unrest, the novel links the deprivation of the workers, starved of jobs and food, to the emotional starvation undergone by the middle-class heroine, Caroline Helstone. The fate of the working class parallels the fate of dispossessed women. Even more radically, *Shirley* offers a positive vision of womanhood, based not on renunciation and passivity, but on action.

The two heroines of *Shirley* represent antithetical models. Caroline Helstone is quiet, dutiful and repressed, the ideal Victorian heroine. It is also not without significance that throughout most of the novel she is depicted as desperately unhappy. Brought up by her stern and detached uncle, she enters into an adult life deprived both of affection and of meaningful activity. This combination of a lack of love and lack of purpose drives her into a classic Victorian decline from which she is only rescued by being reunited with her long absent mother. One derives an impression of overwhelming bleakness from her situation. Yet this misery is shown befalling a heroine who fulfils all the desirable and submissive qualities of the Victorian feminine ideal. The narrative suggests that to live like Caroline Helstone is to be condemned to a living death.

Shirley, a local heiress and landowner, contrasts with Caroline in almost every respect. Wealthy, independent and physically adventurous, she wears men's clothes, she affects masculine slang and is called 'the Captain'. Charlotte appears to be experimenting – uneasily, and one might add, unsuccessfully – with the idea of an independent woman, but can only create a parody of a swashbuckling male. However, Shirley is more interesting than her mannerisms. It is she who imagines an ideal female figure who would not merely be a negation or an imitation of the male.

Chapter 18 of *Shirley* launches what some critics have perceived as a radically feminist discussion. Elegiac in tone, it perhaps fails to attain the universality of theme the text appears to strive for;

what is remarkable is that the scene appears at all. It takes the form of a dialogue in the churchyard, between Caroline and Shirley, while a service is in progress in the church. Their freedom from a male audience is emphasized and they speak frankly: 'we are alone: we may speak what we think.' Shirley begins by criticizing the Christian view of woman based on Eve and, in English culture, on Milton's view of Eve. 'Milton was great but was he good?. . . . Milton tried to see the first woman; but Cary, he saw her not. . . . It was his cook that he saw.' For the Miltonic Eve, Shirley substitutes a Creation myth of female Titans, daring and strong. The first woman, she asserts, was 'heaven born' – that is, made directly from God, not from Adam's rib. Woman, in this vision, does not derive from man. Shirley identifies her Eve with all the living power of Nature. 'I love her – undying mighty being! Heaven may have faded from her brow when she fell in paradise; but all that is glorious on earth shines there still.'

From a feminist perspective, the importance of Shirley's Titan/Eve/Nature image is that it provides a counter-model to the Miltonic/patriarchal/Christian view of women. But Charlotte does not allow her heroines to remain on this visionary plane for long. Their brief moment of freedom 'to speak what they think' is checked by the arrival of Joe Turner, the sanctimonious churchwarden, who lectures them on the weaknesses and inferiority of women, offering a traditional account of their function and capacities. He quotes St Paul: 'Let the woman learn in silence, with all subjection.' Joe Turner performs the function of Everyman, drawing Caroline and Shirley back to 'reality', where women's characters and capacities are defined by men. We perceive two realities existing simultaneously – what women think and say when they are alone, and what they are told to think and say.

The novel's uneasy resolution illustrates a major and unresolved problem in Charlotte Brontë's works. In *Jane Eyre*, the conflict between individual autonomy and the desire for love is more or less successfully resolved. *Shirley*, in spite of the radically feminist vision in Chapter 18, fails to envisage a world in which women could harmonize love with independence. At the novel's close, Shirley's marriage transforms her into a submissive figure, or worse, one who pretends submission. 'She abdicated without a word or a struggle' (Ch. 37). In marriage, Shirley must tacitly be seen to be powerless; dissimulation is the foundation of her relationship with her husband, unlike the frankness of Jane and Mr Rochester. This is a far cry from the fearless Eve–Titan that Shirley had imagined in the churchyard. The conclusion to *Shirley* illustrates not only Charlotte Brontë's own ambivalence about possible, or desirable, female rôles, but the difficulties of defining or imagining a new order.

The Brontës were in no sense public champions of women's rights. However, 'the condition of women question' was central to their work. The fact of their being women and women writers was a major and necessary preoccupation in their novels as in their lives. How and for what were women supposed to live? From the fierce individualism of Catherine Earnshaw in *Wuthering Heights* to the quiet determination of Helen Huntingdon in *The Tenant of Wild-fell Hall*, the Brontës' novels show women struggling with the real, not the ideal conditions of life. The Brontës spoke for those women who were imprisoned by an idealization that rendered their lives a sterile vacuum. Like so many Victorian women, they sought to lead useful lives and nourished ambitions that were unlikely to be fulfilled. They did not challenge the sanctity of domesticity, but they did attack the cult of female idleness:

> For though England held many thousands of women suffering from the same misery, they bore it in solitude and without hope. Had they all met together to make their wants known, and asked for help, no advice could have been given them, except to win a living for themselves, and not beg for it.
>
> (Mary Taylor, *Miss Miles*, London, 1890, p. 420)

The Brontës were fortunate in having the courage and the genius to 'win a living for themselves'. On one level, their novels record the cost of that struggle.

Part Three
Critical Survey

11 Jane Eyre (1847)

The orphan's quest

'I wish you had not sent me *Jane Eyre*,' lamented Thackeray, unable to put the book down once he had started it. Many of Charlotte's contemporaries responded to the novel with the same fascinated enthusiasm. The instant popularity of *Jane Eyre* contrasted sharply with the generally chilly reception afforded *Wuthering Heights* and *Agnes Grey*. Twentieth-century readers, on the other hand, have tended to reverse the process, seeing melodrama and self-indulgence in *Jane Eyre* and masterly artistic control in *Wuthering Heights*.

One way in which *Jane Eyre* differs markedly from *Wuthering Heights* is in its chronological setting. Whereas one can date most of the events of *Wuthering Heights* from internal evidence, *Jane Eyre* is set in an ambiguous time frame. But from the extensive journeys Jane takes by stage coach, we can conclude that the novel is set in a pre-railway age, therefore before the 1830s. As in *Shirley*, where Charlotte made use of the events of the Luddite riots of 1818–19 to dramatize social conditions in the 1850s, so in *Jane Eyre* she raised contemporary questions (governessing, for example), relevant to the 1840s in a period some thirty or forty years earlier. The vagueness of the novel's time frame contributes to the impression one derives from it that the novel operates in the realm of myth, rather than of historical realism, but given many of its themes – the condition of women, the treatment of lunatics and religious ideas – this is a misleading impression. Finally, it seems probable that *Jane Eyre* has suffered in its critical reputation thanks in part to its very popularity, accessibility and even its happy ending. Unlike *Wuthering Heights*, *Jane Eyre* has been given the status of a children's classic, and its more radical implications have been forgotten. But Charlotte's first published novel needs no apologies. The qualities that gripped Thackeray, not an indulgent reader, still legitimately retain their power.

Structure

Jane Eyre functions on one level as a *Bildungsroman* or education novel. The heroine's education takes place in five stages, corresponding with five houses; Gateshead, Lowood, Thornfield, Moor House and Ferndean. Each stage of development is overseen by

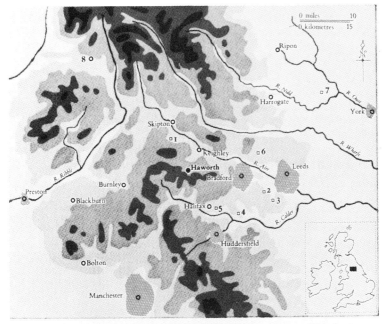

Key to Map numbers

Brontë Country

1. Stonegappe, "Gateshead Hall" of *Jane Eyre*

2. Oakwell Hall, "Fieldhead" of *Shirley*

3. The Rydings, "Thornfield Hall" of *Jane Eyre*

4. Roe Head, Charlotte at School

5. Lawhill, Emily taught at School

6. Upperwood House, Charlotte as governess

7. Thorpe Green, Anne and Branwell stayed

8. Cowan Bridge, "Lowood School" of *Jane Eyre*

Map showing Brontë country

a dominant patriarchal male figure and each home is experienced as an enclosed world from which Jane must break out as, in each case, the promise of protection gives way to the desire for growth and liberty. Jane, an orphan, may be seen as engaged in a quest for her real home. But her story is not a simple progression. She does not merely move from stage to stage as on a chess board, she can also be thought of as oscillating between Romantic feeling and Christian duty and reason.

Jane's education or moral progress is closely linked to the dynamics of Bunyan's *Pilgrim's Progress*, a book universally read in the nineteenth century. The novel falls within the tradition of religious, didactic works, which show a soul struggling between good and evil forces before arriving at the heavenly kingdom: 'I seek an Inheritance incorruptible, undefiled and that fadeth not away' (*Pilgrim's Progress*, Part I). But Jane, unlike Bunyan's Christian, seeks her kingdom in this world, without being elevated into an allegorical or universal figure of passion and reason in revolt. She engages in a quest, for love, justice and legitimate authority. Both are lacking at Gateshead, her Aunt Reed's house, where the novel opens; here the Reed children, especially John, torment and humiliate Jane, the outsider. Jane thinks of herself as a child who cannot please other people or inspire love. The novel focuses on the importance of the child's self-definition for the formation of her adult mind. Jane is torn between the conviction of her incapacity to please and a sense of her legitimate worth. 'I was a discord in Gateshead Hall; I was like nobody there' (Ch. 2). It is significant that at Gateshead Jane effects her first escape from an oppressive reality through the medium of Romantic art, in her reading of Bewick's *British Birds* (see pp. 109–14). Though the importance accorded to childhood in the novel is Wordsworthian, there is no sentimentality about children. Jane, with whom the reader certainly sympathizes, is not a picture of innocence and charm. The opening scene shows young children squabbling with a sort of casual brutality. The description of the poisonous Reed children probably owes a good deal to the Brontës' experiences as governesses in wealthy families. John Reed even strikes Jane, in a display of arbitrary power, clearly based not only on the fact that he is bigger, and a boy, but on class and money. 'You ought to beg', he taunts, 'and not live here with gentlemen's children like us' (Ch. 2).

Mr Reed, who initially gave Jane a home, represents the legitimate authority of the house. Yet Mr Reed is equally a figure of dread; brooding on him when locked in the Red Room, Jane 'sees' his ghost and gives way to nervous terrors. In the context of the novel's theme of spiritual progress, this scene may be interpreted as the equivalent of a trance, the Romantic path to transcendence.

Nevertheless, the story remains within the limits of the probable. Bessie, the family nurse, provides an account of what Jane claims to have seen. 'Something passed her, all dressed in white and vanished' – 'a great black dog behind him' – 'Three loud raps on the chamber door' – 'a light in the churchyard just over his grave' (Ch. 3). Although Jane's ghostly vision is accounted for naturalistically, as the overwrought imagination of a sensitive child, the atmosphere of the supernatural is established early in the novel. Mr Reed represents Jane's belief in a kindly father figure who, if he were alive, would shelter and love her; he is in short, a loving God or patriarch, but absent:

> I thought Mr Reed's spirit, harassed by the wrongs of his sister's child, might quit its abode – whether in the church vault or in the unknown world of the departed – and rise before me in this chamber. I wiped my tears and hushed my sobs, fearful lest any sign of violent grief might waken a preternatural voice to comfort me, or elicit from the gloom some haloed face, bending over me in strange pity.
>
> (Ch. 2)

Gateshead, lacking its legitimate master and ruled by the cold, unmotherly Mrs Reed, who in turn is bullied by her son, John, is no real home.

Jane, of course, lacks a mother as well as a father; the maternal figures in the novel are revealing. Jane's aunt, Mrs Reed, recalls the archetypal wicked stepmother. Bessie, the nurse, though kindhearted, does not treat Jane with any particular favouritism. Miss Temple, at Lowood, succours and consoles her, but her care is limited to what is credible in a teacher. Mrs Fairfax, at Thornfield, a motherly soul if there ever was one, is to Jane's increasingly independent and adventurous mind, good but dull. Given their family circumstances, there is nothing surprising in the fact that the Brontës' novels, generally, lack sympathetic mother figures. In *Jane Eyre* it is nature which functions in the restorative and maternal rôle:

> I have no relative but the universal mother, *Nature*; I will seek her breast and ask repose. . . . Nature seemed to me benign and good; I thought she loved me, outcast as I was. . . . To-night, at least, I would be her guest, as I was her child: my mother would lodge me without money and without price.
>
> (Ch. 28)

Mr Brocklehurst, the headmaster of Lowood School, succeeds Mr Reed as the second example of quasi-paternal authority. Jane's first glimpse of him captures the child's view of a terrifying patriarch, a phallic column:

I looked up at – a black pillar! – such, at least, appeared to me, at first sight, the straight, narrow, sable-clad shape standing erect on the rug; the grim face at the top was like a carved mask, placed above the shaft by way of capital.

(Ch. 4)

Facing up to Mr Brocklehurst, and overcoming his moral black-mail, is Jane's second instinctive act of rebellion, her first being her refusal to submit to John Reed. At Lowood, Mr Brocklehurst unscrupulously employs the language of religion to humiliate his charges. His unctuous speeches betray a fine tinge of sadism:

I have a Master to serve whose kingdom is not of this world: my mission is to mortify in these girls the lusts of the flesh, to teach them to clothe themselves with shamefacedness and sobriety, not with braided hair and costly apparel; and each of the young persons before us has a string of hair twisted in plaits which vanity itself might have woven: these, I repeat, must be cut off.

(Ch. 7)

Mr Brocklehurst is a debased parental figure, his authority little more than sexual tyranny. The symbolic meaning of wishing to cut off the girls' hair, cropping their one ornament to curtail their sexual nature, is evident. Intellectually if not emotionally, it is rela-tively easy for Jane to see through the 'black pillar'. And in spite of her first ominous meeting with Mr Brocklehurst at Gateshead (whose opening conversational gambit is to ask Jane whether she knows where the wicked go after death), Jane looks forward to Lowood as freeing her from the tyranny of her Reed cousins. We notice that, whereas in *Pilgrim's Progress* characters are unambigu-ous, according entirely with their allegorical titles, Mr Brockle-hurst, a clergyman, who allegorically would function as a good man, is intuitively perceived by Jane to be the reverse. Her instinc-tive knowledge, a Romantic quality, remains an important marker, even when she has gained far greater worldly knowledge.

Lowood School for all its horrors, is, in many respects, preferable to Jane's first home. So much emphasis has been placed on the historical basis for Lowood (Cowan Bridge) and the identification of the sanctimonious Brocklehurst with the Reverend Carus Wilson, that we risk forgetting that Lowood is also portrayed positively. Mr Brocklehurst's Evangelical reign of terror is miti-gated to a great extent by Miss Temple's mildness and reason-ableness. At Lowood, Jane finds two moral guides, who have a profound effect on her development. Miss Temple, the headmis-tress, teaches Jane self-control; Helen Burns, the friend who dies, holds up a model of resignation and forgiveness. Helen is like

Bunyan's Faithful, who goes before, to show us the way. Yet another important aspect of Lowood is that in this unprepossessing environment, Jane discovers that she loves study. Her intellectual enthusiasms make even the inadequate food of Lowood irrelevant. 'I would not now have exchanged Lowood with all its privations for Gateshead and its daily luxuries' (Ch. 8).

Jane spends ten years at Lowood, under the benign discipline of Miss Temple. After the latter's marriage, however, Jane finds that a transformation has taken place within herself:

> I imagined myself only to be regretting my loss, and thinking how to repair it; but when my reflections were concluded, and I looked up and found that the afternoon was gone, and evening far advanced, another discovery dawned on me – namely, that in the interval I had undergone a transforming process; that my mind had put off all it had borrowed of Miss Temple – or rather, that she had taken with her the serene atmosphere I had been breathing in her vicinity – and that now I was left in my natural element, and beginning to feel the stirring of old emotions. It did not seem as if a prop were withdrawn, but rather as if a motive had gone: it was not the power to be tranquil which had failed me, but the reason for tranquillity was no more. My world had for some years been in Lowood: my experience had been of its rules and systems; now I remembered that the real world was wide, and that a varied field of hopes and fears, of sensations and excitements, awaited those who had courage to go forth into its expanse, to seek real knowledge of life amidst its perils.
>
> (Ch. 10)

Her decision to leave Lowood is motivated by a desire to 'seek real knowledge of life amidst its perils'. She sets forth on her pilgrimage again, by advertising for a post as governess, and receives a favourable reply from a Mrs Fairfax at Thornfield.

Thus Jane goes to her third 'home' with a profound desire for change; even a new servitude, she feels, is better than a life of inaction. But Thornfield, too, is little more than a peaceful backwater until transformed by the arrival of Mr Rochester (see context passage, pp. 152–5). At Thornfield she discovers Romantic passion, something quite foreign to her experience hitherto. Whereas Jane had rebelled against authority at Gateshead, saying of John Reed, 'Master! How is he my master? Am I a servant?' (Ch. 2), she willingly calls Mr Rochester master and accepts peremptory treatment from him. Jane enjoys Rochester's eccentric manners, a mixture of frankness and authoritarian command. With Rochester, Jane too, is frank. To Rochester's leading question, 'Do you think me handsome?' she replies with an abrupt, indeed tactless, 'No, sir!' (Ch. 14). Like Jane, Mr Rochester is unconventional in both manners and looks. So entirely do Thornfield and its owner appear to be the home and master for which Jane had always longed, that the discovery of his bigamous intentions and her decision to flee represent an emotional uprooting, as much as a disappointment in love. As Jane declares to Rochester, 'Wherever you are is my home – my only home' (Ch. 22).

The problem of mastery, which tormented Jane as a child at Gateshead, is relevant here. On the one hand, she yearns for authority, a master, a legitimizing and caring principle; on the other, authority proves to be arbitrary, unreliable or tyrannical (Mr Brocklehurst, Mrs Reed, John Reed, Mr Rochester, St John Rivers). Though Jane feels her physical inferiority, she is also convinced of her intellectual capacities and spiritual worth. The moral law to which she appeals when she leaves Rochester is not merely a question of obedience to God. By following, no matter how painfully, her inner promptings of conscience, she can attain self-respect and integrity:

> *I* care for myself. The more solitary, the more friendless, the more unstained I am, the more I will respect myself. I will keep the law given by God; sanctioned by man. I will hold to the principles received by me when I was sane, and not mad – as I am now.
>
> (Ch. 27)

Immediately after her trial of strength with Mr Rochester, when he pleads with her to live with him as his mistress, Jane has a dream, which resembles one of her own eerie paintings:

> then, not a moon, but a white human form shone in the azure, inclining a glorious brow eastward. It gazed and gazed on me. It spoke to my spirit. . . . 'My daughter, flee temptation.' 'Mother, I will.' So I answered after I had waked from the trance-like dream.
>
> (Ch. 27)

The border between dream, trance and reality are deliberately blurred, as when Jane hears Rochester calling her at Moor House. But here her unknown mother speaks to re-establish moral authority over the wavering Jane. She is, then, able to defy the third patriarchal authority whom she loves, rather than fears. And like Bunyan's Pilgrim, she sets out on the next stage of her journey, 'a new Road; one I had never travelled'.

Though the element of coincidence strains the patience of some readers, the novel's quest or romance element can be thought to legitimize the discovery of Marsh End and Moor House as Jane's fourth home where she finds blood relations. At Marsh End, Jane discovers the same grouping of siblings as at Gateshead, including herself, three girls and a boy (the same arrangement, of course, as that in the Brontë family). But here the Rivers family represents an ideal of development, instead of the miserable, thwarted, vain and self-indulgent life of the Reed household. Before arriving at this earthly ideal, Jane undergoes severe physical trials of hunger and cold and is forced to beg for food, finally eating burnt porridge destined for pigs. This has the biblical ring of the humiliations suffered by the Prodigal Son as well as reminding us of the inedible food spurned at Lowood, but gratefully eaten here out of necessity. This is Jane's Slough of Despond. In Bunyan's words:

> This miry slough is such a place as cannot be mended. It is the descent whither the scum and filth that attends conviction for sin doth continually run, and therefore it is called the Slough of Despond; for still as the sinner is awakened about his lost condition, there ariseth in his Soul many fears and doubts and discouraging apprehensions, which all of them get together, and settle in this place.

> (Part I)

Like Bunyan, Charlotte provides a moment of physical degradation to mark her protagonist's awakening to her 'lost condition'. And St John Rivers' gesture of rescuing Jane echoes Bunyan's character, Help, who says to Christian, 'Give me thy hand; so he gave him his hand, and he drew him out, and set him upon sound Ground and bid him go his way.'

With the Rivers sisters, Jane enjoys a relationship of mutual respect, where all labour to educate themselves and to help one another. Authority only intervenes in the figure of their brother, St John Rivers, perhaps the most threatening and fascinating of the novel's male figures. His Evangelical enthusiasm and integrity, combined with a fine intellect and physical beauty, make him a redoubtable antagonist. How can Jane refuse his appeal to join in God's work and purpose, which he is so certain that he incarnates?

> I listen to my duty, and keep steadily in view my first aim – to do all things to the glory of God. My Master was long-suffering; so will I be. I cannot give you up to perdition as a vessel of wrath: repent – resolve, while there is yet time. Remember, we are bid to work while it is day – warned that 'the night cometh when no man shall work'. . . . God give you strength to choose the better part which shall not be taken from you.

> (Ch. 35)

St John Rivers' Evangelical enthusiasm, which he intends to apply to the conversion of the 'heathen' in India, reflects the self-assurance of early nineteenth-century missionaries. This is perhaps most tellingly expressed in the hymn by Reginald Heber, later

Bishop of Calcutta, who in 1819 wrote 'From Greenland's icy mountains'. This poem is an example of what now would be thought of as cultural imperialism but which then represented religious devotion:

> From Greenland's icy mountains,
> From India's coral strand,
> Where Afric's sunny fountains
> Roll down their golden sand;
> From many an ancient river,
> From many a palmy plain,
> They call us to deliver,
> Their land from error's chain.
>
> What though the spicy breezes
> Blow soft o'er Ceylon's isle
> Though every prospect pleases
> And only man is vile;
> In vain with lavish kindness,
> The gifts of God are strown
> The savage in his blindness
> Bows down to wood and stone.
>
> Can we whose souls are lighted
> With wisdom from on high,
> Can we to men benighted
> The lamp of life deny?
> Salvation, O Salvation!
> The joyful sound proclaim,
> Till each remotest nation
> Has learnt Messiah's name.

In effect, St John Rivers offers Jane a chance to follow a reliable moral and spiritual guide. What she understands, in spite of her veneration for his calling, is the arrogance of his belief that he is God's interpreter. Applying what he believes is God's purpose to himself is one thing; to impose his law on another person has a flavour of tyranny about it. The power of the religious patriarch satirized in Mr Brocklehurst genuinely terrifies Jane in Rivers, because both her duty and her religious belief seem to urge her to follow him.

A conventional Romantic or Gothic novel would have seen in St John Rivers the answer to a maiden's prayer. Mr Rochester, the Gothic villain, would have given way to the stainless Gothic hero. We notice that in both *Jane Eyre* and *Villette* Charlotte allows her heroine (unusually for the conventions of the day) to consider seriously loving two suitors. Apropos of *Villette*, Thackeray sneered at 'the author's naive confession of being in love with two men at the same time' (letter to Lucy Baxter, 11 March 1853). Since St John Rivers is both morally superior to Rochester and far more handsome, his rejection by Jane is particularly remarkable. She recognizes that Rivers' sense of mission requires a massive egotism that leaves no room for anyone else. Jane knows she will be crushed by him. Rivers is as much a tyrant in his way as John Reed. He is a subtle, intelligent and entirely sincere Brocklehurst. Though Jane can contemplate serving him as a missionary in India, she cannot bear the notion of marrying him without love. 'Can I receive from him the bridal ring, endure all the forms of love . . . and know that the spirit is absent?' (Ch. 34).

Jane's final home or resting place, Ferndean, lies in the heart of a forest, a Romantic labyrinth, which like the similar image in Dante implies the doubts and difficulties surrounding her quest for Rochester:

> I looked round in search of another road. There was none: all was interwoven stem, columnar trunk, dense summer foliage – no opening anywhere. (Ch. 37)

Moor House, by contrast, where Jane found her independence, is set in bracing hilly country. Ferndean, its physical antithesis, shrouded in a deep wood, is a shelter from the world. Perhaps the least satisfying aspect of the novel's happy ending is that the marriage with Rochester is depicted as a relationship of almost suffocating harmony, prefigured by the environment. Certainly the dense wood, the close vegetation, is a favourite Romantic image, and symbolizes Jane's safe return to her Romantic self, though with the sanction of reason and duty.

The five 'homes' in *Jane Eyre*, as a structural and thematic device, mark clear stages in Jane's development. From her turbulent and loveless childhood, she goes in quest of justice, love and religious consolation. True and false guides lead her: Miss Temple, Helen Burns, Mr Brocklehurst, and Rochester himself, who can be both false and true. Jane's rejection of St John Rivers is an acknowledgement that she must be her own guide; that her strength is in herself. She is then free to help Rochester. The novel's conclusion suggests that there is no authority save one's own integrity founded on religious principle. The theme of religion fittingly closes the novel. St John Rivers' single-minded dedication to God, though inhuman in its intensity, remains a troubling instance of the human desire to transcend the world. He is compared to Bunyan's Greatheart, 'who guards his pilgrim convoy from the onslaught of Apollyon' (Ch. 38). Jane, however, chooses the world of flesh and blood. Ferndean attains an Edenic status, as is clear from the Miltonic echo at the close of Chapter 37, reversing, as it were, the expulsion from Paradise. Whereas

Milton's Adam and Eve 'through Eden took their solitary way' into the world of sin and death, Charlotte's closes her chapter with the sentence: 'We entered the wood and wended homeward.' The novel's quest is as much for the true home as for romantic love.

Religion and the supernatural

Religious questions are central to *Jane Eyre*. Broadly speaking, the rigidities of institutionalized religion, in the persons of Brocklehurst or even the admirable Rivers, contrast with a kind of non-institutionalized Wordsworthian version of Protestantism. The moral rigours of the Protestant individual conscience are mitigated by the healing influence of nature. The novel contrasts lived religious experience, linked to nature, mysticism and even the supernatural, with established religion. Mr Brocklehurst is, of course, the primary exemplar of Evangelical hypocrisy masquerading as religious authority. His religion is fundamentally a form of social control. The girls at Lowood School are to be taught humility and self-sacrifice for the good of their souls and the convenience of society. On one occasion, in a scene reminiscent of *Oliver Twist*, he remonstrates with Miss Temple for supplementing the children's inedible breakfast with bread and cheese:

> Oh, madam, when you put bread and cheese, instead of burnt porridge, into these children's mouths, you may indeed feed their vile bodies, but you little think how you starve their immortal souls!
>
> (Ch. 7)

Jane's religion at this juncture is entirely pragmatic. When asked by Mr Brocklehurst how she hopes to avoid going to hell, she replies: 'I must keep in good health and not die' (Ch. 4). In contrast to Mr Brocklehurst, Helen Burns teaches Jane a religion of forgiveness and acceptance, a New Testament conception:

> I hold another creed, which no one ever taught me, and which I seldom mention, but in which I delight, and to which I cling, for it extends hope to all; it makes eternity a rest – a mighty home – not a terror and an abyss. Besides, with this creed, I can so clearly distinguish between the criminal and his crime, I can so sincerely forgive the first while I abhor the last; with this creed, revenge never worries my heart, degradation never too deeply disgusts me, injustice never crushes me too low; I live in calm, looking to the end.
>
> (Ch. 6)

Helen's religious belief gives her hope for the after-life, but it is insufficient for Jane, who also demands justice in this world. (We see why Mrs Oliphant thought she was a dangerous radical.) On the other hand, Helen's lesson is not lost. Jane is capable, as an adult, of forgiving Mrs Reed, for her treatment of her as a child. The novel's moral toughness is perhaps nowhere better displayed than at Mrs Reed's deathbed. Charlotte eschews the temptation to allow Mrs Reed's remorse for having deprived Jane of her inheritance to transform her suddenly into a kindly person. She has never loved Jane; she will not do so now:

> I approached my cheek to her lips; she would not touch it. She said I oppressed her by leaning over the bed. . . . As I laid her down – for I raised her and supported her on my arm while she drank – I covered her ice-cold and clammy hand with mine: the feeble fingers shrank from my touch – the glazing eyes shunned my gaze.
>
> 'Love me, then, or hate me, as you will,' I said at last, 'you have my full and free forgiveness: ask now for God's and be at peace.'
>
> Poor suffering woman! it was too late for her to make now the effort to change her habitual frame of mind: living, she had ever hated me – dying, she must hate me still.
>
> (Ch. 21)

Jane exercises Helen's forgiveness, without expecting anything in return. In Mrs Reed's death, we see the way the novel weaves its themes together. Helen Burns' legacy lives on in Jane, tempered by a moral realism.

Part of the significance of Helen Burns' 'creed', 'which no one ever taught me', reflects a pervasive feeling in the novel, that spiritual truth and organized religion are incompatible. Religion is powerfully associated with Nature (see prose extract, pp. 152–5). Where Jane differs from Mr Brocklehurst, Helen and St John Rivers is in not seeing religion as the antithesis of life. Rivers, for example, represses his natural instincts, his love for Rosamond Oliver, because he believes that religion and instinct are necessarily at odds. Jane describes in one of St John's sermons the essential morbidity, as she conceives it, of his views:

> The heart was thrilled, the mind astonished, by the power of the preacher: neither were softened. Throughout there was a strange bitterness; an absence of consolatory gentleness; stern allusions to Calvinistic doctrines – election, predestination, reprobation – were frequent; and each reference to these points sounded like a sentence pronounced for doom. When he had done, instead of feeling better, calmer, more enlightened by his discourse, I experienced an inexpressible sadness.
>
> (Ch. 30)

In contrast to this doom-laden religion, Helen's creed, which 'extends hope to all', runs like a silver thread through the novel. Jane, who by no means blindly follows her instincts, as we see from the fact that she flees Thornfield, nevertheless finds legitimacy in spontaneous feeling. It is left to the reformed rake, Rochester, however, to express the novel's conclusion on the religious and moral law. Recognizing God's punishment in the burning of Thornfield, Rochester, like Coleridge's Ancient Mariner, learns to pray:

> Divine justice pursued its course; disasters came thick on me: I was forced to pass through the valley of the shadow of death. *His* chastisements are mighty; and one smote me which has humbled me for ever. You know I was proud of my strength: but what is it now, when I must give it over to foreign guidance, as a child does its weakness? Of late, Jane – only – only of late – I began to see and acknowledge the hand of God in my doom. I began to experience remorse, repentance, the wish for reconcilement to my Maker. I began sometimes to pray.
>
> (Ch. 37)

When Jane had first met Rochester at Thornfield, he had lived on a principle similar to Jane's as a child; he was obsessed with the wrongs done to him by others, by his father, brother, wife or mistress. In the end, his Byronic cynicism gives way to religious acceptance and to an acknowledgement of his individual responsibility for his troubles. In *Jane Eyre* the genuinely religious life is not incompatible with whatever human happiness can be attained by our efforts. Nevertheless, the trace of mystical experience, things 'too awful to be communicated or discussed', can be felt throughout. This may explain why the novel ends with a valedictory passage to the problematic St John Rivers. He represents both Bunyan's Pilgrim and, in his missionary work, the nineteenth-century zeal for improvement:

> Firm, faithful, and devoted, full of energy and zeal, and truth . . . he hews down like a giant the prejudices of creed and caste that encumber it. He may be stern; he may be exacting; he may be ambitious yet; but his is the sternness of the warrior Greatheart, who guards his pilgrim convoy from the onslaught of Apollyon.
>
> (Ch. 38)

Rivers offers an uncanny echo of Mr Brocklehurst, in his belief that he is divinely inspired:

> I am the servant of an infallible Master. I am not going out under human guidance, subject to the defective laws and erring

control of my feeble fellow-worms: my king, my lawgiver, my captain, is the all perfect. (Ch. 34)

Rivers, in short, has the inhuman satisfaction of believing he is always right. The narrator records admiration for his faith and purpose, but no love. A religion which excludes human affections is shown as, perhaps, fit for heroes, but it is not, in *Jane Eyre*, a creed to live by. Indeed such a faith kills its adherents.

Point of view

As a first-person narration, *Jane Eyre* conveys a tone of passionate engagement. One may pick out three characteristic aspects of the narrational stance. First, the early chapters powerfully convey the child's point of view. I have already mentioned Jane's meeting with Brocklehurst, when from her diminutive perspective she sees him as an elongated pillar. Though the emphasis on the child's perceptions is Romantic in origin, Jane is not portrayed as a Wordsworthian infant, 'seer blest', 'six year darling of a pigmy size'. She is an angry and difficult little girl. The narrative stresses both Jane's sense of outrage and the intensity of her perceptions. Secondly, Jane, in her rôle as adult governess, observes character and physiognomy. We notice how she 'draws' Rochester or the Ingram ladies. As an observer she is a social satirist, her vision strongly ironic; we note, for example, her narrational treatment of the Miss Reeds, or more kindly, of Miss Oliver. Thirdly, Jane is an acute recorder of natural phenomena. The novel contains more detailed natural description than *Wuthering Heights*, which one often thinks of as being attuned to the elemental. Sensitivity to nature is an important index of character in the novel. In Chapter 34, for example, Jane describes a walk with Rivers during which he is oblivious to his natural surroundings, but which she observes:

> a soft turf, mossy fine and emerald green, minutely enamelled with a tiny white flower . . .

Jane responds to the beauty of the natural world in the present, whereas Rivers, obsessed with his vision of the future, seems to see nothing. Overall, the persona that emerges from the first-person narration is varied: ironic, distanced; passionate or angry; observant and sensitive to natural stimulus, the different narrative voices contribute to our perception of Jane as a complex individual.

What 'kind' of a novel?

Because *Jane Eyre* is set in a recognizable historical period, the early nineteenth century, in a real country, England, and portrays what was a familiar social type, the poor governess, the reader approaches it with broadly realistic expectations. We assume that the novel accords with the conditions of life as most of us experience them. There are a number of ways in which Charlotte Brontë violates these expectations. Some of the sins against verisimilitude commonly listed are:

1 Bertha Mason's madness. This is characterized as pure Gothic, and the burning down of Thornfield, by releasing Jane from the dilemma of what to do about Rochester, too coincidentally convenient: what would she have done if Bertha had not died?
2 Rochester's Byronism,
3 the discovery of Marsh End and Jane's cousins is grossly coincidental;
4 with the bald intrusion of the supernatural (Rochester's voice to Jane at Moor House) our credulity is strained. Generally, the talk of fairies, men in green and so on is seen as a blot on a novel ostensibly set in the realist mode.

It is possible to place *Jane Eyre* within the broad confines of realist fiction, while agreeing that it attempts more than one form of fictional representation. The Gothic element is indeed present, but as I argued in the discussion on Bertha Mason (pp. 131–2), the madwoman had both an historical and a psychological relevance to the novel. We know that in 1845 Charlotte visited North Lees Hall Farm in Yorkshire, owned by the Eyre family, which was said to have a 'mad woman's' room. The hall had been burned down by its insane occupant in the seventeenth century. The year 1845 was also the one which saw the passage of the Lunatics Act, establishing the principle that the community had a duty to provide care for the insane. This act followed the revelations of the Select Committee on Madhouses (1815–16), which exposed the abuse and near starvation of the insane under modes of care then prevalent. 'Single lunatics', locked up by their families, sometimes for no better reason than that the latter wished to get their hands on their property, were by no means uncommon. Charlotte Brontë's introduction of a madwoman in *Jane Eyre* was a theme of topical interest and formed part of a new public awareness of the treatment of the insane. And finally, on a psychological level, Bertha Mason serves as a tangible reminder of Rochester's guilty past that must be confronted and expiated; she is also a warning to Jane of what her future would be if she consulted only her passions.

Similarly, the emphasis on fairy-tale and myth – indeed, the believability of ghosts, in the first instance – can be traced to the Brontës' childhood. Their servant, Tabitha Aykroyd, frequently told the children ghost stories, and a belief in the supernatural would have been common in the country districts of that time. Whether or not Charlotte believed in ghosts herself, she had been subject to hallucinatory moments in relation to her Angrian fantasies and, therefore, the notion of introducing 'voices' into the plot of her novel was perhaps not so astonishing. *Jane Eyre* conveys the feeling that the world is a more complex place than most of our conceptions of it. As Romanticism in the novel counteracts theological rigidity, so the supernatural subverts, to some extent, the purely empirical and utilitarian view of the world. Both Rochester and Jane are spontaneous Romantics, experiencing an almost mystical sense of kinship with one another. As Rochester ironically puts it:

> it is as if I had a string somewhere under my left ribs, tightly and inextricably knotted to a similar string situated in the corresponding quarter of your little frame. . . . I am afraid that cord of communion will be snapped; and then I've a nervous notion I should take to bleeding inwardly.

(Ch. 23)

This spiritual kinship, reminiscent of Cathy and Heathcliff, also recalls Goethe's *Elective Affinities* (1809), possibly known to the Brontës through their German studies. (Schiller is, of course, quoted in *Jane Eyre*.) In this context it may be helpful to think of the example of the German *Novelle*, a fictional form in some respects closer to *Jane Eyre* than the English realist novel. In the *Novelle*, the setting had a largely symbolic function and the action often included episodes not subject to rational explanation. *Jane Eyre* is more realistic than the German *Novelle*, but the use of symbolic settings and the recourse to the marvellous are reminiscent of its conventions. It is tempting to see a connection with German fiction in this aspect of the novel. When we consider the episodes at Moor House where Jane and the Rivers sisters study German literature, we can reasonably suppose that Charlotte discovered in the *Novelle* literary models that allowed her to express elements of romance and of the supernatural which she found appropriate to her story. For example, what the supernatural conveys in relation to the theme of love is the overwhelming sense of the 'rightness' of passion, though on a purely rational level it may seem wrong. In *Jane Eyre* the supernatural functions partly as a metaphor for sexual feeling in a novelistic convention where explicit sexuality could not be expressed.

Probably more difficult for the twentieth-century reader to accept than the telepathic communion of voices is the recourse to bald coincidence. Jane, when starving, happens to collapse on the very doorstep where her as yet unknown cousins live. In addition, her uncle, Mr Eyre, also unknown, who leaves her a fortune, happens to be acquainted with Bertha's brother, and sets in train the unmasking of Rochester. And finally, Jane is able to marry Rochester because Bertha providentially destroys herself in a fire.

One can only say that if the sin of coincidence is to be held against novelists, all the work of Dickens, much of Scott, Thackeray, Hardy, Balzac or indeed the Naturalist, Zola, would have to be sacrificed. Coincidence functions as one of the building blocks of nineteenth-century fiction.

Jane Eyre imagines what might happen if love and justice triumphed in the world. The unlikelihood of this occurring in real life is underscored by Charlotte's recourse to romance and by the analogy to *Pilgrim's Progress*. It is as though she were deliberately showing the gap between romance and reality. In real life, worthy, intelligent but powerless individuals tend not to achieve their desires, unless, of course, they happen to write novels which express their own and their readers' deepest wishes. One can account to some extent for *Jane Eyre's* early and continued popularity by suggesting that the novel resembles Freud's description of the function of a dream: it is a wish fulfilled. Like a dream it is both plausible and implausible; unlike a dream it was the work of a conscious artist, though drawing on material derived from the unconscious mind.

Prose extract and critical commentary

I lingered at the gates; I lingered on the lawn; I paced backwards and forwards on the pavement: the shutters of the glass door were closed; I could not see into the interior; and both my eyes and spirit seemed drawn from the gloomy house – from the grey hollow filled with rayless cells, as it appeared to me – to that sky expanded before me – a blue sea absolved from taint of cloud; the moon ascending it in solemn march, her orb seeming to look up as she left the hill tops, from behind which she had come, far and farther below her, and aspired to the zenith, midnight dark in its fathomless depth and measureless distance; and for those trembling stars that followed her course, they made my heart tremble, my veins glow when I viewed them. Little things recall us to earth: the clock struck in the hall; that sufficed. I turned from moon and stars, opened a side-door and went in.

The hall was dark, nor yet was it lit, only by the high-hung bronze lamp. A warm glow suffused both it and the lower steps of the oak staircase. This ruddy shine issued from the great dining-room, whose two-leaved door stood open, and showed a genial fire in the grate, glancing on marble hearth and brass fireirons, and revealing the purple draperies and polished furniture in the most pleasant radiance. It revealed, too, a group near the mantelpiece. I had scarcely caught it, and scarcely become aware of a cheerful mingling of voices, amongst which I seemed to distinguish the tones of Adèle, when the door closed.

I hastened to Mrs Fairfax's room. There was a fire there too, but no candle, and no Mrs Fairfax. Instead, all alone, sitting upright on the rug, and gazing with gravity at the blaze, I beheld a great black and white long-haired dog, just like the Gytrash of the lane. It was so like it that I went forward and said 'Pilot', and the thing got up and came to me and snuffed me. I caressed him, and he wagged his great tail; but he looked an eerie creature to be alone with, and I could not tell whence he had come. I rang the bell, for I wanted a candle; and I wanted, too, to get an account of this visitant.

(Ch. 12)

CONTEXT   The passage follows Jane's meeting with Mr Rochester in the lane. The association with an uncanny world has already been established by the comparison of the dog with a 'Gytrash' (a fairy-tale creature of Bessie's stories, lion-like, with long hair and a huge head) and will be later reinforced by Mr Rochester's association of Jane with the 'men in green'. Previously Jane had lamented her dissatisfaction with the 'stagnation' of Thornfield, in her placid life with Mrs Fairfax. It is this suffocating atmosphere that she dreads on seeing the gloomy house. Her return, however, signals a profound change in her life, as if in response to her desire for action.

ANALYSIS   Jane comes back reluctantly, imagining the interior of Thornfield dark and silent and 'my own lonely little room'. Enclosure and imprisonment predominate in her imagination, invoked by the phrase, 'viewless fetters'. One underlying irony in Jane's perception of the house is that, in a way unknown to herself, she is correct; the house is a prison for Bertha, if not for her. She longs to be 'tossed in the storms of an uncertain struggling life', an image which acts as a counterpoise to the search for tranquillity in the novel.

Jane contemplates the night sky, which, with the rising moon, seems to express her own aspirations. The rhythms of this paragraph – 'I lingered at the gates; I lingered on the lawn;' – suggest her internal vacillations. The length of the first sentence, punctuated by colons and semi-colons, constitutes a form of interior monologue. What passes as a natural description is, in effect, a painting of Jane's state of mind. The imprisoning house, 'the shutters of the glass doors were close', and the free sky, 'that sky expanded before me', juxtapose constraint and freedom, and suggest an image of innocence, 'a blue sea absolved from taint of cloud'. The religious and moral vocabulary ('absolved', 'taint') is significant. This cloudless sky is more than weather; it represents a realm of innocence and of freedom unassociated with 'storms' of passion, which Jane will discover subsequently. She projects her ambitions upon the moon in a sustained personification; the moon 'seemed to look up', 'aspired to the zenith'. However, she identifies with the stars perceived as frailer than the great moon. 'Those trembling stars' are rendered as the objective equivalent of Jane's own frailty as well as of her ambition. 'They made my heart tremble, my veins glow when I viewed them.' The paragraph closes with the homely intrusion of time. 'Little things recall us to earth: the clock struck in the hall.' The opposition between limitless aspiration and 'the viewless fetters' of time and custom represented by the house ironically undercuts Jane's dreams of grandeur. And though the next paragraph evokes the warmth and geniality which Rochester brings to Thornfield and to Jane's life, the preceding contemplation of the sky, a realm of moral purity and 'trembling' aspiration remain with Jane. This passage then expresses in natural imagery Jane's desire for moral and physical freedom.

The 'glow' of Jane's veins finds an immediate response when she enters the house. Instead of 'the grey hollow filled with rayless cells' which she had imagined the house to be, she is met with warmth and light: 'a warm glow', 'this ruddy shine', 'a genial fire', 'pleasant radiance'. The adjectives reveal the feelings of empathy and ease that she will develop with Mr Rochester. But though he is the cause of the ruddy glow, so welcoming to Jane, this fire also prefigures Rochester's passion as potentially destructive.

THE ROLE OF NATURE The foregoing passage is an instance of Charlotte Brontë's recourse to nature imagery as a language for the inarticulate heart. Jane's habitual reserve and self-effacement are broken when in states of anger (at Gateshead) or under the 'genial glow' of Rochester's affection; but her moments of greatest mental liberty lie in the contemplation of the natural world. Thornfield, though transformed by Rochester's warmth, is still a prison. We remember that during their engagement Rochester showers Jane with expensive gifts, concrete manifestations of the 'viewless fetters'. Ferndean, too, enclosed by trees, is a prison for Rochester when blind. Jane's triumph at the novel's end is to have achieved liberty herself, and in doing so to restore it to Rochester.

The passage of 'entry' to Thornfield reverberates with images and themes informing the novel as a whole. The consistency of tone and compression of feeling achieved in *Jane Eyre* partly arise from the repetition of themes and image patterns and their orchestration at different periods of Jane's existence. The novel's real drama is not the Cinderella rags-to-riches story, but the heroine's triumphs over her own fears and passions. Her resistance to, or rebellion against, Mrs Reed, Mr Brocklehurst, Mr Rochester and finally St John Rivers establishes her independence and her ability to confer strength on another. Nature imagery – storms, the moors, fire and ice, birds (sparrow, linnet, for Jane, the eagle for Rochester, plumy birds for the grand ladies at Thornfield) – is integrated with thematic concerns (Byronism, liberty, self-respect) and with the supernatural which also arises out of the strengthening presence of the natural world. In such passages we are made aware of the Wordsworthian resonances of Charlotte's text. The links between nature and divine purpose (first suggested in Bewick) justify Jane's struggle to maintain her moral code in spite of her adoration of Rochester. On the other hand, the love she feels for him is affirmed to be somehow natural and legitimate. Nature in the above passage, as in the novel as a whole, functions as a guide and a hope.

12 *Villette* (1853)

In *Villette* Charlotte Brontë creates an atmosphere of intensity, suspense and psychological complexity from the seemingly prosaic material of life in a Continental girls' boarding school. But the narrowness of the novel's social range is not its prevailing impression. Although based on Charlotte's eighteen-month stay in Brussels, with many incidents drawn directly from that experience, it brilliantly objectifies its autobiographical origins.

Narrative choices: Brussels transformed

If one contrasts Charlotte's first but posthumously published novel, *The Professor*, with *Villette*, one can more readily appreciate her success in transforming her Brussels' experiences into a mature work of fiction. *The Professor*, dated 1846 but published in 1857, attempted, like a number of Charlotte's juvenilia, to treat auto-biographical experience through the device of a male narrator. William Crimsworth is an unsatisfactory and unconvincing protagonist. His feud with his brother reminds us of the rivalry in Angria between two brothers, Douro and Lord Charles Wellesley, and his gloom and adolescent rudeness further place him in the mannered world of the juvenilia. In *The Professor*, Charlotte was largely unsuccessful in creating a credible male narrator. We feel that the novel's strength lies in its scenes of Low Country life, of the schoolroom which Charlotte remembered from Brussels and the buildings among which she had experienced so much unhappiness. M. Heger is absent as a character, though some critics have identified him, almost certainly erroneously, with the cynical M. Pelet. For a first novel, *The Professor* is not a negligible achievement, but it illuminates, by contrast, how in *Villette* Charlotte succeeded both in distancing herself from, and confronting, the emotional legacy of Brussels. She was at last able to reconcile her imaginative talents with the exigencies of realist fiction. This time she chose a female narrator. The novel takes place on two levels; in a prosaic school-room world and in an almost morbidly sensitive mind. The narrator, Lucy Snowe, draws both points of view together in often painful juxtaposition through an ironic perspective.

Literary and artistic metaphors

As in *Jane Eyre*, *Pilgrim's Progress* runs as a sub-text through *Villette*. In one sense, these echoes of *Pilgrim's Progress* were characteristic of a strain of nineteenth-century optimism. Bunyan's seventeenth-century allegory of salvation, achieved through a series of spiritual and moral tests undertaken in the form of a journey, often became in the nineteenth century not much more than a framing metaphor for individual struggle and success. The pilgrim's journey was all too readily associated with the idea of Victorian material and social progress. Charlotte Brontë appropriated the theme to highlight the psychological and moral struggles of her heroine, but her account of Lucy Snowe's 'pilgrimage' is far from sharing the optimism of her age. Rather than reducing Bunyan's nonconformist intention, she retains his idea of a spiritual, rather than a worldly journey.

The language of *Villette* is imbued with Bunyan's allegorical figures, the personification of abstract qualities (Fate, Hope, Pity, Common sense, Reason):

> That evening more firmly than ever fastened into my soul the conviction that Fate was of stone, and Hope a false idol – blind, bloodless, and of granite core. I felt, too, that the trial God had appointed me was gaining its climax.
>
> (Ch. 15)

Both the personification of Hope and Fate and the reference to life as a trial, appointed by God, emphasize the sub-text. Lucy's early visits with Mrs Bretton are compared to 'the sojourn of Christian and Hopeful beside a certain pleasant stream, with green trees on each bank, and meadows beautified with lilies all the year round' (Ch. 1). When Lucy hopes that M. Paul will find a chance to speak to her before he sails for the West Indies she exclaims:

> Oh! *I* would be ready, but could that longed-for meeting really be achieved? the time was so short, the schemers seemed so watchful, so active, so hostile; the way of access appeared strait as a gully, deep as a chasm – Apollyon straddled across it, breathing flames. Could my Greatheart overcome? Could my guide reach me?
>
> (Ch. 38)

In addition to language and imagery, *Pilgrim's Progress* provides a significant strain of thematic reference. Lucy's life unfolds as a trial or test, whose successful termination may not be in earthly happiness. False hope, suffering and disillusion are conceived of as part of a preparation for the after-life. The vision of a religious pilgrimage relates to important doctrinal conflicts in the novel. Lucy Snowe, a Protestant in a largely Catholic country, struggling to retain her religious identity and mental liberty, anchors her experience in the language of one of the great English Puritans. Overarching the question of her personal destiny, Lucy clings to a belief in God's inscrutable will. Chapter 38, for example, opens with an explicit evocation of *Pilgrim's Progress*, which links the destiny of individuals to the divine order:

> Let us finish our course, and keep the faith, reliant on the issue to come off more than conquerors. . . . WE SHALL NOT DIE!

Bunyan's original version reads:

> Nay, in all these things we are more than conquerors, through him that loved us, and with that Apollyon spread his dragon wings, and sped him away, that Christian saw him no more.
>
> (Part I)

The theme of faith and the equation of Lucy with Bunyan's hero, Faithful, also relate to the theme of love and the problems of narrative expression. Lucy remains faithful to M. Paul, her entire narrative being a commemoration of that fidelity. Unlike Miss Marchmount, whose fidelity to lost love results in a life of bitterness and silence, Lucy, though she mourns M. Paul's shipwreck, does find her distinctive voice. She becomes both the author of her own tale and the recorder of M. Paul's 'heroism'. Her story redeems an otherwise silent life. In telling her story, she also narrates M. Paul's, a voluble man who never wrote anything down:

> M. Emanuel was not a man to write books; but I have heard him lavish, with careless, unconscious prodigality, such mental wealth as books seldom boast. . . . I used to think what a delight it would be for one who loved him better than he loved himself, to gather and store up those handfuls of gold-dust, so recklessly flung to heaven's reckless winds.
>
> (Ch. 33)

Lucy often bemoans her lack of expressiveness. As a child at Bretton, she was outwardly unresponsive. When she arrived at Labassecour, she literally had no voice, being unable to speak French. When M. Paul subjected her to an oral examination (Ch. 35), 'Though answers to the questions surged up fast, my mind filling like a rising well, ideas were there but not words. I either *could* not or *would* not speak.' Yet in her writing and in her teaching, Lucy finds the voice for her needs. Further, under the spur of jealousy and passion, she even finds the voice to tell M. Paul she loves him. In the end, Lucy is truly eloquent. Bunyan's language and theme are part of a literary and religious tradition that helps to give her life a structure and meaning.

The sub-text of *Pilgrim's Progress*, with its idea of a pilgrimage, offers Lucy a heroic model in a society where heroism, at least for women, seems inconceivable. It is implied that her story, like Bunyan's, may serve as a model to others. But what kind of a

'*Apollyon straddles the path*', *from John Bunyan,* Pilgrim's Progress, *J. Clarke, London 1728, p. 68*

model? Lucy's life is, after all, one that many might not wish to emulate. Harriet Martineau found it dreary and dwelling too much on a woman's need for love. In a culture where women were understood as dependent, Lucy strives for both financial and emotional autonomy. Yet the price of her independence may be coldness of heart (her name Snowe and her chilly demeanour underscore this danger); it may be unbearable solitude, which can drive one mad (encapsulated in the dreadful holiday period when she is alone in the pensionnat with only the maid Goton and the imbecile pupil); it may mean the renunciation of the love and comfort of one's fellow creatures. Lucy's desire to retain her integrity conflicts with her human need for love.

Women character models

Though Charlotte's acute eye for social observation allowed her to paint a range of characters in *Villette*, the novel shares a characteristic of *Jane Eyre* in that places and characters have both a realistic and emblematic significance; observation and allegory merge. Ginevra Fanshawe, for example, is both a young society miss, a vain, self-centred if attractive young woman, and an anti-model in Lucy's private drama of self-creation. The female characters in general function as so many analogies for Lucy, examples to follow or to reject. Similarly Lucy is presented with explicit pictorial models on her visit to the Villette portrait gallery, an allegorical device which allows her to examine the conventional ideals for women of her class and period.

None of these female prototypes by which Lucy is confronted appears entirely satisfactory. Beginning with women characters, in the older generation, we find Miss Marchmount, bitter and lonely, the avaricious Mme Walravens, the teachers at the school, especially Mlle Zélie St Pierre, characterized as cold-hearted and scheming for men, Mrs Bretton, kind but egotistically absorbed in her son, and, finally, Mme Beck. The latter, though accomplished, successful, competent and admirable, to Lucy comes to appear manipulative and power-hungry. That Mme Beck, the first to befriend Lucy in a foreign country, is ultimately seen as the arch-enemy is partly a tribute to Charlotte's continued animosity to Mme Heger on whom Mme Beck was based. Mme Beck's relationships with others (save in her dispute with M. Paul, when he strikes her, Ch. 41) are noticeable for their suavity; nothing ripples the smoothness of her deportment. Lucy, by contrast, lacks social ease; her self-possession is often won at the cost of an almost killing self-control.

Another model presented even more ambiguously is that of Paulina Holme (Polly). Like Lucy, she is capable of intense feeling, but she channels her feelings through others; first through her father and subsequently through Graham Bretton. Polly is one of the fortunate ones for whom such immersion in another is possible:

> One would have thought the child had no mind or life of her own, but must necessarily live, move and have her being in another: now that her father was taken from her, she nestled to Graham, and seemed to feel by his feelings: to exist in his existence.

> (Ch. 3)

The characters in the novel who are fated for good fortune – Graham, Polly, Mrs Bretton and even Madame Beck – experience no conflict between their relationships with other people and their own sense of self. They are what they appear to others, even if they are only surface, like Mme Beck. Lucy, by contrast, has a strong sense of her individual identity – often in a negative sense (she is *not* like this or that other person – and no social context to explore her own being. Her childhood with the Brettons is a borrowed one. Even visiting them as an adult, Lucy feels these scenes of warmth, comfort and fellowship are not her own. Her life as a teacher is largely one of self-denial. The theme of disguise which permeates the novel has its origins in this problem of personality.

Pictorial models

In addition to negative or positive female models among the characters, moral analogy also operates in an artistic form, embodied in Lucy's visit to the portrait gallery (Ch. 19). This episode may be compared with *Pilgrim's Progress* where Christian visits the House of the Interpreter. He is shown a portrait and a number of allegorical persons (Patience and Passion, for example) to educate him as to the dangers and errors that may face him on his journey. The portrait has a similar educative function:

> Christian saw a picture of a very grave person hang up against a wall. And this was the fashion of it: it had eyes lift up to heaven, the best of books in its hand, the law of truth was written upon its lips, the world was behind its back, it stood as if it pleaded with men, and a crown of gold did hang over its head.

> (Part I)

Whereas this allegorical figure has a positive lesson for Christian, (for example 'the world was behind his back' indicates that he must leave the world behind him for salvation), the allegories that Lucy will see on her museum tour elicit a negative response. If the Villette Portrait Gallery is the equivalent of the House of the

Interpreter, she emphatically refuses the interpretations offered. In this respect, Lucy is true to the spirit of nineteenth-century individualism.

At the beginning of this museum tour, Lucy warns the reader that she is no art expert. But she immediately rejects, on broadly 'realist' principles 'certain *chef d'oeuvres* bearing great names' because they lack truth to nature:

> Nature's daylight never had that colour; never was made so turbid, either by storm or cloud, as it is laid out there, under a sky of indigo: and that indigo is not ether; and those dark weeds plastered upon it are not trees.

(Ch. 19)

Lucy's naïve demand that paintings should appear life-like has an ironic function. She views the paintings in the Villette gallery with determined literal-mindedness because she dislikes artifice as opposed to art. This attitude is in accord with her moral views generally. She finds artifice of any kind repellent; artifice is what links the otherwise disparate characters of Mme Beck and Ginevra Fanshawe.

A central quality of *Villette*, which is often insufficiently stressed, is its ironic, sometimes comic, tone. So much retrospective emphasis has been placed on the tragic atmosphere surrounding the Brontës, that Charlotte's skill as an ironist has been underrated. The opening of *Shirley* with its scathing parody of the three curates, which made Mr Nicholls roar with laughter, is a good example of Charlotte's gift for broad comedy. But her life provided, in general, little material for hilarity. Harriet Martineau rightly spoke of the 'sense of pervading pain' in *Villette*. Nevertheless, the characteristic tone is one of sustained irony, through Lucy's sardonic voice. Ginevra Fanshawe calls her 'Timon', 'old Crusty', 'old Diogenes' and 'the dragon'. As a detached observer, whether of social behaviour or of artistic splendour, Lucy displays a dry wit. Yet the reader does not draw from *Villette* an impression of easy ironic distance, as, for example, from Jane Austen's novels. This may arise from the fact that in employing a first-person narrator, who is identified with a shrinking, hypersensitive protagonist, Charlotte cannot command the tolerant authority, which assumes a shared world with her audience. Lucy typically experiences isolation. She defines herself against the world, not in harmony with it. Consequently irony functions as a desperate weapon to maintain sanity, to force objectivity. But in spite of this the genuinely exuberant comic response does occasionally arise, as in Lucy's reading of the 'Cleopatra' portrait, an imagined composite of Rubensesque characteristics (see Rubens illustration, opposite):

*Peter Paul Rubens, 'Cimon and Iphigenia', 'that wealth of muscle, that affluence of flesh. . . . She had no business to lounge away the noon on a sofa.' (*Villette, *Ch. 19)*

It represented a woman, considerably larger, I thought, than the life. I calculated that this lady, put into a scale of magnitude suitable for the reception of a commodity of bulk, would infallibly turn from fourteen to sixteen stone. She was, indeed, extremely well fed: very much butcher's meat – to say nothing of bread, vegetables, and liquids – must she have consumed to attain that breadth and height, that wealth of muscle, that affluence of flesh. She lay half-reclined on a couch: why, it would be difficult to say; broad daylight blazed round her; she appeared in hearty health, strong enough to do the work of two plain cooks; she could not plead a weak spine; she ought to have been standing, or at least sitting bolt upright. She had no business to lounge away the noon on a sofa. She ought likewise to have worn decent garments; a gown covering her properly, which was not the case: out of abundance of material – seven-and-twenty yards, I should say, of drapery – she managed to make inefficient raiment. Then, for the wretched untidiness surrounding her, there could be no excuse. Pots and pans – perhaps I ought to say vases and goblets – were rolled here and there on the foreground; a perfect rubbish of flowers was mixed amongst them, and an absurd and disorderly mass of curtain upholstery smothered the couch and cumbered the floor. On referring to the catalogue, I found that this notable production bore name 'Cleopatra'. . . . it was on the whole an enormous piece of claptrap.

(Ch. 19)

In the Cleopatra episode, Lucy ridicules the sensual and aesthetic ideal of woman. We see how far Charlotte had come from her Angrian fantasies in which such a model as Cleopatra might have won approval. Lucy's enumeration of the queen's attributes undermines the eroticism, masked as idealism, of the portrait. How much butcher's meat 'to say nothing of bread, vegetables and liquids – must she have consumed to attain that breadth and height, that *wealth* of muscle, that *affluence* of flesh' [my italics]. The painting offers a sensual ideal of beauty based, as the narrator clearly indicates, on equating flesh with money. Cleopatra's languorous physical attitude is next reduced to absurdity by Lucy's mock-uncomprehending judgement:

She lay half-reclined on a couch: why, it would be difficult to say; . . . she appeared in hearty health, strong enough to do the work of two plain cooks. . . . She had no business to lounge away the noon on a sofa.

(Ch. 19)

Cleopatra's nudity is also ridiculed and with it the convention of female nudes in painting. Why, Lucy enquires naïvely, with some 27 yards of drapery around her, cannot Cleopatra cover herself properly? And finally, what an untidy mess surrounds her. One may contrast the ideal of perfect neatness that Lucy extends to her clothes and surroundings with this 'wretched untidiness, pots and pans rolled here and there, a perfect rubbish of flowers'.

In short, Lucy finds Cleopatra absurd. 'It was on the whole an enormous piece of claptrap.' The object of her mockery is idealized sensuality itself. Lucy, the puritan, finds Cleopatra comic rather than shocking. To her, this nude represents an incomprehensible and supremely ridiculous masculine ideal of the sensual woman, composed, as she unkindly notes, of only too material a flesh: butcher's meat, bread, vegetables and liquid.

M. Paul, who is alive to the erotic implications of the painting, finds Lucy contemplating the Cleopatra, and whisks her away to look at morally improving pictures, which in his view provide suitable models for a young woman's life. These are a set of four didactic paintings entitled 'La Vie d'une femme'. They show women in four stages: the girl, the married woman, the mother and the widow, visual equivalents of the moral tracts that proliferated in the nineteenth century on women's duties as wives, mothers and daughters (see, for example, Bishop Dupanloup, *La Femme studieuse* (1869) or Mrs Sarah Ellis, *The Wives of England*, and *The Women of England, their Social Duties and Domestic Habits*, and the illustration on the next page). To Lucy, M. Paul's didactic models seem 'flat, dead, pale and formal'. If Cleopatra is 'claptrap', these representations of a woman's life make the heart sink:

> The first represented a 'Jeune Fille', coming out of a church-door, a missal in her hand, her dress very prim, her eyes cast down, her mouth pursed up – the image of a most villainous little precocious she-hypocrite.
>
> (Ch. 19)

The correct public attitude for an unmarried girl, as Lucy describes it, necessitating religious observance, primness and so on promotes not virtue but hypocrisy. Proper behaviour for women is, in effect, a training in dissimulation. The second painting, 'Mariée', also conveys an aura of religious hypocrisy, the woman 'showing the whites of her eyes in the most exasperating manner'. The third depicts a 'Jeune mère', 'hanging disconsolate over a clayey and puffy baby' (the joys of motherhood?), and the fourth, 'Veuve', describes a woman and her daughter in mourning, 'a black woman, holding by the hand a black little girl'. In the last example, metonymy reduces the woman and her daughter to a pile of funeral clothes.

Lucy indicts 'La Vie d'une femme' because this prescription for the ideal woman can only produce 'insincere, ill-humoured, blood-

Currer and Ives, 'Stages of a Woman's Life from the Cradle to the Grave', New York, 1850. An example of nineteenth-century didactic painting of women, such as Lucy saw in the Villette Portrait Gallery

From left to right the verses read as follows:

In swaddling clothes
behold the bud
Of sweet and gentle
womanhood.

Next she foreshews
with mimic plays,
The business of
her future days.

Now glorious as a
full-blown flower,
The heart of manhood
feels her power.

A husband now
her arms entwine,
She clings around
him like the vine.

Now bearing fruit
she rears her boys,
And tastes a mother's
pains and joys.

Like sparkling fountain
gushing forth,
She proves a blessing
to the earth.

A busy housewife
full of cares,
The daily food
her hand prepares.

As age creeps on
she seeks for grace
Always to church
and in her place

Now second childhood
loosens all her tongue,
She talks of love and
prattles with the young.

A useless cumberer
on the Earth,
From house to house
they send her forth.

Chained to her chair
by weight of years
She listless knits
till death appears.

less, brainless nonentities' (Ch. 19). Even worse, these 'nonentities' are what they are because they exist as 'unmarried girl', 'wife', 'mother', 'widow' – relative creatures, defined by their relationship to men. Are they, Lucy wonders, what men themselves really want? Clearly M. Paul, who is shown as comically railing against stiff-necked Englishwomen and their astounding insular audacity, admires Lucy because she is the antithesis of these models, sincere and intelligent. Even Graham Bretton, conventional in his attitudes towards women, chooses the well-informed and sensitive Polly in preference to the more decorative but empty-headed Ginevra Fanshawe.

The female models at the art gallery constitute the two poles of women's possibilities within a patriarchal culture, sensual high-priced animal or self-sacrificing angel. As such, Lucy is able to ridicule them with relative ease. A third and more unsettling possibility emerges in the actress Vashti's performance at the theatre, which Lucy is taken to see by Dr John. This is a scene as intense in its way as Jane's vision of Bertha Mason. Vashti personifies passion in a woman:

> Wicked, perhaps, she is, but also she is strong; and her strength has conquered Beauty, has over-come Grace, and bound both at her side, captives peerlessly fair, and docile as fair. Even in the uttermost frenzy of energy is each maenad movement royally, imperially, incedingly upborne. Her hair, flying loose in revel or war, is still an angel's hair, and glorious under a halo. Fallen, insurgent, banished, she remembers the heaven where she rebelled. Heaven's light, following her exile, pierces its confines, and discloses their forlorn remoteness.
>
> Place now the Cleopatra, or any other slug, before her as an obstacle, and see her cut through the pulpy mass as the scimitar of Saladin clove the down cushion. Let Paul Peter Rubens wake from the dead, let him rise out of his cerements, and bring into this presence all the army of his fat women; the magian power or prophet-virtue girting that slight rod of Moses, could, at one waft, release and re-mingle a sea spell-parted, whelming the heavy host with the down-rush of overthrown sea-ramparts.
> (Ch. 23)

By identifying with Vashti, Lucy enjoys a fantasy of terrible revenge on Rubens's fat women as she imagines Moses allowing the Red Sea to drown them. This passage conflates in a powerful way two pictorial models. Rubens is rejected, indeed annihilated, and John Martin, the painter who celebrated a stern biblical vision, implicitly substituted. Martin had painted 'The Destruction of Pharoah's Host', where the prophet is shown standing on a promontory with his staff held high, keeping the waters parted for the Israelite host (see p. 170). In Lucy's vision, the seemingly frail Vashti becomes 'that slight rod of Moses', which has, nevertheless, the power to part the waters of the Red Sea, imbued with 'magian power or prophet-virtue'. But Vashti is more than a symbol of power. She may also be understood as a darker version of the Eve/Titan figure of *Shirley*, a satanic rebel from heaven. 'Fallen, insurgent, banished', this is Milton's Satan in female form. Vashti is a disturbing counter-possibility, one that will nearly absorb Lucy in her nervous jealousy and emotional exaltation. In the portrait gallery and the theatre, Lucy begins to construct a conception of womanhood for herself. For neither the sensuality of the Cleopatra, nor the denial of self-hood (as practised in the didactic paintings) point to an honourable 'vie d'une femme'. What if, however, the self were allowed free development? Would it be as terrible as the Vashti? Ultimately Lucy is capable of constructing herself, by means of a critical awareness of the models surrounding her.

Themes of disguise and concealment: the spy

When Lucy first arrives at Mme Beck's school, she is both shocked and intrigued to discover that Mme Beck spies on her to the extent of searching through her clothes and personal effects (Ch. 8). As Tony Tanner has shown (Penguin Introduction), spying on the one hand and concealment on the other are the stock-in-trade of both sympathetic and unsympathetic characters in the novel. Part of this obsession with secrecy is attributed, probably unfairly by the narrator, to the Jesuitical influence pervading Labassecourian life. Mme Beck, Père Silas and even M. Paul indulge in spying as a way of maintaining control over, or of learning about, other people.

Yet we are aware that Lucy, who struggles against artifice, also spies and dissimulates. Throughout much of the novel she watches and observes; she spies on Mme Beck spying on her; she conceals herself in order to watch and overhear others at the midnight fête, and as narrator, she deliberately withholds information from the reader. In addition, she regularly disguises her feelings in order to mislead – for example, in making M. Paul think she had forgotten his birthday.

In spite of Lucy's hatred of artifice, dissimulation is curiously appropriate to her character and to her narrative strategy. In order to unravel the mystery of others' personalities, Lucy Snowe, as first-person narrator, can only observe, speculate and very rarely intervene. Thanks to her relatively humble social status, she cannot initiate action. Spying, it is true, often leads to comic mistakes. The watcher draws erroneous conclusions. This is graphically illustrated when Lucy spies on M. Paul with his ward, and concludes he means to marry her. The idea of conspiracy in the novel is both true and false. There are individual and collective plots; some are comic like the ghostly nun, some malevolent, like Mme Beck's, some benign like M. Paul's 'plot' to buy a school for Lucy. Where Lucy is able to break through her jealousy and reserve, to abandon disguise, and to confide in M. Paul she ceases to be an actor in others' plots, and can invent her own.

Prose extract and critical commentary

On quitting Bretton, which I did a few weeks after Paulina's departure – little thinking then I was never again to visit it: never more to tread its calm old streets – I betook myself home, having been absent six months. It will be conjectured that I was of course glad to return to the bosom of my kindred. Well! the amiable conjecture does no harm and may therefore be safely left uncontradicted. Far from saying nay, indeed, I will permit the reader to picture me, for the next eight years, as a bark slumbering through halcyon weather, in a harbour still as glass – the steersman stretched on the little deck, his face up to heaven, his eyes closed: buried, if you will, in a long prayer. A great many women and girls are supposed to pass their lives something in that fashion; why not I with the rest?

Picture me then idle, basking, plump, and happy, stretched on a cushioned deck, warmed with constant sunshine, rocked by breezes indolently soft. However, it cannot be concealed that, in that case, I must somehow have fallen over-board, or that there must have been wreck at last. I too well remember a time – a long time, of cold, of danger, of contention. To this hour, when I have the nightmare, it repeats the rush and saltiness of briny waves in my throat, and their icy pressure on my lungs. I even know there was a storm, and that not of one hour nor one day. For many days and nights neither sun nor stars appeared; we cast with our own hands the tackling out of the ship; a heavy tempest lay on us; all hope that we should be saved was taken away. In fine, the ship was lost, the crew perished.

(Ch. 4)

CONTEXT   Lucy is associated with the sea early in the novel. The passage quoted, at the opening of Chapter 4, offers a deliberately ambiguous account of her life after leaving Bretton. Lucy does not describe her original home, except by inference; it is almost certainly the antithesis of Bretton. Instead she veils her subsequent life after leaving Bretton in a sea-shipwreck metaphor. Following this unexplained disaster, she goes to work for Miss Marchmount as a companion.

John Martin, 'The Destruction of Pharoah's Host', 1830. 'The Magian power . . . girting that slight rod of Moses . . . whelming the heavy host with the down-rush of overthrown sea-ramparts.' (Villette, Ch. 23)

IMAGERY   The pictorial source for this passage may well have been John Martin's 'The Destruction of Tyre' (*c.* 1840). That painting shows an ancient city by the sea, its harbour in the convulsions of storm and earthquake, the frail ships being swallowed by the waves. For a novel which takes place largely in the conventual atmosphere of a girls' school, set in an unromantic Labassecourian city, set in turn in a flat Flemish landscape, *Villette* is remarkable for conveying a sense of the power of nature. This is effected primarily through storm and sea description, especially the metaphorical application of storm imagery to psychological states. Thackeray noted Charlotte Brontë's 'remarkably happy way of carrying metaphor logically through to its conclusion' (11 March 1853 to Lucy Baxter).

This extended metaphor of the wreck at sea, prefiguring the wreck at the novel's close, conceals as much as it reveals. Fact is suppressed in favour of feeling. What happened to Lucy and her family emerges only indirectly; but the quality of Lucy's suffering reveals itself through the image of the shipwreck and the storm. It seems likely that the reference to the 'steersman' in the passage was an autobiographical clue on Charlotte's part. The steersman is oblivious to possible danger, 'his face up to heaven, his eyes closed: buried, if you will, in a long prayer'. Though couched in deliberate ambiguity, this reference suggests the withdrawn behaviour of Patrick Brontë towards his family, his eyes closed to Branwell's deterioration; the phrase 'if you will' even suggests doubt about his religious commitment. Whatever his autobiographical origins, within the context of the novel, the steersman is the only clue we have to Lucy's home life.

The passage begins with the reader's 'amiable conjecture', which is, by implication, illusory. The picture of Lucy that the reader is 'permitted' to hold as 'a bark slumbering' is ambiguous. The halcyon weather, the sea of glass are products of the reader's hackneyed imagination, not of Lucy's experience. And, were this period of blissful peace to have existed, the narrator implies, it was not necessarily happy: 'A great many women and girls are supposed to pass their lives something in that fashion, why not I with the rest?' It is as though Lucy were describing the bay at Glass Town. The lulling and, we suspect, deceitful rhythms, 'rocked by breezes indolently soft' are broken by Lucy's rueful comment: 'However, it cannot be concealed . . . there must have been a wreck at last.' The whole function of the metaphor in this case is to conceal rather than to reveal Lucy's personal experience. In the last sentence, the peaceful fiction, 'the amiable conjecture', collapses. 'To this hour, when I have a nightmare, it repeats the rush and saltiness of briny waves in my throat and their icy pressure on my lungs.' The image of the glassy sea, which has been projected on the reader as a

'The Bay of Glasstown', a drawing by Charlotte Brontë after John Martin

harmless fantasy, explodes. The disaster that wrecked Lucy is revealed, not as an historical account (did her family all die, was there some shameful secret attached to this 'wreck'?) but as a feeling, which for Lucy is expressed in the physical agony of drowning. The image that began as a polite adornment suddenly carries the weight of horror. This handling of imagery serves simultaneously to distance feeling and also to expose it, characteristic of Lucy's narrational strategy of concealment and revelation.

One may also note the personality of the 'amiable reader', a figure not unlike Emily Brontë's Lockwood, and serving a similar function. He or she is conventional and thought to be of that fortunate race of mortals, like Graham Bretton or Ginevra Fanshawe, who are not cursed either with much ill-fortune or with a morbid sensitivity. Lucy's fate, by contrast, is to feel too much. The fiction of the 'amiable reader' in *Villette* does not bind narrator to reader; rather, it distances the reader. We are only allowed glimpses, veiled in metaphor, of an emotional reality which our sensibility cannot penetrate. This handling of metaphor further serves to emphasize Lucy's isolation.

Though much of the novel takes place ·in interiors and though the feeling of conventual life is a strong one, nevertheless weather, the sky, land- and sea-scapes play a major part in its drama. Storms are seen as premonitions of disaster – for example, at Miss Marchmount's:

> Three times in the course of my life, events had taught me that these strange accents in the storm – this restless, hopeless cry – denote a coming state of the atmosphere unpropitious to life.
> (Ch. 4)

The novel also contains actual sea- and sky-scapes, notably the Channel crossing, first described poetically by Lucy 'grand with imperial promise, soft with tints of enchantment' and then ironically undercut: 'Becoming excessively sick, I faltered down to the cabin.' The wind plays an epic rôle. Charlotte herself was always racked by the winter east winds in Yorkshire. 'The north and east owned a terrific influence, making all pain more poignant, all sorrow sadder.' The effect of external storm on psychological states is striking:

> I do not know why that change in atmosphere made a cruel impression on me, why the raging storm and beating rain crushed me with a deadlier paralysis than I had experienced while the air remained serene.
> (Ch. 15)

A violent storm also coincides with Lucy's visit to the Basse Ville in her search for Mme de Walraven's house. But most characteristically the imagery of storm is internalized, expressing Lucy's passion, her fears and her jealousy. When she awaits a last message from M. Paul, the hours 'passed like a drift cloud – like the rack scudding before a storm' (Ch. 38).

The novel ends with the great hurricane that destroys Lucy's hopes. Again the ambiguity in the language of the final passage reflects less an effort to console Mr Brontë with something that might resemble a happy ending, than the consistent development of the dynamics of concealment and revelation in the opening chapters. The storm image is by no means entirely negative. It promises freedom and action as well as disaster. More terrible than shipwreck is inaction (we remember the glassy harbour). As an image of energy, the storm is both crushing and liberating. If one compares M. Paul, the little stormy figure, with Mme Beck, the woman of icy calm, the former emerges as preferable. For Lucy Snowe, the risks of the voyage, the shipwreck itself, are better than life in the still harbour. *Villette* can be understood, to use another metaphor, as Charlotte Brontë's escape from Glass Town to confront the dangers of life and real, rather than imagined passion.

STYLE IN *VILLETTE*   *Villette* shows Charlotte Brontë extending her control over language and imagery. The novel possesses a variety of tones, striking in a first-person narration. We have noted the recourse to irony, to extended metaphor and to biblical language. At the same time, Lucy records the minutiae of daily life in the pensionnat, the size and shape of the rooms, the sense of routine and confinement of the school. Further, in contrast to the homely world of the schoolroom one finds passages conveying heightened feeling, the best-known perhaps being the fête-dream sequence in Chapter 38. Here, reflecting the hallucinatory effect of the drug which Lucy has been administered, the language expresses the wonder and hypnotic quality of a dream. Charlotte, as often in her passages of heightened tone, has recourse to a pattern of inversions; 'Voices were there . . . unnumbered; instruments varied and countless', 'Here were assembled ladies, looking by this light most beautiful', or again, 'a garden most gorgeous'. This device, which also occurs in *Jane Eyre*, was, I think, Charlotte's indirect tribute to M. Heger. She employed French cadences and turns of phrase as though she mentally wrote in French and then translated into English. Such expressions and inversions occur throughout, quite apart from the use of French quotations, which are always correct, idiomatic and apt. Charlotte's French constructions resemble an unspoken conversation with her much loved teacher. In her writing generally, the imprint of and immersion in the French language was profound and has been insufficiently noted by critics. The fact that she was an excellent linguist helps to explain her gift for mimicry, if not parody, and the effortless way in which she absorbed and adopted literary sources for her own needs.

13   *The Tenant of Wildfell Hall* (1848)

The Tenant of Wildfell Hall, like *Agnes Grey*, owes much to Anne Brontë's experiences as a governess, coloured by her period with the Robinson family at Thorp Green Hall, Little Ouseden, near York, where she lived between 1841 and 1845 and where Branwell joined her as tutor to the Robinsons' son. *The Tenant of Wildfell Hall* has always been interpreted as Anne's version of Branwell's decline, and it seems clear that the Thorp Green episode and her brother's breakdown did furnish Anne with the core material for her novel. Though she was unlikely to have witnessed much rakish behaviour at Thorp Green, she could observe an unhappy marriage in action. We know, in addition, that Anne and her sisters always believed Mrs Robinson to blame for Branwell's infatuation. In *The Tenant*, Anne dramatized both the problem of incompatibility in marriage, and the incapacity of a self-indulgent individual to deal effectively with his life. Anne probably wrote herself into the novel as Helen, in so far as the latter is the helpless spectator to Arthur Huntingdon's decline. Mrs Robinson appears in the figure of the heartless Lady Lowborough and Branwell as a combination of Lord Lowborough and Arthur Huntingdon.

Nevertheless, critics have been struck by the fact that the excesses of behaviour described in the novel cannot all be reduced to Anne's experience, any more than the kingdom of Gaaldine reflects the tenor of life at Haworth. There are, however, important historical and contemporary analogues that suggest themselves. The kind of marriage entered into by Helen Huntingdon, a high-principled and religious girl who believes she can save a rake, was, as has been suggested, in all probability based on Annabella Milbanke's marriage to Lord Byron. The riotous behaviour of Huntingdon and his friends in *The Tenant* have their models in Moore's *Life of Byron*, which the Brontës owned and read. (The life of the dissolute Earl of Rochester, 1648–80, was another probable source.) Arthur Huntingdon, unlike Byron, is not an intellectual, but in his courting days he displays a good deal of Byronic fatal charm.

The second notorious case of matrimonial disharmony in high society with which Anne would have been thoroughly familiar (a full account and editorial appeared in the *Leeds Mercury* on 24 June 1836) was the case of Caroline Norton and the then Prime Minister, Lord Melbourne. Caroline Norton, a grand-daughter of

Sheridan, famous for her wit and beauty, married in 1827 George Chapple Norton, a barrister and MP for Guildford. The couple had three children. The marriage was far from happy, and Norton showed considerable brutality towards his wife. Caroline moved in the artistic and political circles of London society, outshining her rather pedestrian husband. She had many eminent friends, among them Lord Melbourne, much older than herself. Their behaviour appears to have been at least indiscreet. Lord Melbourne, as an intimate family friend, visited the Norton home at any time he chose. In 1836, Mr Norton brought a suit against Lord Melbourne for adultery, asking for £10,000 in damages, no mean sum in those days. It does not take much imagination to conceive of the scandal which such a case, brought against the Prime Minister of the day, would arouse. At the trial, ending on 23 June 1836, it was shown that much of the evidence against Lord Melbourne and Caroline Norton had been fabricated by disaffected servants. The defendants were vindicated of any impropriety and Norton lost his case. The *Leeds Mercury* rejoiced in its leader column:

We state with inexpressible satisfaction that LORD MELBOURNE, after a long and minute investigation of the charge brought against him touching the HON. MRS. NORTON, has obtained an instant, and we may add, honourable and triumphant *acquittal*. The evidence for the plaintiff was not only full of suspicion, but given in great part by profligate and necessitous witnesses, who had been discarded from Mr Norton's family, and kept for some time, if not schooled, at the seat of LORD GRANTLEY, the brother of Mr Norton. The testimony referred to a period of time *three years back* though the intimacy of LORD MELBOURNE with Mr and Mrs Norton continued up to the present year. Not a single fact was proved on credible testimony, that afforded any presumption of guilt. . . . That there was an imprudent frequency of visits, is almost the only feature of the plaintiff's case that was sustained; but those visits were known to and often shared by Mr NORTON, and never took place at untimely hours: and when the habits of the fashionable circles are considered, as well as MRS NORTON'S literary and public character, especially as a member of the family of SHERIDAN, together with LORD MELBOURNE'S literary, social, and dramatic tastes, and especially when we add that MRS NORTON was to the last an attached wife and mother, and that she was never suspected during an acquaintance of several years, until she was separated from her husband owing to a quarrel of a different character, we cannot hesitate to believe the solemn declaration of LORD MELBOURNE, conveyed through his Counsel, that the charge against him and MRS NORTON is absolutely false and groundless.

(24 June 1836)

The consequences of the case for Caroline Norton were not as happy as the *Leeds Mercury* article might lead one to believe. Her good name in society was ruined, she was separated from her husband and lost the custody of her children, one of whom died when under his father's care. Though she earned some money from writing, she discovered that, as the law stood, her husband had a right to her earnings. She began a campaign to reform the law on child custody in order to allow mothers, in cases of separation or divorce, to have custody of their children. An Infants' Custody Bill introduced to Parliament on 1 February 1834 was finally passed in 1839. Caroline Norton also began to campaign in the long battle, not finally won until 1870, to give married women control over their own property and earnings. She seems particularly apposite as a model for Anne Brontë's heroine because her career combined the glamour of high life with the early struggles concerning married women's property rights and child custody, issues at the heart of *The Tenant of Wildfell Hall*.

Anne Brontë, not externally a rebel, was surprisingly forthright on the subject of sexual equality. She made her point strongly in her Preface to the Second Edition of *The Tenant of Wildfell Hall*, raising, as Charlotte did later, the problem of the double standard applied to male and female authorship:

> I am satisfied that if a book is a good one, it is so whatever the sex of the author may be. All novels are or should be written for both men and women to read, and I am at a loss to conceive how a man should permit himself to write anything that would be really disgraceful to a woman, or why a woman should be censured for writing anything that would be proper and becoming for a man.

(22 July 1848)

Like Charlotte, Anne was arguing for moral equality between the sexes; men and women were to be judged by the same standards in their lives as in their writings. It is this ethical passion, based on the Evangelical search for perfection, that informs *The Tenant of Wildfell Hall*. The bitter tone of much of the novel suggests the human cost of this moral struggle. The novel's generally sombre atmosphere, in spite of its happy ending, accords with its main themes: the effect of uncontrolled appetite and undirected education on the wealthy, and especially its effect on men; the largely unsuccessful attempts of women to 'mould' or reform their husbands; the pitfalls of marriage; the social vulnerability of women and the difficult quest for salvation.

Structure

Comparisons are often drawn between *Wuthering Heights* and *The Tenant of Wildfell Hall*, particularly tempting when one considers the structure. Both have dual narrators, recourse to the diary form, and to letters as narrative devices. The narrative begins, like *Wuthering Heights*, by looking back over a twenty-year period, as Gilbert Markham tells his brother-in-law the story of his courtship. Markham, to a modified extent, plays Lockwood's rôle, and Helen's diary could be seen as the equivalent of Nelly's flashback narration.

Critics vary in their estimate of Anne's success with her handling of the narrative. Some find Gilbert unconvincing as a character and therefore as a narrator, while they are gripped by Helen's diary. Others object to the strained nature of the convention which allows the heroine to give her diary to her suitor to read, rather than telling her story herself. The two narrational voices are attempts at conveying different points of view, particularly with respect to class; yeoman farmer vs. aristocrat. An unspoken assumption in the novel is that Gilbert Markham is a better man than Helen's first husband, because, as a farmer, he has work to occupy him. For all the pettiness of village life as described in the novel's opening (and it is full of backbiting and gossip), the characters are less vicious because less uncontrolled and less powerful than the idle rich of Helen Huntingdon's previous existence. Like *Wuthering Heights*, *The Tenant* contrasts two social worlds within its two narratives.

Characterization

If one compares the male and female characters in the novel, it emerges that its view of men is particularly jaundiced. We find bad women in *The Tenant* (Millicent Lowborough and Miss Myers, both mistresses of Arthur Huntingdon), but the more characteristic women are virtuous, like Helen, Mildred Hattersley and Esther Hargrave, or merely spiteful and silly, like Eliza Millward and Jane Wilson. With the exception of Lady Lowborough, who is both rich and sexually unscrupulous, they do not have the power to do much harm, even if they are not presented as actively good.

The men, who may be no more innately depraved than their female counterparts, form a sad catalogue of insufficiency, self-absorption and brutality. One may take as examples the three men who love Helen Huntingdon. Arthur, her husband, originally loves her but entirely selfishly. Early in their marriage, he accuses her of being too religious. 'You were so absorbed in your devotions that you had not even a glance to spare for me – I declare it's enough to make one jealous of one's maker' (Ch. 23). Huntingdon is entirely a slave to his appetites, without the capacity to adopt a settled course in life, a Branwell-like touch. Helen admits that the leisured ethos expected of a country gentleman exacerbates his weakness. Arthur is fundamentally an infantile character, whingeing and miserable when ill; carefree and bullying when well. Helen's early infatuation in marrying him becomes implausible even to herself. His self-pity and morbidity are characteristics which recall Branwell at his worst.

Hargrave, Helen's neighbour at Grass-dale Manor, cherishes a passion for her over a four-year period. It could be argued that Helen's hostility towards him seems to exceed his deserts. He is intelligent, well-informed and attractive, but precisely because of these qualities, places Helen in a position of moral peril. Hargrave tempts her to revenge herself on her unfaithful husband. Helen's entire lack of sympathy for Hargrave is based on her belief that his passion is not for her good but for his, a selfish love. In this respect he resembles her husband.

Though Helen's third suitor, and eventual second husband, Gilbert Markham, speaks through his own voice, in many ways he too recalls the unlamented Huntingdon. Markham, like Huntingdon, flirts (with Eliza Millward), suspects Helen of infidelity on flimsy grounds, is quarrelsome and violent (his attack on Lawrence), and at home behaves in a small-minded and childish manner. His love is also shown as being fundamentally selfish. Markham's response, on reading the harrowing account of Helen's life, is not to feel for her sorrows but to try to persuade her to become his mistress, precisely the tactic of the despised Hargrave. Aside from his greater sobriety it is difficult to see Markham's superiority over Huntingdon, or to imagine that Helen's second marriage could be much happier than her first. Like Charlotte's William Crimsworth in *The Professor*, Gilbert must be accounted an artistic failure. But he also betrays Anne's depressing view of the egotistical male character.

The vision of human nature presented in the novel is bleak. Women, more curtailed and repressed than men, learn, on the whole, self-discipline, though they may become mere hypocrites. Men, lacking the social constraints required of women, run amok, like Lowborough before his reform or the good-hearted but pathetic Hattersley. 'Goodness' in a man is mocked by society as unmasculine. Thus, when Lowborough refuses to fight a duel with Huntingdon, his friends call him a coward. Similarly, Helen's efforts to instil temperance in her son are ridiculed by Mrs Markham and her circle. Since even Helen's virtue seems life-denying and rigid, no entirely satisfactory moral view emerges in the novel.

Religion

Attention is rightly drawn to the novel's didactic tone and its preoccupation with salvation and the moral life. What is curious, and what links it to *Wuthering Heights*, is the absence of religious consolation derived from church or clergy. Markham, like Helen Huntingdon, goes to church, but to gaze at Helen rather than to hear the sermon. The clergyman, Mr Millward, is represented as a pompous bore, fond of eating and drinking and of distributing advice to his parishioners. 'Mr Millward was mighty in important dogmas and sententious jokes, pompous anecdotes, and oracular discourses' (Ch. 5). This description may have more than a touch of Patrick Brontë about it. The unattractiveness of the clergy in the Brontës' novels (with the exception of Mr Weston in *Agnes Grey*) suggests a commentary on the consolations they could expect to derive from the clerical characters they knew best. Mr Millward is described as:

> a tall, ponderous, elderly gentleman, who placed a shovel hat above his large, square, massive-featured face, carried a stout walking stick in his hand, and encased his still powerful limbs in knee breeches and gaiters. . . . He was a man of fixed principles, strong prejudices, and regular habits, – intolerant of dissent in any shape, acting under a firm conviction that his opinions were always right, and whoever differed from them, must be, either most deplorably ignorant, or wilfully blind.
>
> In childhood, I had been accustomed to regard him with a feeling of reverential awe – but lately, even now, surmounted.
>
> (Ch. 1)

As an unimaginative representative of the Established Church, the Reverend Millward is unlikely to understand or sympathize with the difficulties of Helen's failed marriage and her flight from her lawful husband. The novel's religious vitality is to be found at the level of the individual conscience.

Religion, then, in *The Tenant* is a matter of inner struggle rather than of outward form, though church attendance is represented as important. Helen Huntingdon, in her Gothic castle, a lonely and beleaguered figure, has little support in her struggles of conscience. Even her brother, Lawrence, is a weak reed. In this respect, Helen resembles Charlotte's heroines struggling to create a valid world for themselves in circumstances of personal isolation.

One of the novel's strengths is undoubtedly its portrait of a failed marriage, which Anne depicts as being a dual process of disintegration. Helen's virtue has the perverse effect of driving her husband to further excesses – there is little sense that virtue can have a redemptive function. The bleak setting of *The Tenant*, though less powerfully drawn than that of *Wuthering Heights*, is emblematic of the novel as a whole. Moral perfection only exists in social isolation. Human relations tend to be seen as violent and cruel. Occasionally, as with the Hattersleys, change can be effected, but the novel, in spite of its optimistic ending, gives little impression of hope. One can read *The Tenant of Wildfell Hall* as a more literal version of *Wuthering Heights*. It is as though one were asked to live through the passions of the latter novel, without the distance of Nelly and Lockwood and without the confident egotism of Cathy and Heathcliff. Little wonder that Charlotte reacted to it with hostility. Whereas *Wuthering Heights*, with its blend of realism and Gothic romance has an exhilarating effect on the reader, *The Tenant* speaks predominantly of waste and loss, not least the loss of Helen's admirable, if misplaced, idealism to be replaced by a severe and largely negative virtue. It may, after all, be the most truthful account we have of Branwell's emotional legacy.

14 Emily Brontë's poetry

In May 1846 under the pseudonyms Ellis, Acton and Currer Bell, the Brontës published a book of poems at their own expense. Charlotte paid the publishers, Aylott and Jones, £37. This venture was a luxury permitted by a small legacy from their Aunt Branwell. Of the one thousand copies printed, only two were sold. The collection included sixty-one poems; nineteen by Charlotte and twenty-one each by Emily and Anne. Subsequent scholarship has discovered further poems (see C. W. Hatfield, *The Complete Poems of Emily Jane Brontë*). Whereas from a biographical point of view the poems of all three sisters have interest, it is chiefly Emily's poetry which lays a claim to literary merit.

One can suggest various perspectives from which to approach Emily's poems. The most tempting, but perhaps the least rewarding, is that of a personal confession. Because most of the poems figured in the Gondal saga, they remain largely resistant to biographical interpretation. Emily evidently revelled in imagining extremes of emotion; towering rages, brutal revenge, endless woe and so on. She must have drawn on her own feelings, but in an essentially impersonal mode. Her poetry might be said to illustrate Keats's theory of 'negative capability', the capacity to project oneself imaginatively in another's mind. 'The poet', said Keats, 'has no identity.' Emily's identity cannot be said to emerge from her poetry any more than it emerges from *Wuthering Heights*.

One area of personal revelation that has been extensively canvassed involves the poems reputed to concern Branwell, as, for example, the verse beginning:

> Well, some may hate, and some may scorn,
> And some may quite forget thy name,
> But my sad heart must ever mourn
> Thy ruined hopes, thy blighted fame.

(14 Nov. 1839)

The date alone makes clear that the poem antedated Branwell's death by nine years. Emily was unlikely to have foreseen his dramatic decay quite so clearly, though she may have feared it. The Brontë biographer, Winifred Gérin, suggests that the themes of guilt and disappointment showed a marked increase in her poetry from the time of Branwell's unsuccessful London trip in the summer of 1835 and her own return to Haworth after her short period at Roe Head.

Similarly, 'The Wanderer from the Fold', with its Romantic

evocation of early promise, is dated 11 March 1844, before Branwell's catastrophe at Thorp Green. It is addressed to A.G.A. (Augusta Geraldine Almeda, Queen of Gondal) from E. W. (Lord Eldred W., Captain of the Queen's Guard) and forms part of a lament for Augusta's tragic end:

> Sometimes I seem to see thee rise,
> A glorious child again –
> All virtues beaming from thine eyes
> That ever honoured men –

The identification of Emily's poems with Branwell is not entirely sustainable, although as in Charlotte's juvenilia (we note the figure of the brother and cad, Hastings) the theme of disappointment and waste makes a plausible link with Branwell. Branwell, had, of course, become a family disappointment long before he became a disaster. From as early as 1835, when he failed to enter the Royal Academy, he must have been a worrying preoccupation for them all. But in addition, the idea of the promise of childhood, contrasted with the limitations of adult life, is a peculiarly Romantic theme, which would have appealed to Emily. One recalls Wordsworth's lament in the 'Immortality Ode': 'shades of the prison house begin to close around the growing boy.' Precocious children, the Brontës often found the constraints of adult life unbearable. 'Liberty', said Charlotte of Emily, 'was the breath of her nostrils.' Branwell's decay dramatized in real terms what they had all experienced: 'but my sad heart must ever mourn, Thy ruined hopes, thy blighted fame.' To have imagined oneself a genius, in charge of kingdoms, and to become a governess or a railway clerk must have seemed a bitter decline.

From dating and internal evidence, the majority of Emily's poems can be read as commemorating stages in the career of Augusta Geraldine Almeda (also confusingly called Rosina Alcona) and of her consort, Julius Brenzaida. A.G.A.'s life, as we know, was tempestuous. She took, as lovers, Alexander, Lord of Elbe, then Lord Alfred of Aspin Castle. Lord Alfred, after marrying Augusta, killed himself, presumably a commentary on the conjugal life they enjoyed. She then married Julius Brenzaida, King of Almedore in Gaaldine. With Gerald of Exina, Julius invaded Gondal and took the throne. He was subsequently assassinated. A.G.A. fled, but after a period of exile, eventually regained the throne of Gondal. Following further political intrigues and love affairs, Augusta was finally slain in her turn.

Even this brief and incomplete summary throws up certain key Gondal themes; among them, love, ambition, power, liberty, revenge and death. The characters pursue their own passions, living in an almost entirely amoral universe. Particularly striking are the range and extent of A.G.A.'s love affairs and her ruthless quest for power. She is an untrammelled egotist, a female Byronic 'hero'. Augusta, never subject to the constraints of realist fiction, projects an almost Nietzschean version of the will to power.

The thematic links with *Wuthering Heights* are of great interest. Egotism, revenge, passion and especially the desire for death echo through the poems and prefigure the more concretely realized world of the novel. But although such thematic links can be drawn, differences are equally significant. Emily's novel forswears the self-indulgent Byronism of much of the poetry or projects it upon individual characters, towards whom we take an external view-point. Because no Gondal prose manuscripts survive, we cannot judge their quality, but they, like Charlotte's Angrian tales, were probably conceived as pure fantasy.

Imagination

Two poems of especial interest in this regard deal with the im-agination and its role in the poet's life and are reproduced below:

TO IMAGINATION

When weary with the long day's care.
And earthly change from pain to pain,
And lost, and ready to despair,
Thy kind voice calls me back again –
O my true friend, I am not lone
While thou canst speak with such a tone!

So hopeless is the world without,
The world within I doubly prize,
The world where guile and hate and doubt
And cold suspicion never rise;
Where thou and I and Liberty
Have undisputed sovereignty.

What matters it that all around
Danger, and guilt, and darkness lie,
If but within our bosom's bound
We hold a bright, untroubled sky,
Warm with ten thousand mingled rays
Of suns that know no winter days?

Reason indeed may oft complain
For Nature's sad reality,
And tell the suffering heart how vain
Its cherished dreams must always be;
And Truth may rudely trample down
The flowers of Fancy newly blown.

But thou art ever there to bring
The hovering vision back, and breathe
New glories o'er the blighted spring
And call a lovelier life from death,
And whisper with a voice divine
Of real worlds as bright as thine.

I trust not to thy phantom bliss,
Yet still in evening's quiet hour
With never-failing thankfulness
I welcome thee, benignant power,
Sure solacer of human cares
And sweeter hope, when hope despairs.

(3 Sept. 1844)

'To Imagination' is characteristic of Emily's work on several levels. The tone is intense, announced by the exclamation 'Oh my true friend', the vocabulary generalized but spare. It sometimes borders on bathos ('pain', 'despair', 'lone'). Abstract qualities are personified ('Danger', 'Nature', 'Truth', 'Fancy') and there is some recourse to cliché ('The flowers of Fancy newly born'). Nevertheless the poem achieves a powerful tension in the ambiguous feelings aroused by Imagination. The poet's relationship with her equivalent of the Muse is problematic. Imagination is simultaneously a solace, a strange visitant and an integral part of herself ('Thou and I and Liberty'). Against the realm of freedom in the mind, the poet unfavourably contrasts the world, distinguished by 'guile', 'hate', 'doubt', 'cold suspicion', 'danger', 'guilt' and 'darkness'. Yet Truth and Reason testify against 'the bright untroubled day' created by the Imagination. The pull between opposite poles operates strongly in the last two verses. On the one hand, 'but thou art ever there to bring the hovering vision back' and, on the other, 'I trust not to thy phantom bliss'. Belief and scepticism are finely balanced. An overriding despair in the real world is the poem's other dominant theme, 'So hopeless is the world without'. The temptation merely to retreat from reality is resisted, however; the claims of Truth and Nature are acknowledged.

The second poem on the same theme is simply entitled 'Stanzas':

Often rebuked, yet always back returning
To those first feelings that were born with me,
And leaving busy chase of wealth and learning
For idle dreams of things which cannot be:

Today, I will seek not the shadowy region:
Its unsustaining vastness waxes drear;
And visions rising, legion after legion,
Bring the unreal world too strangely near.

I'll walk, but not in old heroic traces,
And not in paths of high morality,
And not among the half-distinguished faces,
The clouded forms of long-past history.

I'll walk where my own nature would be leading:
It vexes me to choose another guide:
Where the grey flocks in ferny glens are feeding;
Where the wild wind blows on the mountain side.

What have those lonely mountains worth revealing?
More glory and more grief than I can tell:
The earth that wakes *one* human heart to feeling
Can centre both the worlds of Heaven and Hell.

The first verse raises the problem of the poet's failure to adapt to the world. In the realm of the imagination, she makes a distinction, not apparent in the previous poem, between what Coleridge termed the primary and secondary imaginations. 'Those first feelings born in me' suggest an authentic self which has been dominated by the 'clouded forms of long-past history', presumably the kingdom of Gondal. The poet goes on to affirm the primacy of imagination grounded in nature and to offer a foretaste of the achievement of *Wuthering Heights*: 'I'll walk where my own nature would be leading'. This world is explicitly that of Emily's Haworth surroundings 'where the grey flocks in ferny glens are feeding'. The final verse encapsulates the feeling of paradoxes locked in strife that pervades *Wuthering Heights*; glory opposed to grief, Heaven to Hell. Both aspects are envisaged as necessary to the whole, both centred on the earth ('what have those lonely mountains worth revealing?'). It is evident that for the poet, all meaning is to be found in the natural world. The poem expresses powerfully what is often referred to as Emily Brontë's pantheism. Also significant here is the extent to which she abandons the world of Fancy. Like Charlotte, she seems to have felt the need to repudiate her adolescent fantasies. Yet, as Charlotte put it, 'when I depart from these [her Angrian characters] I feel almost as if I stood on the threshold of a home and were bidding farewell to its inmates. . . . Still, I long to quit for awhile that burning clime where we have sojourned too long' ('Farewell to Angria', 1839). 'Often Rebuked' affirms the creative power of the imagination linked to nature, while evoking with nostalgia the world of Gondal.

Death is perhaps the most pervasive theme running through Emily's poetry. In this she shows herself a child of the Romantic movement with its sometimes obsessive delight in contemplating mortality and decay. Even poems which begin by celebrating the natural world do so in order to contrast the transience of life with the permanence of death:

The linnet in the rocky dells,
The moor lark in the air,
The bee among the heather-bells
That hide my lady fair.

(1 May 1844)

This lyric records a lament for Augusta Almeda over her grave.
The song birds, the linnet and the moor lark, contrast with the
silent dead. Undying desire endlessly survives the death of the
individual loved, prefiguring Heathcliff's obsession with the dead
Cathy. Separation of lovers also emerges in Augusta's mourning
for her lost love, Julius. In addition, death of the beloved is
portrayed as a kind of betrayal, recalling Heathcliff's anger with
Cathy when she dies. Emily understands the egotistical element in
the composition of grief, as in 'The Appeal' (18 May 1840):

If grief for grief can touch thee,
If answering woe for woe,
If any ruth can melt thee,
Come to me now!

I cannot be more lonely,
More drear I cannot be!
My worn heart throbs so wildly,
T'will break for thee.

And when the world despises,
When heaven repels my prayer,
Will not mine angel comfort?
Mine idol hear?

Yes, by the tears I've poured thee,
By all my hours of pain,
O I shall surely win thee,
Beloved, again!

The insistent repetitions ('if', 'if', 'if'; 'grief for grief'; 'woe for
woe'; 'more and more') convey the obsessive nature of Augusta's
passion. The economy of the short lines and the shortened fourth
line suggest a catch at the heart, the physical pain of heartbreak.
In spite of some banal phrases ('drear', 'my heart throbs so
wildly') the poem speaks convincingly of painful longing. As in
many of the poems of mourning, the final object of desire becomes
death itself. Heaven 'repels' the poet's prayer; the angel invoked
is not a heavenly angel.

The attraction of death is also the theme of Rosina Alcona's
lament to Julius Brenzaida (3 March 1845). Here the grave is seen
as the place of reunion; the world is empty since the loved object
who gave it meaning has vanished. Heathcliff's declaration, 'The

entire world is a dreadful collection of memoranda that she did exist, and that I have lost her' (Ch. 33) suggests a similar sense that the death of the beloved cancels life's significance and leaves the world a void:

> Cold in the earth – and the deep snow piled above thee!
> Far, far removed, cold in the dreary grave!
> Have I forgot, my Only Love, to love thee,
> Severed at last by Time's all-severing wave?

The last verse reads:

> And even yet, I dare not let it languish,
> Dare not indulge in Memory's rapturous pain;
> Once drinking deep of that divinest anguish,
> How could I seek the empty world again?

In the poetry as a whole, the natural world is understood as a spectacle of conflicting forces, where the end product of conflict is annihilation. Emily's dramatic rendering of a summer storm in her earliest known poem (13 Dec. 1836) expresses in its rhythms and language this sense of a destructive but exhilarating process:

> High waving heather, 'neath stormy blasts bending,
> Midnight and moonlight and bright shining stars;
> Darkness and glory rejoicingly blending,
> Earth rising to heaven and heaven descending,
> Man's spirit away from its drear dongeon sending,
> Bursting the fetters and breaking the bars.

The apocalyptic tone and galloping rhythms suggest biblical parallels in the *Book of Revelations*, or a verbal rendition of a John Martin landscape.

Emily's last known poem, published posthumously by Charlotte, is remarkable for forging, beyond the sometimes facile Romantic identification with death, a statement of individual religious belief:

NO COWARD SOUL IS MINE

> No coward soul is mine
> No trembler in the world's storm-troubled sphere
> I see Heaven's glories shine
> And Faith shines equal arming me from Fear.

> O God within my breast
> Almighty ever present Deity
> Life, that in me has rest
> As I Undying Life, have power in Thee.

188

Vain are the thousand creeds
That move men's hearts, unutterably vain,
Worthless as withered weeds
Or idlest froth amid the boundless main

To waken doubt in one
Holding so fast by thy infinity
So surely anchored on
The steadfast rock of Immortality.

With wide-embracing love
Thy spirit animates eternal years
Pervades and broods above,
Changes, sustains, dissolves, creates, and rears.

Though Earth and moon were gone
And suns and universes ceased to be
And thou wert left alone
Every Existence would exist in thee.

There is not room for Death
Nor atom that his might could render void
Since thou art Being and Breath
And what thou art may never be destroyed.

(2 Jan. 1846)

'No Coward Soul is Mine' expresses with a proud stoicism the scorn Emily felt for doctrinal debates. Her religious beliefs, from the evidence of this poem, bore little resemblance to orthodox Christianity. There is no mention of Redemption through Christ, rather an affirmation of God's presence in all aspects of his created universe. Anne Brontë, as we have seen, conveyed a similar universalism in *The Tenant of Wildfell Hall*, invoking the 'God who hateth nothing that He hath made' (Ch. 49). Emily creates a vision of time within eternity; the meditation on change and permanence is brilliantly evocative: 'Thy spirit animates eternal years/ Pervades and broods above,/ Changes, sustains, dissolves, creates, and rears.'

In its affirmation of faith as an essentially creative principle, this poem renounces the death obsession of much of the earlier poetry: 'There is not room for Death'. The universe is conceived as a plenitude of life. Even process, change and struggle partake of the 'Almighty ever present Deity'. God is understood as part of the poet's being, but also separate, a rôle similar to that of Imagination in 'Often Rebuked'. Here, the Romantic ego is simultaneously preserved and overcome.

If Emily had not written *Wuthering Heights* her poetry might have gone largely unremarked. Though tightly controlled and with a musical sensitivity to language, it remained tied to the private world of Gondal. Neither she nor her sisters experimented widely in poetic form and the imprint of Scott and Byron is frequently too apparent. Her poems are, nevertheless, a remarkable legacy and remind us that *Wuthering Heights* did not arise from nothing. Heathcliff's lament for Cathy was already written years before the novel:

O come again; what chains withhold
The steps that used so fleet to be?
Come, leave thy dwelling dank and cold
Once more to visit me.

15   *Wuthering Heights* (1847)

'A strange, inartistic story' (*Atlas*, 22 Jan. 1848)

Though many readers have found *Wuthering Heights* strange, modern critics, unlike the *Atlas* reviewer, have stressed Emily Brontë's artistry. But the *Atlas* may well have used the phrase, 'inartistic story' to express the effect *Wuthering Heights* has on its readers of making us feel we are confronted with a violent natural phenomenon like a hailstorm or a tornado. Charlotte was among the first to depict her sister's novel as the product of untutored genius. In her portrait of Emily, she drew a kind of noble savage figure:

> In Emily's nature the extremes of vigour and simplicity seemed to meet. Under an unsophisticated culture, inartificial tastes, and an unpretending outside, lay a secret power and fire that might have informed the brain and kindled the veins of a hero.

(19 Sept. 1850)

Or again:

> *Wuthering Heights* was hewn in a wild workshop, with simple tools, out of homely materials.

(1850, 'Preface')

In addition, Emily's virtually pathological reticence has given her life an aura of mystery that spills over into her one novel. Whereas Charlotte's novels suffer, if anything, from over-interpretation on the biographical level, Emily's work continues to present a personal conundrum. Whatever the source for *Wuthering Heights* in Emily's own life, her great achievement was to give a sense of natural inevitability to what is in reality a complex and contrived tale. Though it may have been hewn with 'simple tools', the novel is anything but simple.

Structure: time, narration and place

Wuthering Heights has a highly developed structure worked out with scrupulous accuracy in relation to its time scheme. All the major events can be dated from internal evidence (see C. P. Sanger's unsurpassed analysis, 'The Structure of *Wuthering Heights*', 1926).

WUTHERING HEIGHTS.

Top Withins, the setting for Wuthering Heights

Though the story is told as a series of flashbacks with overlapping time frames, it demonstrates remarkable chronological consistency and clarity. *Wuthering Heights* recounts the lives of two families unfolding over three generations. The Linton and Earnshaw family pedigrees shown below demonstrate how the families are linked and the structural symmetry which familial relations lend to the novel.

The Linton–Earnshaw family tree

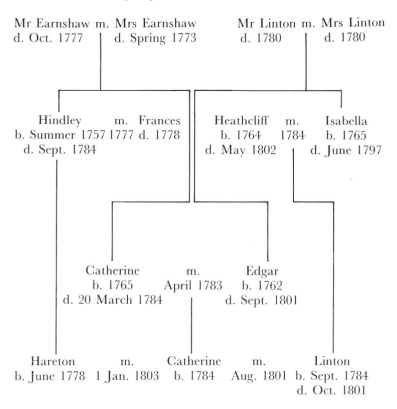

Mr Earnshaw m. Mrs Earnshaw
d. Oct. 1777 | d. Spring 1773

Mr Linton m. Mrs Linton
d. 1780 | d. 1780

Hindley m. Frances
b. Summer 1757 1777 d. 1778
d. Sept. 1784

Heathcliff m. Isabella
b. 1764 1784 b. 1765
d. May 1802 d. June 1797

Catherine m. Edgar
b. 1765 April 1783 b. 1762
d. 20 March 1784 d. Sept. 1801

Hareton m. Catherine m. Linton
b. June 1778 1 Jan. 1803 b. 1784 Aug. 1801 b. Sept. 1784
d. Oct. 1801

TIME   This genealogy demonstrates the fact that *Wuthering Heights* is the story, not primarily of two individuals but of three generations, the conflicts of one generation being worked out in the next. There is a tendency, fostered perhaps by Hollywood, to think that the novel's subject is Cathy Earnshaw's and Heathcliff's passion. Normally sober critics have recourse to vermilion prose when focusing on this aspect of the novel ('Cathy scorning the pusillanimous Edgar to cry across the moor to her demon lover', Thomas Moser, 'What is the Matter with Mary Jane?' *Fiction*, June 1962).

It seems more useful, however, initially, to look at the drama in terms of family rivalries. We see that the Earnshaws and Lintons each have two children, one son and one daughter, a symmetry upset when Mr Earnshaw adopts Heathcliff. The Linton son, Edgar, marries the Earnshaw daughter, Cathy; they have a daughter, Cathy Linton. In the course of the novel, Heathcliff loves and loses Cathy Earnshaw, first to marriage, then to death. He marries Isabella Linton, the sister of Edgar, who leaves him after becoming pregnant with their only son, Linton. Heathcliff pursues a vendetta both against the Earnshaw heir, Hindley, and his son Hareton, whom he beggars. After becoming master of Wuthering Heights, Heathcliff marries his young son, Linton, to Cathy's and Edgar's daughter, Cathy Linton. He eventually dies with the prospect before him that his revenge on the houses of Earnshaw and Linton will be nullified by Cathy the second's coming marriage to Hareton Earnshaw. The second Cathy, we note, marries twice, each time her first cousin. For a novel with a long time frame (30 years), the linkage of generations by the theme of revenge provides both intensity and consistency. An almost suffocating atmosphere is created thanks to the tensions within and between families.

NARRATION   The other key structural device is provided by the two narrators. *Wuthering Heights* is a frame tale in which most of the significant events have already happened. Emily faced the problem of relating a history of Angrian or Gondalian intensity, in many respects a Romantic extravaganza, in such a way as to carry conviction. One device that helps to domesticate the strange world of the Heights is her choice of narrators. The first, Lockwood, who plays at being a Romantic misanthrope, functions as the outsider unused to rural ways. He prepares to find Yorkshire life and its eccentricities picturesque and discovers instead that he is confronting life and death directly, in the shape of snarling dogs, dead rabbits, a blizzard, a savage landlord and even a ghost. Lockwood's mannered language – for example, 'you are the favoured possessor of the beneficent fairy', 'a capital fellow', 'fascinating creature', 'head over ears', 'the sweetest of all imaginable looks' (Ch. 2) – places him as someone ill-adapted to understand the dour inhabitants of the Heights. Lockwood reminds one of Charlotte's narrator in the juvenilia, Charles Wellesley, a highly pretentious individual. One wonders whether Emily was having a quiet joke at her sister's expense. In any event, Lockwood's very fatuousness has the paradoxical effect of making the reader more sympathetic towards the other characters. But Lockwood also speaks for the outside world of normal expectations and therefore, as a narrator, is to be believed. By setting the frame for the tale, Lockwood engages our assent as readers to suspend our disbelief.

The second narrator, Nelly Dean, is to some extent an actor in the drama; but as a servant, though of a superior standing, she observes events rather than initiates action. She, too, radiates normality as she prepares to tell her story: 'I'll just fetch a little sewing, and then I'll sit as long as you please. But you've caught cold; I saw you shivering, and you must have some gruel to drive it out.' It is as though Sheherezade were to bring gruel and sit doing the mending while recounting *The Arabian Nights*. Emily anchors her novel in prosaic and homely details. Because Nelly is originally in the rôle of foster-sister to the Earnshaw family, she views the children without sentiment or astonishment. By the adoption of the common-sense narrator, distanced from but familiar with the action, Emily to some extent 'naturalizes' the excesses of both Heathcliff and Cathy.

Further variety in narrative voices occurs with the insertion of passages from Cathy Earnshaw's diary (Ch. 3), Heathcliff's account of looking in the window of Thrushcross Grange (Ch. 6), and Isabella's letter and narrative (Ch. 13 and 14). Cathy's diary, read by Lockwood, brings her clearly into the narrative as an individual voice, renders vivid the atmosphere of the Heights under Hindley's and Joseph's baleful management, and is the trigger for Lockwood's dream. This dream, in turn, is a form of sub-narrative, falling into two parts. In the first, Lockwood dreams of an interminable Calvinist sermon preached by Jabes Branderham, and then hears Cathy's ghost crying to be let in through the window.

The vicious persona that the well-behaved and conventional Lockwood discovers in himself is perhaps the most surprising constituent of the dream:

> The intense horror of nightmare came over me. I tried to draw back my arm, but the hand clung to it, and a most melancholy voice sobbed, 'Let me in – let me in! . . . terror made me cruel; and, finding it useless to attempt shaking the creature off, I pulled its wrist on the broken pane, and rubbed it to and fro till the blood ran down and soaked the bedclothes.
>
> (Ch. 3)

One effect of Lockwood's dream is to suggest that the drama, which we are to see unleashed, is less particular than universal. If the conventional Lockwood can dream so cruelly, the violent and often sadistic world of Wuthering Heights may lie in us all. Secondly, the dream lends credibility to the ghost theme. Though Lockwood explains his ghostly nightmare naturalistically (the branch scratching on the window pane), Heathcliff's extraordinary reaction to Lockwood's account strengthens the ghost's reality for the reader:

He got on to the bed, and wrenched open the lattice, bursting, as he pulled at it, into an uncontrollable passion of tears. 'Come in! come in!', he sobbed. 'Cathy, do come. Oh do – *once* more! Oh! my heart's darling! hear me *this* time – Catherine, at last!'

(Ch. 3)

Heathcliff, for one, clearly 'believes' in Catherine's ghost. Thus the complex layering of narrative voices, Lockwood, his dream persona, Nelly's story, Cathy's journal, Isabella's story and letter all combine to provide a rich variety of witnesses to the tale. The last witness, the weeping shepherd boy who 'saw' Cathy's and Heathcliff's ghosts on the moor, is, in some respects, the most telling of all. Nelly says:

I was going to the Grange one evening – a dark evening, threatening thunder – and, just at the turn of the Heights, I encountered a little boy with a sheep and two lambs before him; he was crying terribly. . . . 'What is the matter, my little man?' I asked. 'They's Heathcliff, and a woman, yonder, under t'Nab', he blubbered, 'un' Aw darnut pass 'em'.

(Ch. 34)

Overall, Emily Brontë achieves, through her use of multiple perspectives, an effect of authorial impersonality. Take my story or leave it, she seems to say – believe it or not as you wish.

In this regard an aspect of *Wuthering Heights*, which has attracted both praise and blame, is its air of moral neutrality. If we think of narrative voices in the English novel from Fielding to George Eliot, we find a vein of explicit moral direction in their narrational control. Emily Brontë is perhaps best compared in her authorial detachment with later novelists like Conrad or Flaubert. The narrative structure of *Wuthering Heights* ensures that the narrators, while convincing, are only partial witnesses. None holds overall moral authority or omniscience. Nelly, for example, though good and faithful, is also capable of duplicity in her own or others' interests. Of course values do emerge from the novel by other means. The moral positives – affection, warmth, spontaneity and plain-speaking – arise incidentally, but it is difficult to speak with the certainty that some critics have of any controlling moral vision. So convincingly does *Wuthering Heights* depict the elemental aspects of human passion and natural life that we may feel that its moral structures operate merely to impose an arbitrary pattern, like the seventy times seven sins of Jabes Branderham's discourse.

PLACE   The dual mode of narration is also borne out in the novel's dual topographical structure. This is based on the setting in two houses: Thrushcross Grange (modelled on Ponden House two miles from Haworth), lying in a valley; and Wuthering Heights, thought to be based on Top Withins, a rugged farmhouse in the hills. Polarities extend to the atmospheres generated by the two dwellings. Thrushcross Grange is grand but cold (Lockwood finds the fire extinguished), whereas Wuthering Heights boasts the huge fireplace in which warm embers always glow even at night. It is not the case that the elemental qualities of Wuthering Heights are painted as agreeable. Life there appears remarkably unpleasant, but it is at least life, not convention. The inhabitants of the two houses are in harmony with their surroundings; the gentle, moral Edgar Linton of the Grange contrasts with the malevolent and magnetic Heathcliff. We become aware that the dualistic structure, in time, family rivalry and place, offers a world of endlessly developing conflicts where it is difficult to imagine resolutions even in death.

Love and death

Though the novel is tied to the notion of a family saga, it is also true that the Cathy/Heathcliff relationship is at its core. Cathy survives her death in Heathcliff's passionate remembrance of her, and, whether supernaturally or psychologically, is the cause of his death. What concept of love does Emily Brontë dramatize and how are we to understand Cathy and Heathcliff? Most interpretations agree that the intensity of this central passion in the novel cannot be explained as straightforward sexual attraction, particularly taking into account Emily's own limited experience of life and the sexual conventions of her day. On the other hand, any study of Emily's poetry or of Charlotte's juvenilia convinces us that the Brontës revelled in tales of adulterous passion. Charlotte's Zamorna, with his faithful wife and adoring mistress, both of whom he systematically deceives, gives one some idea of the erotic dreams of the Brontës' adolescence. Similarly, Emily's Gondal heroine, Augusta Almeda, ate, as one might say, men for breakfast. Remembering that the Brontës read one another's juvenilia, it is clear that Victorian conventions and the narrowness of social life at Haworth did not inhibit their sexual imaginations. In comparison with the juvenilia, the Cathy–Heathcliff relationship could be said to be quite tame. However, it bears many of the characteristics of the juvenile writings, notably the fascination with death.

If one adopts a broadly psychoanalytic interpretation, one can suggest that the primary relationship between Cathy and Heathcliff defines itself in childhood when they stand in the relation of sister and brother. As in *Jane Eyre*, the importance of childhood in shaping character is a crucial factor in *Wuthering Heights*. Though initially both Earnshaw children react cruelly to Heathcliff and exhibit classic symptoms of violent sibling jealousy, Cathy quickly becomes his ally. Her pairing off with Heathcliff reminds one of the Brontë children's pairing, first Charlotte–Branwell, Emily–Anne and subsequently Emily–Branwell. This sense of family ties lies at the core of the novel's concept of love. One need not take the view that *Wuthering Heights* is chiefly an incest drama to suggest that the passions generated can be understood not so much on the level of adult sexuality as in the unregulated but intense feelings of childhood, the strong bonds and rivalries of brothers and sisters.

Such psychoanalytic readings are closely related to the novel's mythic or fairy-tale elements. When Mr Earnshaw returns from Liverpool with gifts promised for Hindley and Cathy, they find that Hindley's fiddle has been crushed and Cathy's whip lost; the gift they receive is Heathcliff, the 'gipsy brat', as Mrs Earnshaw dubs him. As if in response to his worst fears, Hindley is duly supplanted in his father's affections by Heathcliff, the latter even being given the name of a son who had died in childhood. The origin of conflict, as in so many fairy-tales, lies in the rivalry between two brothers (a theme also exploited by Charlotte in *The Professor*), in Hindley's sense of being usurped by a stranger, and in Heathcliff's experience of rejection by the Earnshaw children. Emily Brontë allows us to see the conflict from all points of view, the justice and injustice of each. The dynamics of these early hostilities generate all subsequent conflicts. It is a family romance founded on the fairy-tale theme of the three gifts.

An historical interpretation, on the other hand, might focus on the Heathcliff–Cathy relationship as reflecting contemporary social conflict (see, for example, Terry Eagleton, *Myths of Power, A Marxist Study of the Brontës*, London, 1975). In this view, Heathcliff, the urban waif from a Liverpool slum, a representative of the landless poor, is thrown into Cathy's rural world of minor landed gentry. Her rejection of Heathcliff for Edgar Linton, a local landowner, can be interpreted as an assertion of her class privilege. Heathcliff's demonic revenge is then explained as that of the dispossessed and vengeful proletarian class. We notice that the question of property and property rights and the acquisition of land are without doubt major issues in the novel. Heathcliff is not merely content to see his enemies, Hindley and Edgar, die; he also wants their property. Heathcliff understands that the power Hindley and Edgar once had over him was based on landed wealth. Such an interpretation sees Emily Brontë conveying, in symbolic terms, the effect of class conflict. The novel, instead of being read as a timeless rural idyll, is seen to reflect the major tensions between urban and rural life arising during the Industrial Revolution.

These interpretations are not mutually exclusive and agree on

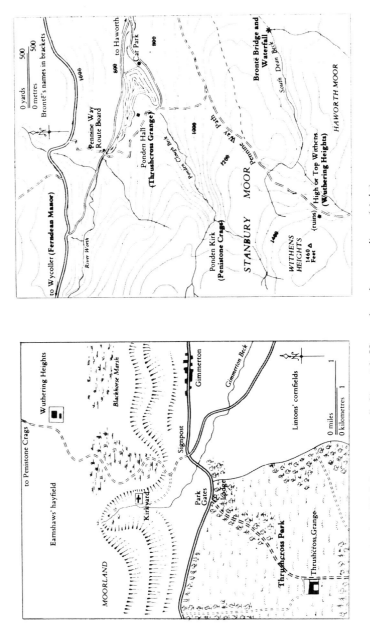

Map of *Wuthering Heights country (left), with Haworth and surroundings (right)*

Left map:

MOORLAND

to Penistone Crags

Wuthering Heights

Earnshaws' hayfield

Blackhorse Marsh

Kirkyard

Signpost

Park Gates

Lodge

Thrushcross Park

Thrushcross Grange

Gimmerton

Gimmerton Beck

Lintons' cornfields

0 miles 1

0 kilometres 1

Right map:

0 yards 500

0 metres 500

Brontë's names in brackets

to Wycoller (Ferndean Manor)

River Worth

Pennine Way Route Board

Ponden Hall (Thrushcross Grange)

to Haworth

Car Park

Ponden Kirk (Penistone Crags)

Ponden Clough Beck

STANBURY MOOR

Pennine Way

High or Top Withens (Wuthering Heights)

(ruins)

WITHENS HEIGHTS
1460 △ Feet

Brontë Bridge and Waterfall

South Dean Beck

HAWORTH MOOR

the irreconcilable nature of the conflicts generated in the novel. Emily Brontë seems to offer no possible social world in which love as understood by Heathcliff and Cathy could prosper. Love, indeed, generates a desire for death as dramatized by Heathcliff's final wasting away (a curious male variant of the Victorian female decline). In this respect their love affair is characteristic of the Romantic death wish associated with the concept of love. In effect, when Heathcliff seeks to reunite himself with Cathy's ghost, one could suggest that he is seeking to regain his childhood, his lost paradise. Whereas critics like Queenie Leavis have stressed the vitality of life at the Heights, and the healing and affirmative ending, with the second Cathy's and Hareton's marriage, one could argue that the opposite pole pulls equally strongly. Death is the great attraction, not as an escape into a better life, but as representing the possibility of reunification with one's childhood self. *Wuthering Heights* powerfully renders the Romantic attraction to death. Heathcliff's necrophiliac attempt to embrace Cathy's body in her grave, and Nelly's account of his grinning corpse at the end are part of the Romantic–Gothic focus on decomposition and death. Where the novel is superior to many of its models is in the psychological and social credibility that it lends to these themes.

Another Romantic legacy with which *Wuthering Heights* is imbued is that of Byronism. Byron popularized outlaws, bandits and exiles as the heroes of his tales. His characters, like Cain and Manfred, are scorned by society. In the Byronic manner, Emily gave her hero–villain a mysterious origin, and made him a satanic rebel against convention. But at the same time she presented him as a working Yorkshire farmer and business-like landlord. Social reality to some extent tames the exotic in *Wuthering Heights*, though it does not do away with it.

Religion

As in all the Brontë novels, religion plays an important role. However, Emily contributes her own idiosyncratic gloss. One can identify three major religious themes: Calvinism, satirized in Joseph and the Jabes Branderham sermon; a more hopeful or char- itable Christian orthodoxy, exemplified by Nelly Dean; and a strain of religious mysticism more pagan than Christian (Cathy and Heathcliff). In Joseph, Emily mocks some of the worst aspects of Calvinism, a spiteful, self-righteous fanaticism. To be fair, his is virtually the only voice to be raised consistently against the dramatic excesses of the other characters. In an odd way, Joseph does represent moral stability. Yet Ellen and Cathy, one feels, rightly castigate him as a hypocrite, because he clothes his natural meanness in the language of religious justification. His exhortations are portrayed as ineffective, since his puritanical restraints on Cathy and Heathcliff only goad them to rebellion. As a lay preacher, he subjects them to a three-hour sermon at home on a rainy Sunday, in addition to forcing religious tracts on them ('The Helmet of Salvation', 'The Broad Way to Destruction'). Joseph speaks constantly of the sin and damnation he foresees for everyone except himself. Nevertheless, in spite of his sanctimoniousness, he remains a fixture at the Heights, railing against the behaviour of its inmates but tolerated by them. He sees the drama of sin and damnation (or salvation) being played out everywhere around him, with Heathcliff functioning as a kind of Satan figure. 'Heathcliff, indeed, stands unredeemed; never once swerving in his arrow-straight course to perdition', wrote Charlotte in the 1850 Preface. We notice that Joseph has the last word over Heathcliff's corpse:

'Th' divil's harried off his soul,' he cried, 'and he muh hev his carcass intuh t'bargain, for ow't Aw care' . . . but suddenly composing himself, he fell on his knees, and raised his hands, and returned thanks that the lawful master and the ancient stock were restored to their rights.

(Ch. 34)

For Joseph, there is an overriding moral-divine purpose manifesting itself in human affairs. Though his final prayer of thanksgiving has a certain dignity, the text does not here mitigate his characteristic spite. Overall, in *Wuthering Heights*, Calvinism emerges as an aggressive, inhibiting, though not a ridiculous creed.

Nelly's Christianity, while lacking Joseph's punitive harshness, seems to have equally little relevance to the lives of the chief characters. She believes that good will be rewarded and evil punished, and that we may all meet again in a better world. Nelly speaks of forgiveness and repentance on the occasion of Cathy's and Heathcliff's deaths, but neither the conventional nor the rebellious characters appear to derive much comfort from her assurances. On one occasion, however, Nelly does reflect on the spectacle of death and offers a vision of tranquillity that goes beyond her conventional set pieties, reminding one of Helen Burns in *Jane Eyre*:

I see a repose that neither earth nor hell can break; and I feel an assurance of the endless and shadowless hereafter – the Eternity they have entered – where life is boundless in its duration, and love in its sympathy, and joy in its fulness.

(Ch. 16)

This vision of a generous redeemer, an eternity not based on the idea of punishment, recalls Emily's poem 'No Coward Soul is Mine' (see pp. 188–9) and prepares us for Lockwood's final meditation on 'the sleepers in that quiet earth'.

Mysticism and nature

One can easily exaggerate the pantheistic qualities of *Wuthering Heights*. However, in spite of relatively sparse descriptions of nature, we find that the characters seem aware of mystical links between themselves and their surroundings. When confronted with the theological views of Joseph, Nelly or the shadowy curate, Heathcliff or Cathy or indeed Hindley simply find them irrelevant. They are not materialists in that they believe in some form of spiritual reality, but their belief does not exist within the context of orthodox Christianity. Nature (see passage for commentary) is felt as a dominant presence, partly because, except by Lockwood, it is never portrayed as picturesque. Nature *is*, rather than is reflected upon. Nor does nature necessarily relate to, or suggest, a moral scheme of things. It is simply *the* profound reality. In this respect Emily Brontë departs from the self-conscious Romantic contemplation of nature and approaches what Schiller called the 'simple' as opposed to the sentimental attitude towards the natural world. Unlike Charlotte in *Jane Eyre*, or Wordsworth in *The Prelude*, there is little sense in *Wuthering Heights* that the elemental forces of nature coincide with the moral law.

Prose extract, Cathy's vision, and critical commentary

'I thought as I lay there, with my head against that table leg, and my eyes dimly discerning the grey square of the window, that I was enclosed in the oak-panelled bed at home; and my heart ached with some great grief which, just waking, I could not recollect – I pondered, and worried myself to discover what it could be; and most strangely, the whole last seven years of my life grew a blank! I did not recall that they had been at all. I was a child; my father was just buried, and my misery arose from the separation that Hindley had ordered between me, and Heathcliff – I was laid alone, for the first time, and, rousing from a dismal dose after a night of weeping – I lifted my hand to push the panels aside, it struck the tabletop! I swept it along the carpet, and then, memory burst in – my late anguish was swallowed in a paroxysm of despair – I cannot say why I felt so wildly wretched – it must have been temporary derangement for there is scarcely cause – But, supposing at twelve years old, I had been wrenched from the Heights, and every early association, and my all in all, as Heathcliff was at that time, been converted, at a stroke, into Mrs Linton, the lady of Thrushcross Grange, and the wife of a stranger; an exile, and outcast, thenceforth, from what had been my world – You may fancy a glimpse of the abyss where I grovelled! Shake your head as you will, Nelly, *you* have helped to unsettle me! You should have spoken to Edgar, indeed you should, and compelled him to leave me quiet! Oh, I'm burning! I wish I were out of doors – I wish I were a girl again, half savage and hardy, and free ... and laughing at injuries, not maddening under them! Why am I so changed? why does my blood rush into a hell of tumult at a few words? I'm sure I should be myself were I once among the heather on those hills. ... Open the window again wide, fasten it open! Quick, why don't you move?'

'Because I won't give you your death of cold,' I answered.

'You won't give me a chance of life, you mean,' she said, sullenly. 'However, I'm not helpless yet, I'll open it myself.'

And sliding from the bed before I could hinder her, she crossed the room, walking very uncertainly, threw it back, and bent out, careless of the frosty air that cut about her shoulders as keen as a knife.

I entreated, and finally attempted to force her to retire. But I soon found her delirious strength much surpassed mine; (she was delirious, I became convinced by her subsequent actions and ravings).

There was no moon, and everything beneath lay in misty darkness; not a light gleamed from any house, far or near; all had been extinguished long ago; and those at Wuthering Heights were never visible ... still she asserted she caught their shining.

'Look!' she cried eagerly, 'that's my room, with the candle in it, and the trees swaying before it ... and the other candle is in Joseph's garret ... Joseph sits up late, doesn't he? He's waiting till I come home that he may lock the gate. Well, he'll wait a while yet. It's a rough journey and a sad heart to travel it; and we must pass by Gimmerton Kirk, to go that journey! We've braved its ghosts often together, and dared each other to stand among the graves and ask them to come ... But Heathcliff, if I dare you now, will you venture? If you do, I'll keep you. I'll not lie there by myself: they may bury me twelve feet deep, and throw the church down over me; but I won't rest till you are with me ... I never will!'

She paused and resumed with a strange smile. 'He's considering ... he'd rather I'd come to him! Find a way, then! not through that Kirkyard ... You are slow! Be content, you always followed me!'

(Ch. 12)

CONTEXT   The extract from Chapter 12 occurs about halfway through the novel. Cathy, after exacerbating a quarrel between her husband, Edgar, and Heathcliff, tells Ellen that she plans to frighten Edgar by making herself ill; 'I'll try to break their hearts by breaking my own.' Cathy locks herself in her room for three days; the quoted passage reflects the state of mind into which she has fallen during her self-imposed solitude.

TONE   This directly reported conversation portrays both the clarity and confusion of her perceptions. Though cogent, the sentences are broken and frequently separated by dashes. Cathy's passionate and exclamatory monologue alternates briefly with Nelly's down-to-earth remark, 'Because I won't give you your death of cold.' Nelly's editorial gloss ('she was delirious, I became convinced') offers a rational explanation for Cathy's prophetic vision, without undermining its plausibility in the reader's mind.

SUBJECT MATTER   From an external perspective, Cathy's behaviour is that of a spoilt child throwing a tantrum because she cannot have everything she wants, a view established by Nelly's narration. This extended direct quotation, however, allows us to experience Cathy's point of view. Particularly interesting is the way that Cathy's state of mental distress conflates periods of time. From her anger at Edgar ('I couldn't explain . . .') that leaves her in a kind of inarticulate fit, she describes how her mind transported her into the past where she experienced a similarly intense grief. She recollects the 'oak-panelled bed at home'. The reader is already familiar with the bed, so like a coffin, from Lockwood's dream and will see it again at the novel's end, containing Heathcliff's grotesquely grinning corpse. The state of grief which Cathy feels on waking is equated not with its immediate cause, her quarrel with Edgar, but with separation from Heathcliff after her father's death. We notice that her grief is not for her father but 'my misery arose from the separation that Hindley had ordered between me, and Heathcliff'. She feels the temporal and spatial connections between her present and past self abolished and speaks of an abyss (a language also used by Heathcliff after Cathy's death) and herself as an exile, a stranger, an outcast. She wishes to become a child again and evokes her girlhood as a time of freedom, the antithesis of the room in which she now has shut herself, emblematic of her married life. Her hysterical desire to reach the window is part of the Romantic yearning for liberty in nature: 'I'm sure I should be myself were I once among the heather on those hills.'

The second part of her monologue, introduced by Nelly ('There was no moon') becomes more uncanny, moving from a contemplation of the past to the future. As past time is brought into the present through the mechanism of grief, so the future is made visible. Emily Brontë makes an essentially Gothic vision of the future credible in psychological terms, showing that the mental reality of time is very different from our normal chronological sense. Cathy's soliloquy becomes a prophecy: 'We must pass by Gimmerton Kirk, to go that journey.' The journey to be reunited with Heathcliff, she now accepts, cannot be undertaken in this world; it is a journey towards death. She foretells that her return to the Heights will only be accomplished as a ghost, a prophecy we have already seen 'confirmed' in Lockwood's dream. By seeming to see the light at the Heights which cannot actually be seen, Cathy's second sight is established. Whether one chooses to regard it as delirium, or vision, is left up to the reader. Recollection joins with prophecy in her memory, as she and Heathcliff dare one another to call the ghosts in the churchyard ('We've often braved its ghosts . . . and dared each other . . . to ask them to come.'). Cathy then, foretells her own death and her power over Heathcliff to drag him to the grave after her. She appears to be in telepathic communication with him ('He's considering . . .'). Her monologue prefigures the whole second half of the novel. Her will is seen to control Heathcliff's ('they may bury me twelve feet deep, and throw the church down over me; but I won't rest till you are with me . . . I never will.'). One can suggest that Cathy, not Heathcliff, is the great Byronic egotist of the novel. Heathcliff is possessed by her as by a medieval succubus. She, not Heathcliff, is the true demon lover. The spectre of Augusta Geraldine Almeda lives on in Cathy Earnshaw.

FUNCTION   This passage performs a number of important functions. Initially it lets us into Cathy's mind, much as her confession to Nelly in Chapter 9 clarified the nature of her bond with Heathcliff ('My love for Heathcliff resembles the eternal rocks beneath – a source of little visible delight, but necessary'.). Thus her histrionic behaviour, which has alienated everyone, including, perhaps the reader, in this scene, becomes comprehensible. The passage further has a pivotal function in structural terms. Her breakdown frees her from the constraints of time and place, bringing back the past and making the future accessible. Cathy, we learn, plans to haunt Heathcliff many months before she dies. Though dying in childbirth, the impression that she wills her death remains strong. Death is conceived of not so much as a reunion with Heathcliff, as with a lost time and place. But above all it is her will that dominates his ('Be content, you always followed me'). Heathcliff's obsession with Cathy in the second half of the novel thus becomes credible.

To the extent that dreams and presentiments are 'true' in *Wuth-*

ering Heights, Cathy when 'mad' speaks the truth, by recognizing the implications of her bond with Heathcliff. The mind in its affections, griefs and hatreds knows no time. Cathy's freedom from rational constraints in her illness enables her to see that which eludes others – namely, the past and the future. Her desire for liberty (from marriage, adult life, pregnancy, social conformity, her own mistakes) is articulated in the impossible desire to become a child again, before the period of adult sexuality, when she and Heathcliff were not lovers but brother and sister. The passage gives credibility to the ghost theme, reinforces the novel's sense of timelessness, while underlining chronological time (seven years), and dramatizes, in particular, the characters' Romantic death wish.

16 Conclusion

Wuthering Heights has been the subject of an extensive and often contradictory range of critical opinion, a tribute both to the novel's fascination and enigmatic power. In spite of incorporating substantial passages of Yorkshire dialect, it has dated far less than most other regional novels – for example, those of Scott, in which colloquial speech is used in a similar way. In her one work of fiction, Emily Brontë succeeded in finding a form in which to objectify those passions that she had expressed in the rather sibylline utterances of her poetry. Concrete, spare and emotionally driven, the novel harries the reader, rather as Joseph envisaged the devil harrying off Heathcliff's soul.

Contrasted with Emily, it could be said that Charlotte did not achieve in her novels the degree of unselfconsciousness or directness that her sister displayed in *Wuthering Heights*. The elder sister always – and rightly, one feels – evinced a certain awe for Emily. Charlotte's genius developed in the direction of increasingly complex analyses of inner experience, most highly articulated in *Villette*. Finally, Anne, critically the least regarded of the three sisters, showed, in *Agnes Grey*, a remarkable gift for social observation which, in *The Tenant of Wildfell Hall*, she enriched with a religious fervour and controlled anger. Like Emily and Charlotte, she had a gift for comic or ironic observation, a quality generally undervalued in estimates of the Brontës.

Though chronologically Victorians, the Brontës were true children of the Romantics, making their inner lives the authentic subject of their writing. As in Wordsworth's poetry, their personal vision arose from a strong sense of place and local attachment. The novels combine the personal, the homely and the archetypal; they fuse an almost bewildering variety of levels of perception. Nelly or Zillah seems to potter away in the kitchen while the turbulent passions of the 'geniuses' seethe around them. Such must have been the 'ordinary' life of the Haworth parsonage during the Brontës' childhood:

> It is past twelve o'clock. Anne and I have not tid[i]ed ourselves, done our bedwork, or done our lessons and we want to go out to play. We are going to have for dinner Boiled Beef, Turnips, potatoes and apple pudding. The kitchen is in a very untidy state. Anne and I have not done our music exercise which consists of b. major. Taby said, on my putting a pen in her face, 'Ya pitter pottering there instead of pilling a potatate.' I

answered, 'O Dear, O Dear, O Dear, I will directly.' With that I get up, take a knife and begin pilling.

(Emily Brontë's diary paper, Nov. 1834)

This record of a moment of daily experience shows us how the children's heightened imaginations were nurtured. Emily's gleeful list of undone household tasks, her absorption in writing, the understandable wrath of the long-suffering Tabitha and the way the diary paper catches her idiomatic turn of phrase reveal both the tensions between the life of the imagination and ordinary life, as well as pleasure in both levels of existence. In the case of Charlotte, Emily and Anne, it was these ultimately fruitful tensions which culminated in a body of fiction of quite extraordinary power and intensity.

Part Four
Reference Section

Brief biographies

TABITHA (TABBY) AYKROYD   Servant in the Brontë family from 1824 until her death in 1855. She worked as cook and maid-of-all-work, initiated the children into a rich variety of fairy and ghost stories and gave them the 'mothering' that their Aunt Branwell failed to provide.

HONORÉ DE BALZAC, 1799–1850   French novelist, author of a series of linked novels, *La Comédie humaine*. *Le Père Goriot* (1834) chronicles the adventures of an impecunious but well-born law student who attempts to conquer Parisian society.

THOMAS BEWICK 1753–1828   Artist, born at Ovingham, Northumberland, he was apprenticed to a wood engraver in 1767 at Newcastle. In 1790 he published the *General History of Quadrupeds* which ran to eight editions by 1824. He was remarkable for his drawings observed from life. His *History of British Birds* was issued in two volumes: vol. I, *Land Birds*, 1797, with a text by Ralph Beilby; and vol. II, *Water Birds*, 1804, text supplied by the Reverend Mr Cotes, of Bedlington. Bewick was determined to 'stick to nature as closely as he could'. In addition to the verisimilitude that he lent to the birds themselves and the scenes in which they were depicted, the volumes were rendered enormously popular by the vignettes which he included at the end of each entry. They show humour, pathos and a keen sense of observation. Bewick's love of nature, his knowledge of country life, as well as of natural history, and his dedication to his craft made his drawings remarkable. He revived the craft of wood engraving in Britain.

MARTHA BROWN, b. 1828   Servant in the Brontë family, daughter of Mr Brontë's sexton, John Brown, she first came to work for the family on washing days at the age of ten. She was interviewed by Mrs Gaskell for *The Life of Charlotte Brontë*.

JOHN BUNYAN, 1628–88   Author and Baptist preacher. A tinker by trade, he was ordained as a preacher in 1657 and imprisoned in 1660, under the Restoration of Charles II, for attempting to preach as a nonconformist. He remained in prison for 12 years. His best-known work, *The Pilgrim's Progress*, was published between 1678 and 1684.

GEORGE GORDON, 6TH LORD BYRON, 1788–1824 Poet, eccentric peer, pugilist and athlete (though suffering from a club foot), Byron was as renowned for his amorous adventures as for his writing. Among the former were his affair with Caroline Lamb, wife of Lord Melbourne, and with his half-sister, Augusta Leigh. His most famous works include *Childe Harolde's Pilgrimage* (Cantos i–ii, 1812, iii, 1816, iv, 1818), *The Giaour (1813)*, *The Corsair* (1814), *Manfred* (1817) and *Don Juan* (1824). He died of fever in Greece while engaged in the struggle for Greek independence.

RICHARD HURRELL FROUDE, 1803–36 Fellow of Oriel College, Oxford, he became an influential member of the Oxford movement. Though he was anti-Protestant in the sense of hating Evangelical reform and was a high Tory, he continued to oppose Romanism and, unlike his colleague, Newman, remained an Anglican.

ELIZABETH CLEGHORN GASKELL, 1810–65 Novelist. In 1832 she married the Reverend William Gaskell, minister of Cross Street Unitarian Chapel, Manchester. Her published works include: *Mary Barton* (1848), *North and South* (1855), *Ruth* (1853) and *The Life of Charlotte Brontë* (1857).

CONSTANTIN HEGER, b. 1809, and CLAIRE ZOË HEGER, née PARENT, b. 1804. Zoë Parent followed in the footsteps of her aunt, Anne Marie Parent, in setting up a girls' school at 32 rue d'Isabelle, Brussels, after the 1830 revolution. She met Constantin Heger in 1834, then a teacher at the Athenée Royale. He had been married to Marie-Josephine Noyer, and had a child, both of whom died in the cholera epidemic of 1834. He and Zoë Parent married in 1836 and had six children. Their school acquired an excellent reputation. Mrs Gaskell visited M. Heger in 1856 to gather material for her *Life*, when she saw Charlotte's indiscreet letters to her former teacher.

HENRY HUNT, 1773–1835 Radical politician who organized the Bristol Patriotic and Constitutional Association for electoral reform. He presided at the public meeting at St Peter's Fields, Manchester, on 16 August 1819, in which the troops fired on the crowd and which became known as the Peterloo Massacre. Hunt served a two-year prison sentence. He won a seat in Parliament in 1831, moved for the repeal of the Corn Laws and presented the earliest petition in favour of women's rights.

SIR JAMES PHILLIPS KAY-SHUTTLEWORTH, 1804–77 A medical doctor, active in the great cholera epidemic of 1832 in Manchester, he campaigned for improved living and working conditions for the poor, parliamentary reform and the repeal of the Corn Laws. His principal contribution, however, was in education where he developed a system of national education and teacher training. He founded the first teacher training college at Battersea in 1839–40 and inaugurated the system of public inspection and pupil-teacher training. It was at his holiday home on Lake Windermere that Charlotte Brontë met Mrs Gaskell.

JOHN KEBLE, 1792–1866 Fellow of Oriel College, Oxford, Professor of Poetry and author of the enormously successful collection of religious verse, *The Christian Year*. He was one of the founder members of the Oxford movement in July 1833 with his sermon, 'National Apostasy'.

WILLIAM LAMB, 2nd Viscount Melbourne, 1779–1848 Whig politician who served in a succession of ministries as Irish Secretary, Home Secretary and Prime Minister. His private life was colourful. In 1805 he married Lady Caroline Ponsonby from whom he separated in 1825 after her scandalous liaison with Lord Byron. Melbourne twice appeared as a co-respondent in actions for divorce, once in 1829, against Lord Brandon, and on 22 June 1836 in the Norton vs. Norton case. The first case was discontinued, the second won by the defendants.

GEORGE HENRY LEWES, 1817–78 Critic, novelist, biographer of Goethe, philosopher and writer in the natural sciences. From 1854 until his death, he lived with Mary Ann Evans (George Eliot). He reviewed Charlotte Brontë's novels and corresponded with her. Their relationship was stormy, but his face, she said, reminded her strongly of her sister Emily.

JOSEPH BENTLEY LEYLAND, 1811–51 Halifax sculptor. Friend of Branwell Brontë. He studied in London under Benjamin Robert Haydon and exhibited in Manchester in 1832. He is best known for his sculpture of African bloodhounds, praised by Landseer. Most of his work has been lost.

JOHN MARTIN, 1789–1854 Painter of landscapes and historical canvases. Martin began as an apprentice to a miniature painter, but in 1812 he exhibited his first large painting, 'Sadak in Search of the Waters of Oblivion'. Other famous works include: 'Joshua Commanding the Sun to Stand Still' (1816), 'The Bard' (1817) and 'Belshazzar's Feast' (1821). His 'The Fall of Nineveh' was bought by the Belgian government and exhibited in Brussels, where Charlotte and Emily may have seen it. His pictures were widely copied as engravings and enjoyed a huge popularity.

HARRIET MARTINEAU, 1802–76 Author of *Illustrations of Political Economy*, an immensely popular series of tracts on economic questions. She published a novel, *Deerbrook*, in 1839, wrote her *Autobiography* in 1855 and lived for a further 20 years. From a Unitarian background, Martineau became a freethinker. She wrote widely and fearlessly on a range of contemporary issues such as women's rights, slavery and education. Suffering from almost complete deafness, she overcame her handicap to achieve economic independence through her writing. She eventually settled in the Lake District where Charlotte Brontë visited her.

ANNE ISABELLA (ANNABELLA) MILBANKE, Lady Byron, 1792–1860 A precocious child, she studied philosophy and mathematics but had little experience of fashionable society. She married Byron in 1815, bore him a daughter, Augusta Ada, and left him, on grounds of brutality, on 15 January 1816.

HARRIET TAYLOR MILL, 1807–58 Her long friendship with John Stuart Mill, whom she married in 1851, after her first husband's death, is described in Mill's *Autobiography*. She published articles on women's emancipation, for example, 'On the Enfranchisement of Women' (1851), read by Charlotte Brontë. Her daughter, Helen, became a women's rights campaigner and in 1885 became the first woman to attempt to stand for Parliament.

JOHN STUART MILL, 1806–73 Philosopher. The eldest son of James Mill, a Utilitarian philosopher, J. S. Mill widened and humanized the Utilitarian ethic (the idea of the greatest happiness for the greatest number) and wrote widely in philosophy and political economy. Some of his best-known works are: *Principles of Political Economy*, 1848, *On Liberty* (1859), *Utilitarianism* (1863), *The Subjection of Women* (1869), *The Autobiography of John Stuart Mill* (1873).

THOMAS CAUTLEY NEWBY Anne and Emily Brontë's publisher, Cavendish Square, London. He tried to pass off *The Tenant of Wildfell Hall* as written by the author of *Jane Eyre*.

JOHN HENRY NEWMAN, 1801–90 Fellow of Oriel College, Oxford. In 1833 with Keble, Pusey and Hurrell Froude, he founded the Oxford movement. He published a series of pamphlets defending the High Church position, *Tracts for the Times*. In 1845 he joined the Roman Catholic Church and in 1864 published his *Apologia pro vita sua*, an account of his spiritual history. He was made a cardinal in 1879.

ARTHUR BELL NICHOLLS, 1818–1906   Born in County Antrim and educated at Trinity College, Dublin. He became Patrick Brontë's curate in 1845, married Charlotte in 1854 and remained at Haworth until Patrick's death. He returned to Ireland, married his cousin, Mary Bell, and settled down as a farmer.

FLORENCE NIGHTINGALE, 1820–1910   Though from a wealthy middle-class background, she disliked fashionable life and in 1845 decided on a career in nursing, an occupation of very low status at that period. She organized nursing care for the victims of the Crimean War, which led to a reorganization of hospital services in the British Army, and she founded the Nightingale Training School for Nurses in 1860, succeeding in establishing nursing as a serious profession with high standards. She then turned to the task of reorganizing the War Office.

CAROLINE NORTON, 1808–77   Poet and polemicist, who campaigned for the rights of divorced women. She was not, however, an advocate of sexual equality. She gained social and literary success from the publication of her poem, 'The Sorrows of Rosalie' (1829). She supported herself, after her separation from her husband, George Norton, a barrister, by her publications. In 1839, the Infant Custody Act, for which she had campaigned, was passed. Her most polemical and influential work was a review of contemporary law affecting women, *English Laws for Women in the Nineteenth Century* (1854), which demonstrated how little protection married women enjoyed under English law.

THE NUSSEYS   A large family (13 children) of cloth manufacturers from Rydings in Yorkshire. One brother, Henry, who became a vicar, proposed to Charlotte and was probably a model for St John Rivers. The youngest, Ellen, born 1817, was Charlotte's school friend and remained her steady correspondent and confidante until the latter's death in 1855. Though she rather disapproved of Charlotte's choice of husband, Ellen attended Charlotte's wedding and was active in promoting her literary reputation after her death.

EDWARD BOUVERIE PUSEY, 1800–82   Fellow of Oriel College, Oxford. He collaborated with Keble and Newman in *Tracts for the Times*. In 1843 he was charged with heresy and suspended as university preacher. Unlike Newman, he did not leave the Church of England, maintaining High Church views, but opposing secession to the Church of Rome.

THE REVEREND EDMUND ROBINSON and his wife, LYDIA (later Lady Scott), of Thorp Green, Yorkshire. Anne and Branwell both worked for the Robinsons as governess and tutor, respectively (1841–45). The revelations in Mrs Gaskell's *Life* about Mrs Robinson and Branwell led to a threatened lawsuit by the now Lady Scott and to a withdrawal of the first edition.

WILLIAM ROBINSON, 1799–1839   Leeds artist and portrait painter who gave lessons to Branwell Brontë.

CHARLES SIMEON, 1759–1836   Fellow of King's College, Cambridge, he had strong Evangelical convictions. Known as a leader among Evangelical churchmen, he founded the Church Missionary Society in 1797. He also founded a body for acquiring church patronage and was able to fill many livings with vicars who supported his Evangelical views. Patrick Brontë came under his influence while at Cambridge.

GEORGE MURRAY SMITH, b. 1824   Head of the publishing firm of Smith, Elder and Co., 65 Cornhill, London, who became Charlotte Brontë's publisher. He entertained her and Anne royally on their first London visit and remained a loyal friend to Charlotte, introducing her to his family and to established authors like Thackeray and George Henry Lewes. He and his mother are usually considered the models for John Graham Bretton and Mrs Bretton in *Villette*.

ROBERT SOUTHEY, 1774–1843   Poet. With Coleridge, he wished to form an ideal community, a 'pantisocratic settlement', a plan never realized. He was made Poet Laureate in 1813. Like Wordsworth, he overcame his earlier radicalism and espoused conservative ideas. Byron attacked him comprehensively in *The Vision of Judgment* (1821) as a political renegade.

JAMES TAYLOR   Member of the publishing firm Smith, Elder and Co. Taylor went to India in 1851, proposing marriage to Charlotte Brontë before he did so. She appears to have admired him but to have found him personally antipathetic.

MARY TAYLOR, 1817–93   School friend of Charlotte Brontë, living at Red House, Gomersal. Her father, a cloth manufacturer and banker, had suffered financial reverses. He was a man of advanced Radical views and Mary seems to have absorbed his unconventional attitudes. After studying in Belgium (where her sister, Martha, died in 1842) and in Germany, Mary Taylor emigrated to Wellington, New Zealand, in 1845, where she opened a general store and prospered. She destroyed her correspondence with Charlotte, but provided some crucial material for Mrs Gaskell's *Life*.

Her own published works include: *The First Duty of Women* (1865–70), *Swiss Notes* and a novel, *Miss Miles* (1890).

WILLIAM MAKEPEACE THACKERAY, 1811–63   Journalist and novelist. He wrote for *Fraser's Magazine* and *Punch*, for which he contributed the series *The Snobs of England*. His novels include: *Vanity Fair* (1847–48), *Pendennis* (1848–50), and *Henry Esmond* (1852). Charlotte Brontë idolized him, but they did not, in the event, get on well when they met.

CHARLES WESLEY, 1707–88   Co-founder with his brother, John Wesley, of a 'methodist' society for revitalizing religious observance. Along with George Whitfield, the preacher, they were the driving force of the Methodist movement. Charles is particularly remembered as a composer of hymns.

JOHN WESLEY, 1703–91   Leader of the Evangelical or Methodist movement of religious revival in the Church of England. He took orders but dissented from the doctrine of predestination. He undertook extempore prayer and open-air preaching and formed a strong band of missionary preachers among the laity.

WILLIAM WEIGHTMAN   One of Patrick Brontë's many curates, and certainly the best-liked by the family, he served at Haworth between 1839 and 1842. Charlotte called him 'bony, pleasant . . . careless, fickle, unclerical'. He died of cholera on 6 September 1842.

WILLIAM WILBERFORCE, 1759–1833   Philanthropist and member of Parliament, he campaigned for the abolition of the slave trade. A Bill abolishing the slave trade was passed by Parliament on 25 March 1807. He was a member of the Clapham Sect, an Evangelical group, which campaigned for Christian social reforms.

WILLIAM SMITH WILLIAMS   A reader for Smith, Elder and Co., Williams was present when Charlotte and Anne Brontë revealed their identities to their publisher. He corresponded regularly with Charlotte.

THE REVEREND CARUS WILSON   Vicar of Tunstall, Yorkshire. Clergyman and philanthropist, he founded the Clergy Daughters' School at Cowan Bridge that Maria, Elizabeth, Charlotte and Emily Brontë attended with such tragic results. His reputation was much tarnished by *Jane Eyre* and the revelations in Mrs Gaskell's *Life* that Cowan Bridge was the model for Lowood School and he for Mr Brocklehurst.

NICHOLAS PATRICK WISEMAN, 1802–65   Cardinal and Archbishop of Westminster. He was the first English cardinal of the restored English Catholic Church. Wiseman's appointment outraged extreme Protestants who complained of 'papal aggression'. Wiseman served at Westminster for 14 years and outstayed the public's indignation.

MARGARET WOOLER, b. 1792   Headmistress of Roe Head School, later moved to Dewsbury Moor, Yorkshire, the school attended by Anne, Charlotte and Emily Brontë. She corresponded with Charlotte for many years and was one of the two guests at her wedding, where she gave away the bride. Charlotte admired her as a model of the independent single woman.

Further reading

Original MSS and collections

For the best discussion of the problem of Brontë sources, see Tom Winnifrith, *The Brontës and Their Background*, London, 1973. Major collections of Brontë manuscripts, letters, juvenilia and so on are held in the Brontë Parsonage Museum, the Brotherton Library, Leeds, the Fitzwilliam Museum, Cambridge, the British Library, and a host of American collections, one of the best-known being the Bonnell Collection, Philadelphia. Fully reliable editions of the letters do not exist. T. J. Wise's 4-volume edition, *The Brontës, Their Lives, Friendships and Correspondence*, The Shakespeare Head Brontë, Oxford, 1932, is still the best general collection. T. J. Wise and J. A. Symington issued *The Miscellaneous and Unpublished Writings of Charlotte and Branwell Brontë* in 1934. Clement Shorter, *The Brontës' Life and Letters*, London, 1908, also contains valuable material. The main periodical devoted to Brontë studies is *The Transactions of the Brontë Society*.

The novels

The Brontës' novels have been continuously republished since their first appearance. Both Oxford and Penguin issue a complete collection with critical introductions and notes. Many other inexpensive editions are also available, a witness to the Brontës' continuing popularity. The most scholarly contemporary edition is the Clarendon Edition of the novels of the Brontës, General Editors I. and J. Jack, Oxford University Press.

Poems

Wise and Symington published in their Shakespeare Head Edition, *The Complete Poems of Emily Jane and Anne Brontë*, in 1934 and *The Poems of Charlotte and Patrick Brontë*, also in 1934. The latter have been re-edited in two separate volumes by Tom Winnifrith, *The Poems of Branwell Brontë*, 1983, and *The Poems of Charlotte Brontë*, 1984. The definitive edition of Emily's poetry was edited by C. W. Hatfield, *The Complete Poems of Emily Jane Brontë*, New York, 1941. Among collections of Brontë poetry one may mention Stevie Davies, *The Brontë Sisters, Selected Poems of Charlotte, Emily and Anne Brontë*, Cheadle, 1976, and Juliet R. V. Barker, *The Brontës' Selected Poems*, London, 1985, as well as M. R. D. Seaward (ed.), *Poems by the Brontë Sisters*, London, 1985.

Biographies

There exists a wide range of biographical and semi-biographical work on the Brontës. In many respects, Mrs Gaskell's *Life of Charlotte Brontë*, 1857, reissued by Penguin, has not been surpassed, though it has been criticized for its inaccuracy (the Robinson imbroglio) and for perpetrating too pessimistic a view of the Brontës' lives. But it remains a compelling account, and Mrs Gaskell was scrupulous in consulting most known first-hand sources. A sympathetic view of Patrick Brontë can be found in John Lock and W. T. Dixon's *A Man of Sorrow*, London, 1965. The Brontës' major twentieth-century biographer is Winifred Gérin, who has published separate works on each of the Brontës: *Anne Brontë*, London, 1951; *Branwell Brontë*, London 1961; *Charlotte Brontë, the Evolution of a Genius*, London, 1967; and *Emily Brontë*, Oxford, 1971. Gérin draws on an impressive range of sources. Nevertheless, these biographies tend to interpret the works in terms of the lives, and where information is scanty on the lives, to infer facts from the works. To some extent, the Gérin *oeuvre* illuminates the elusiveness of the Brontës.

Criticism

Students of the Brontës are assisted by a number of modern collections of critical essays, both past and present, among them: Miriam Allott (ed.), *The Brontës, the Critical Heritage*, London, 1974; I. Gregor (ed.), *The Brontës, a Collection of Critical Essays, Twentieth-Century Views*, New Jersey, 1970; Miriam Allott (ed.), *Charlotte Brontë, Jane Eyre and Villette, a Casebook*, London, 1974; and on Emily: Miriam Allott (ed.), *Wuthering Heights, a Casebook*, London 1970; A. Everitt, *Wuthering Heights, an Anthology of Criticism*, London, 1967; J. P. Petit, *Emily Brontë, a Critical Anthology*, Penguin, 1973; and T. A. Vogler, *Twentieth-Century Interpretations of Wuthering Heights*, New Jersey, 1968.

On the juvenilia, the pioneering study was that of Fanny Ratchford, *The Brontës' Web of Childhood*, New York, 1964. It has been superseded by Christine Alexander's scholarly and engaging study, *The Early Writings of Charlotte Brontë*, Oxford, 1983. A selection of Charlotte Brontë's and Jane Austen's juvenilia is available in Penguin, and a number of separate works and short novels have also been re-edited – for example, W. Gérin, *Five Novelettes*, London, 1971. Another excellent study of the Brontës' early development can be found in Enid Duthie's *The Foreign Vision of Charlotte Brontë*, London, 1975.

On the Brontës' novels, the range of critical material is vast; the following titles are intended to suggest types of critical approaches.

Among Marxist studies, the most impressive is Terry Eagleton's *Myths of Power, a Marxist Study of the Brontës*, London, 1975, which persuasively argues an historical-materialist interpretation. Another work in the same vein, dealing in part with the Brontës, is Igor Webb's *From Custom to Capital*, Ithaca, New York, 1981. A major area of interpretation of the Brontës has been broadly psychoanalytic, including modern feminist criticism. Thomas Moser, 'What is the Matter with Mary Jane?', *Nineteenth-century Fiction*, 14, June 1962, a Freudian study of Emily, is almost a parody of the genre ('inhibited spinster', 'she did not know what she was doing') and raises all the problems of modern critics who extend critical patronage to the Brontës. Far more impressive in this field are, John Maynard, *Charlotte Brontë and Sexuality*, Cambridge, 1984; James Kavanagh, *Emily Brontë*, Oxford, 1985; and Dianne Sadoff, *Monsters of Affection*, Baltimore, Maryland, 1982. Important feminist psychoanalytic studies include: S. M. Gilbert and S. Gubar, *The Madwoman in the Attic*, London, 1979; Helene Moglen, *Charlotte Bronte, the Self Conceived*, New York, 1976; Pauline Nestor, *Charlotte Brontë*, London, 1987; and Margaret Homans, *Women Writers and Poetic Identity*, Princeton, New Jersey, 1980, which considers Emily's poetry. One of the best studies of Emily Brontë, concentrating on religious themes, is Jacques Blondel's *Emily Brontë, expérience spirituelle et création poétique*, Paris, 1962–63.

Among numerous stylistic or thematic critical studies one may include: Enid Duthie, *The Brontës and Nature*, London, 1986; John Hewish, *Emily Brontë, a Critical and Biographical Study*, London, 1969; Karl Kroeber, *Styles in Fictional Structure*, Princeton, New Jersey, 1971; Q. D. Leavis's essays on the Brontës (see *Collected Essays*, vol. I, Cambridge, 1983); Margot Peters, *Charlotte Brontë, Style in the Novel*, Madison, Wisconsin, 1973; and C. P. Sanger, 'The Structure of Wuthering Heights', *Hogarth Essays*, XIX, 1926. There tend to be fewer works about Anne Brontë than about her sisters. Recent studies are: A. C. Bell, *Anne Brontë, The Tenant of Wildfell Hall*, Ilkley, 1974; Ada Harrison and Derek Stanford, *Anne Brontë, Her Life and Work*, London, 1959; and P. J. M. Scott, *Anne Brontë, a New Critical Assessment*, London, 1983.

History

Some useful background studies are: G. M. Young, *Portrait of an Age, Victorian England*, Oxford, 1971; and Walter Houghton, *The Victorian Frame of Mind*, New Haven, Connecticut, 1963. On religion in nineteenth-century England, see: Owen Chadwick, *The Victorian Church*, London, 1966; A. O. J. Cockshut (ed.), *Religious Controversies in the Nineteenth Century*, London, 1966; and Robert Lee Wolff, *Gains and Losses: Novels of Faith and Doubt in Victorian England*, London, 1977.

On the 'Condition of Woman Question' and its relation to the Brontës, see: Joan N. Burnstyn, *Victorian Education and the Ideal of Womanhood*, London, 1980; Inga-Stina Ewbank, *Their Proper Sphere*, London, 1966; Lee Holcombe, *Victorian Ladies at Work, 1850–1914*, London, 1973; Martha Vicinus (ed.), *Suffer and Be Still*, Bloomington, Illinois, 1972; and Martha Vicinus, *A Widening Sphere*, London, 1977.

Finally, it may be mentioned that Charlotte's friend, Mary Taylor, was herself a novelist and essayist. Her novel, *Miss Miles*, London, 1890, is unfortunately out of print. It paints a moving picture of women's economic vulnerability in the early nineteenth century. She also wrote a number of feminist essays published in the *Victoria Magazine*. Her life and times in New Zealand are chronicled by Joan Stevens, *Mary Taylor: Friend of Charlotte Brontë, Letters from New Zealand and Elsewhere*, Oxford, 1972.

General index

Index of Brontë works

The characters are listed alphabetically under the novels.